William Chadwick

King John of England

A History and Vindication Based on the Original Authorities

William Chadwick

King John of England

A History and Vindication Based on the Original Authorities

ISBN/EAN: 9783743401679

Manufactured in Europe, USA, Canada, Australia, Japa

Cover: Foto ©ninafisch / pixelio.de

Manufactured and distributed by brebook publishing software (www.brebook.com)

William Chadwick

King John of England

KING JOHN OF ENGLAND:

A HISTORY AND VINDICATION,

BASED ON

THE ORIGINAL AUTHORITIES.

BY

WILLIAM CHADWICK.

"*King John.* What follows if we disallow of this?
Chat. The proud control of fierce and bloody war,
   To enforce these rights so forcibly withheld.
King John. Here have we war for war, and blood for blood,
   Controlment for controlment: so answer France.
Chat. Then take my king's defiance from my mouth,
   The farthest limit of my embassy.
King John. Bear mine to him, and so depart in peace;
   Be thou as lightning in the eyes of France;
   For, ere thou canst report, I will be there,—
   The thunder of my cannon shall be heard."
                        KING JOHN, *Act* i., *Scene* 1.

"Let time's black hand blot out the memorie
   Of that vile age: and let it not be said
That *John* did ever guide this empire.
   That future time with shame may not upbraid
   This nation's name, by whom I was betray'd;
And say, that subjects yet did never bring
Such grievous wrongs upon a wretched king."
                        KING JOHN—*A Mirrour for Magistrates.*

LONDON:
JOHN RUSSELL SMITH, 36 SOHO SQUARE.
1865.

PREFACE.

In undertaking to penetrate the foggy atmosphere of the Magna Charta period of English history, I had in view the opening out of a very obscure, benighted period of our national existence.

I had often heard of the "old Barons of Runnemead" and "the glorious sheet-anchor of our liberties," &c. &c. &c.; but I wished to investigate for myself whether the Barons were '*old*,' and also whether the sheet-anchor were really as '*glorious*' as what it was pretended to be.

I wished to know what a '*libere tenens*' or freeholder in England was, and also what a copyholder was. I wished to compare the two, and judge for myself which was which.

I did not know the value of the forty-shilling freehold-limitation Act of Henry VI., and the foundation on which it stood. I wished to know this; yea, I was desirous of examining the concreted rock-work of that foundation for myself. I have done this, and my book gives the result.

In seeking information, I began with the Chronicles of the thirteenth century, and I read them all, but to very little purpose; for I soon found that, from the death of the truthful chaplain of Henry II.,—Roger de Hoveden, —in the year A.D. 1201, we have not one Chronicler of the early Plantagenet period who can be relied upon.

Breaking down completely in History, (so-called,) I turned my attention to the Tower Records; and from them I learned that the extant history on the Magna Charta period was not only doubtful, but flagrantly and maliciously false, and that the writers were, to a man, Benedictine monks and priests, who wrote their mendacities and frivolities to serve the cause of the Church of Rome, as opposed to the Civil Power in England.

I respectfully invite attention to what I have presented; and perhaps my comments on the facts, real and alleged, may interest a few. Not Cromwell, not any one of the great leaders of "The Commonwealth," has been more misrepresented than King John. I hope that I furnish a contribution at any rate, toward casting off the immense guano-piles of slander and caricature, bigotries and prejudices, that have for centuries lain upon his illustrious memory. If in any degree I do so, I shall be abundantly rewarded for much unthankful toil. *Contigimus portum, quo mihi cursus erat.*

WILLIAM CHADWICK.

ARKSEY, DONCASTER, *Feb.* 18, 1865.

☞ By an oversight in numbering the Chapters, Chap. XIII. has been missed. It will be understood that it is merely in the heading, not in the matter.—C.

CONTENTS.

CHAPTER I.
BOYHOOD SLANDERS—HENRY AND RICHARD—EARL JOHN, . 1

CHAPTER II.
JOHN CREATED KING BY ELECTION, . . . 7

CHAPTER III.
KING JOHN REALLY GOVERNS—HIS INTENSE APPLICATION—HIS JOURNEYS, ... 15

CHAPTER IV.
THE OFFICIALS OF JOHN—HIS AUTHORITY REAL, . . . 29

CHAPTER V.
DIFFICULTIES IN NORMANDY AND DEATH OF ARTHUR, 43

CHAPTER VI.
THE DEATH OF HUBERT WALTER, ARCHBISHOP OF CANTERBURY, . 58

CHAPTER VII.
ELECTION OF A SUCCESSOR TO HUBERT WALTER, ARCHBISHOP OF CANTERBURY, ... 61

Contents.

CHAPTER VIII.
CHARTER "WORRY"—LANGTON AGAIN, . . 79

CHAPTER IX.
MAGNA CHARTA TREASON—INVASION BY LOUIS, . 84

CHAPTER X.
"IN THE SHADOWS:" DEATH, ... 122

INTER-CHAPTER.
ACCESSION OF HENRY, ... 126

CHAPTER XI.
THE BARONS, . . . 131

CHAPTER XII.
TITLE OF "MAGNA CHARTA" INVALID—NOBLE "BROKERS"—DETAILS OF CHARTER EXAMINED, ... 141

CHAPTER XIV.*
FEUDALISM—VASSALAGE—COWARD-CHARGE, . . . 158

CHAPTER XV.
FEUDAL SYSTEM—WRITS—JOHN'S VIGILANCE, . 163

CHAPTER XVI.
SPORTS—HUNTING—DOGS, . . . 173

CHAPTER XVII.
ALLEGED PROFLIGACY OF KING JOHN, . . 186

---

* See note at end of Preface.

CHAPTER XVIII.

JOHN'S ALLEGED CRUELTY TO THE JEWS, . . . 204

CHAPTER XIX.

JOHN'S ALLEGED SKULKING IN ISLE OF WIGHT, . . . 221

CHAPTER XX.

JOHN'S CARE FOR THE POOR, . . . 224

CHAPTER XXI.

KINGLY KINDNESS REWARDED WITH TREASONOUS INGRATITUDE, 229

CHAPTER XXII.

JOHN'S ALLEGED LOW ASSOCIATES—LUPESCAIRE AND ALGAIS, . 246

CHAPTER XXIII.

'WALLET' OF HISTORICAL MEMORABILIA, . . . 262

NOTE A, . 287

INDEX OF CHIEF MATTERS, ... 289

KING JOHN OF ENGLAND.

CHAPTER I.

BOYHOOD SLANDERS—HENRY AND RICHARD—EARL JOHN.

IN all the family contentions and plottings of the household of Henry II., the Queen and three elder sons, Henry, Richard, and Geoffrey, largely participated; and this entirely to the exclusion of the *boy* John.

Attention to dates alone suffices to acquit John. He was born on Christmas eve, A.D. 1166–7, at the King's manor-house in Oxford. He was thus, throughout these domestic squabbles, a mere boy, younger by ten years than his brother Richard, (born 1157.) Yet does History (so-called) even thus early slander him: and, oblivious of chronology, impute to him the crimes and vices of his seniors.

John was knighted at Windsor by his father, in the 13th year of his age, in April 1180 ['1185']; and, according to many "Chronicle" writers, he proceeded to Ireland as " King."

Arriving there, he "employed"—so they mendaciously tell—" the money destined for the troops that accompanied him, for the gratification of his own covetousness." Precocious "covetousness" indeed! no less precocious "sovereignty!" As to the latter, when he went to Ireland, he was in his 19th, not 13th year.

John was the favourite child of his parents at home; but how he could be sent out with a few scores of knights and soldiers to

A

take upon himself the sole sovereignty of Ireland, we are puzzled to make out. Is there any solution of the difficulty? Let us see: Giraldus Cambrensis was there, as guardian of the whole expedition! The vanity of this man was such, that he might persuade the court of Henry II. that he, related in blood, and doubly related by alliance, to all the old Kings of Ireland, and such of the old nobility as were worth being related to, could induce them to submit to the rule of this boy and *his guardian and chaplain!!* Here, I believe, we have the origin of the conquering kingly expedition to Ireland by John. Here, likewise, I find the explanation of the many libels on our King in relation to this expedition. Giraldus writes concerning it, and gives as the cause of its utter failure, the reckless, prodigal living, and folly of John and his knightly followers, when in garrison at Dublin Castle. They never took the field against any enemy, but spent their days and nights in folly and "riotous living;" till, on the expiration of eight months, Earl John returned to England, leaving his chaplain to bring over the people and their rulers to submission to English rule by his powers of persuasion!

But what are the facts to be placed over-against the peevish nonsense of the monk? The Irish "Annals" inform us that John complained heavily to his father of Hugo de Lacy, the Viceroy of Ireland, being jealous of his superseding him in his sovereignty, and of his throwing every obstacle in the way of his success as a conqueror of Ireland.

In consequence of these representations made to his father in England, John obtained his recall, when the entire administration of affairs, with the chief command of the forces, was given to the brave John de Curcy; with a recall for Hugo de Lacy, the Viceroy of Ireland, who was then exercising a power independent on, and opposed to that of, the crown of England: which recall Hugo de Lacy treated with contempt—he remaining in Ireland, and exercising kingly authority notwithstanding.

No sooner had Henry II. closed his mortal career, by a sudden and mysterious death, in Normandy, A.D. 1189, than Richard, his son, succeeded to the throne of England, and his father's possessions in Normandy and other provinces in France.

One of the first acts of his reign was to give to his brother John the earldom of Gloucester, with the heiress of Robert, Earl of Gloucester, together with the castles of Marlborough, Lutegarshale, Bolsover, Nottingham, and Lancaster; with the honour of William Peveral, and also the counties of Cornwall, Devon, Somerset, and Dorset. Soon after this, or in five months from his coming to the crown of England, on December 11th, Richard sailed from Dover to Calais, on his way to Paris, there to meet his fellow-crusader, Philip Augustus, King of the French, in whose company he set out for the Holy Land, at the head of three or four hundred thousand men of all arms, and the usual tag-rag of camp-followers.

To govern the kingdom of England, with the dependencies in Normandy and neighbouring provinces, Richard appointed William Longchamp, Bishop of Ely, his Chancellor, and the Bishop of Durham, as Regents of the kingdom.

No sooner had Richard left the shores of England for the Holy Land, than William of Ely, the Regent and Chancellor, revoked the King's grants made to his brother Earl John; and even laid siege to Nottingham Castle,[1] and refused to surrender to him the several castles [2] which the King had given to him.

Whatever may have been the origin of this dispute between the Chancellor (of whom much onward) and Earl John, it soon assumed a national importance, and required a great council of the Barons of the realm to settle it; when the following agreement was come to:—"That the dispute between Earl John and William of Ely, the Chancellor, should be set at rest, through the mediation of the Archbishop of Rouen, and the Bishops of Durham, London, Winchester, Bath, Rochester, and Coventry, with other faithful servants of our Lord the King." I relegate details to a note.[3]

---

[1] Roger de Wendover, vol. ii. pp. 78-86.   [2] Hoveden's Annals, vol. ii. p. 225.
[3] See Appendix, Note A.

Suffice it here to say, that this man and Earl John came to such a deadly feud, that blows were struck by the adherents of each party, and a knight of Earl John's killed. On this, Earl John, supported by William Marshall, Earl Striguil, called a national council in St Paul's Churchyard in London, and with it a "*Folkmote*" of the citizens of London. At which great national council and Folkmote, the Chancellor was formally deposed from his office; which deposition affords the first example recorded in English History of a minister of the Crown being made responsible to the people of England for the advice which he might give to his sovereign. Thanks for this to William, Earl Marshall; the ever-to-be-remembered Earl of Pembroke. This churchyard council and Folkmote of the citizens was reported by his basely faithful Chancellor to King Richard, then in the hands of the Emperor of the Romans, and calling vehemently upon his ministers, earls, barons, and loyal subjects to ransom him. It excited and exasperated his Majesty.

At this painful juncture of Richard's career, Hubert Walter, the great and enlightened statesman of John's reign,—he being a crusader and prisoner to the Emperor, along with his master,—came to England with Peter de Rupibus, another of the leaders in the succeeding reign, to raise the required ransom for the deliverance of the King. As for William, Bishop of Ely, the Chancellor and Regent, the King took his part altogether, and stood by him, as long as he lived, which was for seven years after this.

Earl John with his supporter William Marshall was to be blasted by the royal displeasure. John was "traitor," leagued with the King of France, against his "King and brother;" and at home "worse than traitor," charged, as he was, by this Chancellor with "having designs upon the Crown, as supposing that his sovereign and brother would never be able to return to England." No sooner had Richard returned to England, which he did immediately, the ransom having been forwarded, than he made an attack upon Earl John and his castles, commencing with the siege of Nottingham Castle, which he took; and put the prisoners to ransom at fixed prices.

Soon after this, Richard carried his arms against France, and there he ended his miserable and disastrous life. He was mortally wounded by the arrow of Bertram de Gurdun at the siege of the castle of Chalus. Seeing his end to be drawing nigh, he began to turn his thoughts to the disposition of his kingdom of England, and his other possessions.

To his brother John he left his kingdom, with his possessions in France; and ordered all those then present to do homage for the same. He also commanded his castles to be given to him, with three-fourths of his treasure. Surely we have in all this evidence that the dying Richard saw through the slanders and the slanderers of his brother John!

In leaving his kingdom of England to John his brother, instead of to Arthur his nephew, Richard committed an irregularity; but such a one as had been not infrequent. This Arthur, Duke of Brittany, was so completely French, and so much under the control of Philip, the King of that nation, whose daughter Mary he had married, that he would have been rejected by the English nobility and people. It is quite certain that Arthur, the boy-tool and son-in-law of Philip the King of the French, never would have been acknowledged as King of England and Duke of Normandy by the nation.

Arthur, though only a boy of fifteen years, had already been in arms, under French colours, against the English king in Normandy, in the year A.D. 1196, when Constance, his mother, (a French princess,) aiding the same cause, was taken prisoner, and placed in confinement by her husband, Randulph Blandeville, Earl of Chester.

Although Earl John had been disgraced at court, and William

his Chancellor, they yet lived in the affections of the people of England for the part they had taken in opposing the measures of the tyrannous reign of that king.

At the death of Richard I., Earl John, soon to become KING JOHN, was idolised by the people of England of all classes, and was, moreover, the most popular Earl in Europe, wherever the tyrannies of William Longchamp, Bishop of Ely, the chief minister of Richard I., were known.

So that it is not difficult to see here, if, on the one hand, there was forethought and a dying instinct on the part of Richard in setting aside Arthur, his nephew, there was likewise a tacit admission that Earl John was the name that would rally the nation around the throne. It was a noble heritage on which John entered; and <u>nobly did he discharge to the darkened close its difficult and overwhelming duties</u>.

CHAPTER II.

JOHN CREATED KING BY ELECTION.

ON the 6th day of April A.D. 1199, Earl John, the younger brother of the just deceased, King Richard I., and sixth and youngest son, and a dutiful and affectionate son too, of Henry II., succeeded to the Crown of England and its dependencies (the guerdons half of heritage and half of conquest) in Anjou, Touraine, Maine, with Poictiers, Normandy, and Guienne.

The designation of John by Richard was ratified by the ELECTION OF THE NATION, which had not forgotten the St Paul's Churchyard council and public meeting of the citizens of London, nor the Earl's brave-hearted resistance to the Chancellor, to the verge of treason.

This power of election was familiar to England, both in the Saxon, Danish, and Norman times. Even Alfred (it needs not to name him "great," for the world knows but one) was the fourth son of Ethelwolf, and succeeded Ethelbald, Ethelbert, and Ethelred, his brothers, all his nephews (of whom there were many) being thus ignored. Who doubteth the wisdom of the precedent? We know what England got in her Alfred! We know what she would *not* have got in either of Ethelbert's two sons, or Ethelred's sons or daughter. It will be seen what the gain or loss was in passing by the boy-duke of Brittany.

Besides the designation by Richard, the new King occupied his throne with the sanction of the nobles, prelates, ministers of state, and the other "heads" of the "inviolate kingdom." THE

PEOPLE were as yet without voice; nevertheless, the succession sprang out of national choice, as well as regal inheritance.

This starting-point, *a designated succession*, I would have merely noticed, had not coincident occurrences happened to bring into relief every fact and act in the reign of John. Even herein historians and their simple readers have blamed and accused him. What is the secret of the accusations that nestle, newt and toad-like, here? King John would be "King of England" from the first,—no vassal, much less slave! Ha! he dared to assert his prerogatives within his own dominions. Against whom? Against the boldest priest that ever pretended to hold the keys of heaven and hell from Peter, the fisherman of Galilee. John was King of England when Innocent III. ("impious *innocent*," Pericles iv. 4) was Pope. If disaster came, flinging huge shadows over a noble name, —if lies, all too readily credited, have distorted the scoundrel Pope's betrayed opponent,—have we not a key here? John was the proud son of a proud mother, a Norman princess of great wealth and power. He had no doubt been reared in the belief, that as Canterbury was in England, the King of England must be King of Canterbury. John had to proclaim this, and priestly tools were forward to oppose. This will emerge.

On 25th May 1199, a few weeks only after his succession, (no lack of energy, no vacillation in this, certainly!) John was in Normandy taking possession of his late brother the King's treasures, and the "duchy" itself. Old chroniclers give us a glimpse of much pomp and splendour around the new King, himself girt with "sword of state," not as a toy, but to be gripped and used. It needeth not that we tarry in Normandy, save that still we have to remark no trace of that "feebleness" which "historians" are swift to allege against John.

On the same day, at the close of the festival, he again sailed for England, and landed at Shoreham, in Sussex, setting out for London next morning, May 26th.

On the 27th, he was crowned at Westminster, in presence of

the earls, barons, prelates, and a vast assembly of other notables by Hubert Walter, Archbishop of Canterbury, and Chancellor to the late King, William Bishop of Ely having died two years before—England being well rid of the flagitious priest!

The Archbishop made a speech on the occasion. It may in fragments be spelled out in mediæval Latin still. . I grasp one fact in it that he delivered before the audience, that John was elected King by the national will. One likes the ring of the olden words, "AB UNIVERSITATE REGNI."

To this declaration of national *election* John assented.

Then thundered, as only English lungs could, or can do now, "Long live the King." This coronation was more than a pageant. It was a great national council, attended by all the magnates of the realm, with the Archbishop of Canterbury and Chancellor at their head, though Geoffrey Plantagenet, the Archbishop of York, the king's base brother, was absent designedly, as will appear in the sequel,—the two brothers being through life on the worst of terms. John soon took note that Geoffrey Plantagenet was Archbishop of York through purchase, and High Sheriff of Yorkshire, also through the same corrupt means. He was king not by purchase, but by election.

On this great day King John bound William Marshall, Earl of Striguil, (a name not met with in society since the Churchyard gathering, held six years before,) and Geoffrey Fitz-Peter, Earl of Essex, with their counties' swords.

John was crowned by Hubert Walter, Archbishop of Canterbury, on the day of the ascension of our Lord; the transactions of which Roger de Hoveden thus relates:—"Therefore, there being assembled at London in expectation of the coming of the aforesaid Duke, Hubert the archbishop, John of Dublin, the Archbishop de Raguse, William of London, Gilbert of Rochester, John of Norwich, with others, High Church dignitaries too numerous to mention, with earls, and barons, and knights innumerable; amongst whom stood Earls Robert of Leicester, Clare, Tutesbury,

Warren, Salisbury, Striguil, Warwick, Bigot, Arundel, Chester, &c.—Philip, Bishop of Durham, protesting that the coronation should not take place in the absence of Geoffrey, Archbishop of York."

We may look at the scene as placed on record by Roger de Wendover, Monk of Saint Albans. It were to spoil the old chronicler's narrative, as coarse fingers spoil the a-dust auricula, in anywise to change the writing, half inarticulate and stammering though it be. It gladdens a reader in the nineteenth century to find double witness to the broad principle of "elective" monarchy, such as is borne by the Archbishop of Canterbury's noteworthy words, than which worthier have not been heard in old Westminster. The Hebraic historic reference to Saul and David was meet from priestly and arch-priestly lips. But now turn we to Roger de Wendover. "Wherefore, there being assembled against his coming, archbishops, bishops, earls, and barons, and all those who ought to be at that coronation; the Archbishop of Canterbury standing in the midst of all, said:—'Hear ye! all of you! Your discretion should have known that no one can succeed to the kingdom of another by any previous agreement or arrangement, unless chosen unanimously by the whole commonwealth or community of the kingdom, the favour of the Holy Spirit being supplicated upon the transaction, and (præ-electus) pre-eminently chosen for an example and similitude to Saul, the first anointed king whom the Lord placed over His people, not the son of a king, nor one sprung from a royal race. In like manner, after him David, the son of Semei; this because valiant and fitted to the royal dignity: that because sanctified and humble; that so he, who excelled all others in the kingdom in his valour, should be placed before all, both in power and government. But if any one of the race or family of the deceased king shall excel others in virtue, without hesitation and immediately his election is to be consented to forthwith. Therefore we have said these things for the excellent Earl John, who is now present, the brother of our most illustrious King Richard, now dead, an heir proceeding from his own body, who was provident, and energetic, and manifestly noble, whom we, the blessing of the Holy Ghost being invoked, have universally and unanimously elected, as much on account of his own merits, as from his consanguinity to the late king.'"

Words these very memorable, and not to be forgotten by any one who really wishes to get at the man, King John, as he seemed to those nearest him. They were not courtly, idly spoken words. I would have them weighed.

Let us cull the more remarkable. "Pre-eminently *chosen* for *the eminency* of *his morals.*"[1] Fine tautology that, of the old monk! "We have said these things for the *excellent Earl John,* who is now present." "Wanted an heir who was provident and *energetic* and manifestly *noble.*" Ha! then, King John, by attestation of the Holy Ghost, *was* manifestly noble—unanimously elected as much on account of *his own merits,* as for his consanguinity. In this coronation King John bound himself with a triple oath, to wit, "That he would delight himself in the sacred Church and its ordinances, and would preserve it intact from depredations of the malignant; and that bad laws being destroyed, he would substitute good ones, and exercise true justice in the kingdom of England.

"Afterwards he was sworn by the same Archbishop, on the part of God, and strictly forbidden to presume to receive this honour unless his mind were fully made up to carry out in full operation that which he had sworn to carry out or fulfil.

"To this he, responding, promised that he, by the assistance of God, in good faith would perform those things which he had sworn to perform.

"On the morrow, therefore, homages and fealties being accepted, he, a pious devotee, sought, for the sake of his declaration, the

---

[1] Roger de Hoveden's Annals, vol. ii. p. 115.

happy Albanus, the proto-martyr of England. And so making a very short stay in England, and leaving those things which were appointed in his kingdom with his council of great men, he departed for Normandy to settle his affairs there."

One's eyes brim with tears, even at this late day, in reading this solemn narrative of mutual vow and oath. I have said those were not courtly or merely flattering words which the Archbishop spoke. In proof, hear what the same Roger de Wendover says of the speaker of them :—" This Archbishop," he tells us, "was a man of a profound depth of character: and in the kingdom was a column of singular stability and incomparable wisdom. Nor did others, *as yet*, doubt on these matters; knowing, as they did, that he would not have or defined this business had he not sufficient cause." I have italicised two little ominous words "as yet," small, but suggestive of coming shadows. But the good, stout Archbishop's speech had welcome from Earl John, "the King" now, and from all.

We learn from these old words under what sanctions and in what spirit King John placed the crown of England on his forehead; learn that it was with a profound sense of duty, not less than with manly dignity. It were to malign our common nature to suppose for a moment that the pageant was a pageant only, or the vows and oaths and announced purposes unreal. To those who have accepted a low view of John, the shadow of awe in his coronation responses, and his voluntary adhesion to his great council, must seem out of accord. But as we proceed in our inquiry, it will be found that the afterlife went (if I may be allowed the word) on the same plane of projection.

Thus King of England, John had scarcely ascended the throne when he sued a divorce from his ~~second~~ wife Isabel, third daughter of the Earl of Gloucester. She was "barren." The pretext, common in that age, was too close consanguinity in blood. They were in the *third* degree of kindred; whereas the Pope prohibited all marriages within seven degrees of kindred. I state the fact, I do not vindicate it. But I cannot measure it by a nineteenth century standard.

Morality is eternal; but conscience is educated in the progress of the ages.

He married, upon his divorce, Isabella or Avis, daughter of the Earl of Angouleme. This "fair ladye" had previously been contracted to Hugh le Brun, Count de la Marche, a gallant Troubadour. From the moment of the royal marriage, the Count became a deadly enemy of the King.[1] Here, again, I pause to ask my readers to observe another of the after-meshes in which John was involved; another element toward a proper estimate of himself and his circumstances alike.

By Isabella John had issue, Henry—afterwards King of England as the third of that name, and whose life-story, equally with his father's, has been darkened and confused by calumny—Richard, Earl of Cornwall, and Eleanor, who was married twice; first, to William Marshall the younger; and secondly, to one who lives for "all time" in the page of Joanna Baillie's magnificent drama— Simon de Montfort, Earl of Leicester, who fell at the battle of Evesham. He had other two daughters.

The King having been in France for four months, looking after

---

[1] Randulph de Diceto, Dean of London, 1200, when writing on King John's matrimonial alliance, in his *History* or *Imagines Historiarum*, observes in vol. i. page 709 :—"Lord John, King of England, having in intent to take for his wife the daughter of the King of Portugal, whose fame had won over his affections, he sent from Rouen, to inquire about her, illustrious and stately men, as the Bishop Lisoiensis, William de Stagno, Randulph de Ardene, Hubert de Burgh, and many others, as well from England as from Normandy. But he by chance, consulting less their honour than became the royal dignity, while they were on their journey, nay, without securing their support, married Isabel, the only daughter and heiress of the Earl of *Engolismensis*, who before had been contracted to a certain nobleman of Poictiers—namely, Hugo le Brun; on which business afterwards there arose the greatest misunderstanding amongst themselves. He made her to be crowned Queen at Westminster by Hubert, Archbishop of Canterbury, on the 8th of the ides of October, when he himself was crowned."

his affairs there, returned to England on the 6th of October A.D. 1200,[1] and was crowned again at Westminster, along with his wife, by Hubert, the Archbishop, in the presence of the nobles of the kingdom, including Geoffrey of York, who had become reconciled to the King.

Immediately after the coronation ceremony had been gone through in Westminster Abbey, King John made the above statesman his Chancellor, in the place of William Longchamp, Bishop of Ely, the hero of Saint Paul's Churchyard, who had been Chancellor for most of the reign of Richard the First, to the great dissatisfaction of the nation.[2]

---

[1] Itinerary of King John, anno regni 2.   [2] Roger de Hoveden.

CHAPTER III.

KING JOHN REALLY GOVERNS—HIS INTENSE APPLICATION—HIS JOURNEYS.

IMMEDIATELY after his coronation, King John crossed the sea for Normandy, sailing from Shoreham in Sussex, on the 20th of June, and arriving at Roche-Orival on the 29th. He remained in Normandy and his other provinces in France for eight months, arriving at Portsmouth, on his return to England, on the 27th day of February A.D. 1200.

At this time he continued in England two months, or to the 28th day of April, when he again sailed for Normandy.

The alterations in the law courts, and general administration of justice—the innovations of Henry II.—threw a great weight of personal attention to the Circuits of Assize upon the reigning sovereign, who frequently presided in the law courts, supported by the judges.

King John, quite aware of the great responsibility involved in his coronation oath, set himself worthily to fulfil the duties involved in that oath. He personally perambulated the country with the judges in their circuits of assize, in a manner which no king of England ever did, before or since his time. He was a very slave to the public service; for during the two months of his sojourn in England, from February 27th A.D. 1200, we find him at Portsmouth for two days, including Romsey; Winchester, one day; Freemantle, one day; Windsor, two days; Westminster, three days; Woodstock, six days, including part of a day at Silverstone; Northampton, three days; Clipstone, one day; Tichhill, three days;

York, three days, and one day between York, Brotherton, and Doncaster; Bolsover, one day; Derby and Burton-upon-Trent, one day; Burton-upon-Trent, one day; Lichfield, three days, including part of a day at Brewood; Kinfare, one day; Worcester, six days; Farringdon, one day; Windsor, two days; Westminster, three days; Fulham, one day; Guildford, two days, with part of one of them at Alton; Porchester and Bishop's Waltham, one day; Bishop's Waltham and Porchester, one day; Porchester and Portsmouth, one day; Porchester and Southwark, one day; and Porchester, one day.

In the year A.D. 1199-1200, the first year of John's reign, besides the sittings in Westminster, we have three iters; which is to say, that besides the ordinary sittings by the Judges of the King's Bench, and Barons of the Exchequer in Westminster, there were three journeys or circuits undertaken by the itinerant Justiciaries.

1st Iter, that of Simon de Pateshull and his companions, Justices of our lord the King, sat at Oxford, Gloucester, Hereford, and Worcester; the Abbot of Tewkesbury sat on this one occasion as a Justice on the iter.

2d Iter, the Archdeacon of Ely, with other Justices accompanying him, sat at Leicester and Nottingham.

3d Iter, the Bishop of Winchester and other Justices sat at Winchester. *Godfrey de Lucy*

After another absence of five months in France, John returned to England on the 6th day of October A.D. 1200; for on that day we find him at Freemantle; and during the eight months of his sojourn in England at this time he visited, with his judges, chamberlains, treasurers, secretaries, and even huntsmen and hounds, during the hunting season, Freemantle for one day; Westminster for one day; Guildford and Ashley, two days; Ashley, two days; Clarendon, two days; Marlborough, two days; Cricklade and Chelsworth, one day; Chelsworth, one day; Malmesbury and Bradenstoke, one day; Bradenstoke, one day; Stanley, one day; Melksham, one day; Winterbourne and Berkeley, one day; Gloucester, two days, including Westbury; Westbury, one day; St Briavells, two days; Hereford, one day; Ledbury, one day; Upton-Bishop, one day; Feckenham, two days; Bridgenorth, four days; Haywood, one day; Burton-upon-Trent, one day; Melburn, three days, with Nottingham; Clipstone, one day; Lincoln, six days, including Sleaford; Sleaford and Stamford, one day; Geddington, one day; Northampton, three days; Abingdon, two days, with Bedwin; Ludgershall, three days; Clarendon, three days; Canford, four days, with Christchurch; Marlborough, three days; Freemantle, three days; Farnham, three days; Guildford and Reading, two days; Woodstock, six days; Silverstone, three days; Geddington, three days; Bourne, three days; Lincoln and Stow, two days; Stow, one day; Lowth, four days; Beverley, three days, with Driffield; Driffield and Imingham, one day; Pickering, one day; Scarbro', one day; Egton, one day; Guildsborough, one day; Stockton, one day; Durham, two days; Newcastle-upon-Tyne, two days; Belford, one day; Alnwick, one day; Bamborough, three days; Rothbury and Hexham, one day; Hexham, three days; Irthington, one day; Carlisle, three days; Kirkoswald and Morton, one day; Morton and Ravensworth, one day; Ravensworth, one day; Allerton, one day; York, two days; Brotherton, one day; Conisbrough, one day; Clipstone, one day; Bolsover, one day; Nottingham, three days; Aslacton, one day; Geddington, two days, with Kimbolton; Kimbolton, one day; Bernewell, one day; Bury St Edmund's, one day; Sudbury, one day; Chelmsford, one day; Faversham, two days, with Canterbury; Canterbury, three days; Westminster, three days; Windsor, three days; Freemantle, with Marlborough, one day; Marlborough, three days, with Ludgershall, one day; Ludgershall, two days; Cranborn, one day; Dorchester, two days; Bridport, one day; Exeter, one day; Woodstock and Tewkesbury, one day; Tewkesbury, one day; Cirencester, one day; Marlborough, with Ludgershall, two days; Ludgershall,

---

[1] Itinerary of King John, by Thomas Duffus Hardy.

one day; Winchester, two days; Porchester, five days; and Portsmouth, one day.[1]

This kind of thing runs through John's whole reign of eighteen years. Excepting when troublous times come on, his sojourn at Dover was usually two or more months instead of two days, and so of Rochester, Rouen, and other places, where danger invited him.

John again left Portsmouth for France on the 13th day of May, A.D. 1201, and remained abroad thirty-one months, or above two and a half years, till the 28th day of November, A.D. 1203. William d'Albini, Earl of Arundel, was with the King in Normandy, and signed the first document after landing in England at Marlborough Castle, the King's favourite residence, on the 6th day of December, A.D. 1203.

Having got the King once more in England, we will follow him in his truly kingly pursuit of visiting his subjects, along with his judges, ministers, chamberlains, &c., for the carrying of justice to the houses of all,—the most wonderful part of the reign.

It is necessary to shew who travelled with the King, or were his associates in these Circuits of Assize. We will take the earlier years of the reign,—the first three years only at this time, in order to keep down the numbers within manageable limits for the pages of our Vindication:—[1]Roger, Earl Bigot; Geoffrey Fitz-Peter, Chief-Justiciary, who signed fines for fourteen years at intervals, to the time of his death, A.D. 1214; Simon de Pateshull, a judge who attested the fines from the seventh year of Richard I. to the sixteenth year of John; Richard de Heriard; Richard Barre, Archdeacon of Ely; William de Warren; Geoffrey de Bocland; William Briwere, treasurer, from the seventh of Richard I. to the fourteenth of John; John de Gestling, attested fines for ten years of John's reign; James de Potternie, attested from the ninth of Richard I. to the sixteenth year of John; Stephen de Turnham, Richard of Flanders, Randulph de Welford,

---

[1] Preface to " Fines sive Pedes Finium," by Joseph Hunter, p. lxiii.

Robert Fitz-Roger, Geoffrey de Insula, William d'Albini, Earl of Arundel; Alan, Abbot of Tewkesbury; Henry, Archdeacon of Stafford; Henry de Wicheton, Eustace de Faucunberg, Robert de Braibroc, Hugo de Bobi, Henry de Furmans, Walter de Crepping, William de Falaise, Martin de Pateshull, Alan Basset, Randulph Hareng, Stephen de Segrave, Simon de Insula, Stephen de Clay, Randulph Morin, Randulph de Stok, John, Bishop of Norwich; Reginald de Augentoun, Reginald de Cornhill.

These were the judges, and others, eminent lawyers of sufficient standing in the law, to be allowed to preside in the Law courts during the first three years of the reign of John. I have not taken one name commencing with year four of the reign. Some, from their names, must have been connected with the Law courts of Normandy.

As the King, his court and judges travelled frequently thirty, forty, fifty, and even more miles in one day, and these distances taken three or four times in a week occasionally, we must shew how the journey could be performed, by so numerous and august a party, on roads by us supposed to be bad.

The "Tower Records," published by the Royal Commission, afford us ample information on this subject, and give us such an insight into the manners and customs of the time, as cannot be found in any other documents.

The whole subject being both new and interesting, I wish to go into it at this place fully, which shall suffice me for the whole travelling, its expenses and preparations, of the whole reign of King John. It is very evident that the carriages, horses, grooms, vadlets, and others, increase in numbers as the reign progresses.

On the 7th day of November, A.D. 1200, the King and his legal attendants were at Upton-Bishop, in Gloucestershire, on circuit, when the King himself wrote to the constable of Bristol, ordering him "to have made for the use of our Chancery two new carriages, and one 'barhutum,' and eight collars, and eight backbands, and to deliver them to Stephen our coachman; and what expenses he might be put to, in providing these things, should be computed to him at the Exchequer. '*Teste me ipso.*' I myself attesting this, at Upton, vij day of November. By Peter de Rupibus."

The above carriages, and harness for eight horses, were required of the King by Peter de Rupibus, the chief official or minister in attendance, to convey the King and his judges on circuit; the "*barhuch,*" perhaps, taking the four horses, and the two carriages the other four horses between them. We may trace, by the Itinerary, the track of these carriages conveying the King's Chancery on circuit. On Tuesday, November 7th, they were at Upton-Bishop, in Gloucestershire; on the next two days, the 8th and 9th, they were at Feckenham, in Worcestershire; on Friday, the 10th, they were travelling; and on the 11th, 12th, and 13th, they were at Bridgenorth, in Shropshire; on Tuesday, 14th, they were travelling, and on the following day, Wednesday, 15th, were at Haywood, in Herefordshire; and on the Thursday, 16th, they were at Burton-on-Trent, in Staffordshire, and the next two days and a half at Melbourne, in Derbyshire; and on the 19th, Sunday, they were at Melbourne in the morning, and at Nottingham in the evening, from which it would appear that they travelled on Sundays; on Monday, 20th, they were at Clipstone, and for the five following days at Lincoln, till we come to Sunday again, the 26th, when we find the party at Lincoln in the morning, and at Sleaford in the afternoon; and the following day, Monday, at Sleaford and Stamford, and so forward. I should not have noticed this, had not the carriages and the harness for eight horses induced me to ask, Where could they be going to?

"On the 8th of November 1200, the King and his Justiciaries-Itinerant were at Feckenham, in Worcestershire; from which place his chief Justiciary of England, Geoffrey Fitz-Peter, Earl of Essex, wrote to the Vice-count of Worcestershire, to request him to furnish the bearer with one new carriage for the conveying our huntsman, with the requisite number of men to drive the said carriage, and the cost would be defrayed at the Exchequer."[1]

"The King, et cetera, to the Barons of the Exchequer at Westminster, et cetera. — Reckon to the Vice-counts of London xxxviij shillings and ix pence, which they have expended in finding harness for the carriage of the Queen, our wife, and her pack-saddles.—Attested by myself at the Tower of London, on the xxiij day of January, by Robert de Veteriponte, (A.D. 1204.)"

"The King, et cetera, to the Bailiffs of Sorham, et cetera.— Find ye, without delay, for Peter de Leon, our clerk, carriage and safe conduct for transferring, even to London, our rolls and charters, which he has brought from Caen, and it shall be reckoned to you at the Exchequer, et cetera.—Attested by Geoffrey, Earl of Essex, at Werdham, on the xxj day of May, (A.D. 1204.)"[2]

"On the day of Mercury, on the morrow of Saint Michael, (September 30th, 1209,) at Marlborough, for the expenses of iiij coachmen and vij carriage-horses, for two days, who had come even to Marlborough, and from thence were sent to Bridport, because . . . iij shillings and viij pence."[3]

"The King, et cetera, to the Vice-counts of London.—Health in the Lord. Provide ye, from your farm, for the harness for our steward's carriage, now being built, xix shillings and ix pence halfpenny; and for the harness of our butler's carriage, xxxviij shillings and viij pence; for the harness of our kitchen carriage, and for pans, kettles, and pots, for our kitchen carriage, viij pounds and viij shillings and vij pence and a halfpenny; for the harness of the carriage of the huntsman, xiij shillings and iij pence and a halfpenny; for the conveyance of our wine from London, even to Northampton, vj pounds and x shillings and v pence; and it shall be reckoned to you at the Exchequer.—Attested by Peter de Stoke, at the Tower of London, on the xxix day of January. *Per eundem*, (A.D. 1204,) and the 5th year of the reign."[4]

---

[1] Rotuli de Liberate, p. 9.
[2] Ibid., p. 102.
[3] Rotulus Misœ, p. 132, (A.D. 1209.)
[4] Rotuli de Liberate, p. 80.

"For (the posting with post-horses) from Windsor even to London, with three carriages, for two horses, each ij shillings and vj pence, (10d. each, a day;) and from London, even to Rochester, for the same carriages, &c., ij shillings and vj pence. Also, in posting two carriages and two horses each, from Rochester even to Canterbury, xx pence. Also, for one hunting carriage posted from Canterbury even to Rochester, x pence. Also, for the same from Rochester even to Havring, x pence." [1]

"For one carriage with two horses, bearing the fruit of the wardrobe, for five days, iiij shillings and ij pence, (October 15.)" [2]

"On the day of Venus, (July 24th, A.D. 1209,) at Danecaster, for the running of one carriage bearing the harness of the garderobe for v days, iiij shillings ij pence."

"On the same day, (Thursday, Nov. 19th, 1209,) at the same place, (King's Cliffe,) for the expenses of xxix horses of the King, and xxiiij boys for three days, at Rockingham, with the shop, (fabrica for shoeing the horses, and perhaps other mendings in harness,) carriages, *et cetera*, xxiiij shillings and v pence. For the expenses of xlj horses of the King, and xxxv boys, for five days at King's Cliffe, and for the expenses of xl horses and xxxiiij boys at the same place, for one day, Lxxj shillings vj pence halfpenny. Also, for the expenses of xxxviij horses and xxxij boys for one day, at Nottingham, x shillings and v pence halfpenny, freed to Walter, the clerk of Nicholas de Well, by Walter de Saint Andoenus." [3]

Another. "The King, *et cetera*, to the Vice-counts of London.—Health in the Lord. Seek ye from your farm, to prepare a carriage for our kitchen; and for preparing the same carriage, xxj shillings and viij pence; and for preparing the carriage and harness of Stephen the coachman, xxviij shillings and viij pence; and for wax brought to Northampton, ix shillings, and for the sack in which that wax was placed, ij shillings, and for the carriage of the

---

[1] Rotulus Misæ, p. 133. [2] Ibid., p. 134. [3] Ibid., p. 140.

same wax, xij pence, and it shall be reckoned to you at the Exchequer.—I myself attesting at the Tower, London, on the xxx day of May, by Peter de Stoke."[1]

"On the day of Jove, in the Vigil of Saint Laurence, (Thursday, August 9th, A.D. 1212,) at Woodstoke, for the expenses of one esquire of the household, and six boys, and six horses of the Lord the King, and four coachmen of the hunting-carriages, and eight horses of the carriages for hunting; delaying at Winchester, on the Sabbath next after the Feast of St James, during one night, by command of the King; in hay, oats, small payments, and straw-litter for the men, wax-light, and straw-litter for the horses; the sum of five shillings and three pence, freed to Walter, the clerk of the stable, by the King."

"On the day of Venus, in the Feast of St Laurence, (Friday, August the 10th, A.D. 1212,) at the same place, (Silverstone, in Devonshire,) for the expenses of twelve coachmen and twenty-eight carriage horses: namely, for one carriage for the accounts of expenses, for one carriage of the butler, for two carriages of the kitchen, for two carriages for hunting equipments; delaying at Bridgenorth, by command of the Lord the King, for one night; in small payments, and hay, oats, straw for the horses, wax-lights, and straw-litter for the men; the sum of seven shillings and four pence, freed to Walter, clerk of the stable, by the King. On the same day, at Northampton, for one saddle for the load of arms, and for six supercingles for the use of the Lord the King, and for the scabbard to sheathe the arms of the Lord the King, bought by the hand of Walter de Saint Andoen, the sum of eight shillings and four pence, freed to Walter, clerk of the stable, by the King.

"On the same day, (Monday, July 23d, A.D. 1212,) at Bradenstoke, (in Wiltshire,) in the conveyance of the harness of the garde-robe, which was accustomed to be conveyed upon the long carriage of the garde-robe, which was broken, near to Easton, for

---

[1] Rotuli de Liberate, p. 104.

the expenses of xij horses of the King and xxxv boys, for five days, at King's Cliffe, and for the expenses of xl horses and xxxiiij boys, at the same place, for one day, Lxxj shillings and vj pence halfpenny."

"Also for the expenses of xxxviij horses and xxxij boys, for one day, at Nottingham, x shillings and v pence halfpenny, freed to Walter, the clerk of Nicholas de Will, by Walter de Saint Andoenus, (an esquire of the stable.)"[1]

"On the same day, (Friday, Dec. 14th, A.D. 1212-13,) and the 14th year of the reign, at the same place, (Caneford,) in expenses of xv horses of the Lord the King, and two esquires—namely, Hugo de Saint Andoeno and Galfridus Walens, and xiij boys of the stable, and two sumpters, namely, the sumpter of the arms and the sumpter of the closet; tarrying at Warham, by command of the Lord the King, on the Lord's day next after the Feast of Saint George, when the Lord the King went to Corfe; in small payments, hay, oats, straw for litter, and lights, v shillings and x pence halfpenny."[2]

"On the day of Jove next, (Thursday, August 2d, A.D. 1212,) at Bridgenorth, (in Shropshire,) for the expenses of Thomas Marescall and Robin Maresco, who tarried at Gillingham, on the Lord's-day after the Feast of Tiburc and Valerian, and five sumpters of the garde-robe, and one sumpter of the chamber, and ten men of the carriages of the royal palace, and twelve boys having the care of the palfreys of the Lord the King, and fifty-two horses—namely, palfreys, sumpter-horses, and carriage-horses; delaying, at the same place, on the same Lord's-day, by the command of the Lord the King, the sum of twelve shillings and ten pence halfpenny. At the same place, for the expenses of twelve coachmen of the household, and four boys of Robin de Samford, and thirty horses,—of which twenty-six are carriage-horses, and four are Robin de Samford's; delaying at London, when the King went from the Tower of

---

[1] Rotulus Misæ, p. 140.   [2] Ibid., p. 260, (A.R. 14.)

London even to Rochester, against the Earl of Boulogne, for two days; in oats and hay, and straw, and small expenses in fees, the sum of sixteen shillings and two pence."

"At the same place, (Bridgenorth,) for the expenses of three carriages,—to wit, two of the major-domus and butler, and one of the huntsman, and six coachmen, and thirteen carriage-horses, delaying in London during one night, namely, the day of Venus next after the Octaves of Saint Trinity, (Friday, June 1st, A.D. 1212,) when the Lord the King went from Chertsey even to Ditton; in oats and hay, and straw, and small payments, the sum of three shillings and seven pence."

"For the expenses of xxvj horses and xxiiij boys, delaying for one night at Gravesend with Walter de Saint Andoenus, (the vadlet of Henry the King's son,) viij shillings and xi pence."

"At the same place, (Bridgenorth,) for the expenses of two carriages of the huntsman, with four men of the carriages, and eight horses of the carriages; going from Freitmantell even to Odiham, and delaying at the same place during one night, namely, on the day of Mercury next after the Octaves of Saint Trinity; in oats, hay, straw, and small payments, the sum of two shillings and four pence. At the same place, for the expenses of Thomas de Landa, and nine boys of the stable, and nine horses of the Lord the King; delaying at Buckingham, (on the 13th-14th of July, A.D. 1212,) when the Lord the King was at Wakefield, in Buckinghamshire, for two nights; in hay and oats, and straw for litter for the horses, and small payments, and straw-litter for beds for the men, the sum of seven shillings and five pence halfpenny."

"On the day of Venus next, (Friday, August 3d, A D. 1212,) at the same place, for the expenses of Ado the coachman, as well as four coachmen of the garde-robe, and John Coinstance and Hugo, sumpters of the garde-robe, and twelve horses, as well as ten horses for the carriages, which have eleven bushels of oats, and two sumpter-horses of the garderobe; delaying at Winchester during one day, namely, the day of the Sabbath next after the Feast of

Saint James, (Saturday, July 28th, A.D. 1212;) in oats, hay, straw for bedding for the horses, small payments, and straw-litter for the beds of the men, the sum of three shillings and eight pence."

As this system of going on the circuit by educated Judges, supported in the Courts by educated barristers, and educated attorneys or clerks, was the first thing on which the whole clerical opposition to John and his reign, and his father's reign too, turned, we must endeavour to do full justice to it, by shewing what it really was. We have seen the names of the Judges in the first five years of the reign, and we have indicated their labours on circuit. We will now take the list of Judges in the fifteenth year of the reign, and their field of action, in proceeding through the country from one mote-hall to another.

A.D. 1212-13. Geoffrey Fitz-Peter, Chief-Justice, sat at Westminster in the winter, accompanied by Richard de Marisco, William Briware, Pateshull, Potterne, and Huscarl. The King also sat in person on the morrow of the Ascension, and in Trinity, Michaelmas, and Hilary terms. In Trinity term, the King also sat at Odiham and Winchester.

In the autumn, the King sat at Durham, York, Knaresborough, Doncaster, Nottingham, Northampton, Abingdon, Reading, Wilton, and Ludgershall.

The Justices Pateshull, Potterne, Pont-Audemer, were with him.[1]

In no year does it appear that such extensive peregrinations and rapid transits of the King took place, from one part of the kingdom to another, as are shewn by this roll, (A.D. 1213.)

King John appears to have visited, besides other places, the following principal towns and cities of his kingdom, during the year to which this roll refers, at the dates mentioned :—

Alnwick, Jan. 28.
Bristol, July 26, Oct. 18, March 13.
Cambridge, Jan. 4.

---

[1] Sittings of the Curia Regis, Finis, by Josh. Honiton, p. lix.

Canterbury, May 4.
Carlisle, June 23.
Christchurch, Oct. 12, Dec. 16.
Colchester, Sept. 28.
Denham, June 28, Sept. 3, Jan. 24.
Devizes, July 27.
Dover, April 26, May 13.
Guildford, May 13.
Hereford, Nov. 14.
Hertford, Feb. 27.
Knaresborough, June 13, Sept. 7.
Lambeth, May 3, 15, 22, Oct. 2.
Lincoln, Jan. 9, Feb. 15.
London, May 4, June 2, Sept. 20, Oct. 28, March 1, 27, April 16.
Newcastle, Jan. 25.
Northampton, July 13, Dec. 2.
Nottingham, July 6, Aug. 14, Sept. 9, Nov. 24, Feb. 16.
Pontefract, July 3, Aug. 29.
Rochester, April 12, May 2.
Scarborough, Jan. 18.
Southampton, Sept. 21.
Saint Albans, Sept. 20.
Warwick, Nov. 20.
Winchester, May 9, July 28, Oct. 29, Dec. 6, 19, March 7, April 4, 20.
Windsor, May 18, Nov. 3, March 5.
Woodstock, July 20, Aug. 6, Dec. 4.
Worcester, Aug. 1.
York, Aug. 30.

It must have been a year of incessant movement. Three times the King was at the extremities, northern and southern, of his kingdom—at Winchester and at Durham: very rarely does he appear to have stayed a week in one locality. The journeys from day to day seem to have averaged between twenty and thirty miles, but oftentimes more.

He was at Lincoln on the 15th of February, and on the following day, the 16th, at Nottingham—a distance of nearly forty miles; on the 3d December at Northampton, on the 4th at Woodstock; on the 6th September at Durham, and at Knaresborough on the 7th—sixty-five miles distant.

The roads could not have been of a mean order, to have allowed this rapid and constant locomotion.[1]

Let the intelligent reader decide for himself if all this intensity of action, energy of movement, ubiquity of oversight, reality of " governing," at all correspond with the King John of History so-called.—So much for this.

---

[1] Preface to Documents Illustrative of English History in the Thirteenth and Fourteenth Centuries, by Henry Cole, p. xi.

CHAPTER IV.

THE OFFICIALS OF JOHN—HIS AUTHORITY REAL.

HAVING King John in the character of Justice-Itinerant, we must now inquire who were his ministers, privy-councillors, and coadjutors in the Government. They may bear comparison with any. Geoffrey Fitz-Peter, Earl of Essex, was at the head, as Chief Justiciary. He entered upon his office at the coronation, when he was girt with the sword of the county of Essex. He held the office until A.D. 1214, when he died. He was succeeded by Peter de Rupibus, Bishop of Winchester, who held the office at the time of King John's death. Peter de Rupibus had been Treasurer of Pictavia as long as Pictavia had any treasures to need a treasurer.

Hubert Walter, the foster-child and disciple of the great lawyer and crusader Randolph de Glanville, was Archbishop of Canterbury. He was appointed Chancellor at the great national council of the coronation-conclave adjournment, and held his office till the monks of Canterbury induced the Pope—Innocent III.—to remonstrate with him on holding such an office with the archbishopric of Canterbury, when he resigned the chancellorship in the first year of the reign. He was succeeded by Simon, Archdeacon of Wells, who, however, held the office for two or three years only, when he resigned to Hubert Walter, who held it to the day of his death, A.D. 1205. J. de Bromcestre, Archdeacon of Worcester, succeeded him as Chancellor, but only for a few months; for we find Walter Gray held the office in October A.D. 1207. In October

A.D. 1217 Richard de Marisco, Archdeacon of Richmond and Northumberland, surrendered the "Great Seal" at Ospreng.

On the 22d of December, it was given to the Lord Bishop of Winchester, Peter de Rupibus; Randulph de Nevill acting as his deputy. At the time of John's death, Peter de Rupibus was Chancellor.

King John very frequently changed his Chancellor, but rarely any other minister. Could the temper and dignity of position, in Geoffrey Fitz-Peter, Chief Justiciary, have anything to do with the former? Was the Earl of Essex too haughty for his fellow-ministers? Was he too despotic?

The position of Chief Justiciary was a declining one, while the position of Chancellor was a rising one. Was there clashing in point of precedency and dignity?

On this, Madox, in his "History and Antiquities of the Exchequer," observes:—"The chancellorship, from a small beginning, became in process of time an office of great dignity and pre-eminence. When the number of royal charters began to multiply, when the pleas and causes in the King's courts grew numerous, and when the grandeur of the High Justiciary came to decline, the power of the Chancellor waxed (as it seems) greater than it had formerly been; and (if I have observed right) the Chancellor's office received a considerable accession of power and dignity from the greatness of some of the persons who had borne it. In this conjecture, I have been somewhat the more confirmed, because I find *Paulus Æmylius* makes the like observation concerning the chancellors of France. And it seems the chancellors in other countries acquired by degrees the like addition of greatness and pre-eminence." [1]

William of Ely (Briwere) was Treasurer in England for the whole reign.

Hugo de Nevill was Chief Justiciary of the Forests for the

---

[1] Chapter ii., page 62.

greater portion of the reign—the latter part of it, if not the whole.

William Marshall, Earl of Pembroke, was Mareschall of England for the whole reign.

Robert, Earl of Leicester, was Seneschall or Steward of England. On Robert's death, Simon de Montfort, who had married one of his two daughters, took the title with the emoluments of the county of Leicester, and became Seneschall or High Steward of England. This nobleman's son married King John's daughter—the widow of William Marshall the younger.

John Gray, Bishop of Norwich, was Viceroy of Ireland.

Meiller Fitz-Henry was Judiciary of Ireland.

Peter de Stoke was a Baron of the Exchequer.

Hubert de Burgh, Earl of Kent, was a Baron of the Exchequer.

Peter de Maulay was a Baron of the Exchequer.

Robert Fitz-Roger was a Baron of the Exchequer.

Richard Ducket was a Baron of the Exchequer.

William de Saint Michael was a Baron of the Exchequer.

Henry Fitz-Gilbert was High Chamberlain of the Exchequer, or Master Sergeant of Wapontake.

Peter de Pateshull was a Baron of the Exchequer. All the Justices and Barons of the Jews' Court of Exchequer were Barons of the King's Court of Exchequer, and acted under, and in concert with, the above Barons of the King's Exchequer.

These ministers of the Jews' Court were appointed by the King, by letters under the "Great Seal." They exercised "jurisdiction in the affairs of *Judaism;* namely, in the accounts of that revenue, in pleas, upon contracts made with the *Jews;* in causes or questions touching their lands or chattels, their tallages, fines, forfeitures, and the like."[1]

These Justices of the Jews were a reality in the Government, as honourable members thereof; as the following example will

---

[1] Madox's History of the Exchequer, chap. 7, sect. 3, p. 234.

shew, which I take from Madox's History:—" In the reign of King John, Geoffrey Fitz-Peter (Earl of Essex, and Chief Justiciary of England) recovered certain houses in *Saint Laurence Jury, in London*, before Simon de Pateshull, and his fellows (Justices also) the Justices of the Jews."[1] My object here and now is not to go into the Jew question, but merely to shew that the ministers of the Crown were, in the reign of John, a reality, and not a sham.

" The Justices of the Jews recorded in the Great Exchequer, as there was occasion, things within their cognisance relating to the *Judaism.* They made their record or declaration, before the Barons of the Exchequer, in the case hereunder mentioned : and the Barons adjudged thereupon. In fine, the Justices of the Jews were looked upon to be members or officers of the Great Exchequer, and entitled to the privileges belonging to the persons resident there."[2]

There were also *Custodes Judæorum* in *Normandy*. King John, by writ-patent, commanded the Seneschall of *Normandy* and the *Custodes* of the *Jews* there, to forbear vexing wrongfully *Morell* the *Jew*, saving to the King, his rights and duties.[3]

In the fourth year of the reign of John, Reginald de Cornhull was Sheriff of Kent.

In the tenth year, William Briwerr, the Treasurer, was Sheriff of Wiltshire.

William Marshall was Sheriff of Gloucestershire for the whole reign.

In the fifteenth year of the reign, when Master Richard de Marisco exercised the functions of Chancellor, he only did it as deputy[4] to John Gray of Norwich, who was Chancellor, but absent abroad on a mission to the Court of Rome. On returning from Rome, he

---

[1] Madox, chap. 7, sect. 3, p. 235.   [2] Ibid., chap. 7, sect. 3, p. 236.
[3] Ibid., chap. 7, sect. 3, p. 237.
[4] Description of the Patent Rolls of the Tower of London, by Thomas Duffus Hardy, F.S.A., Introduction, p. 6.

died near Poictiers, November 1, A.D. 1214, and was buried in his own church of Norwich.

In the third year of the reign, William de Stutevill fined in £500 to have the custody of Yorkshire, as Sheriff, for as long a time as he should serve well, and should duly render the ferm and other issues of the county, — William de Perci and Walter de Bovinton being admitted under-sheriffs.

The counties of Dorset and Somerset were fined in £100, that William de Wroteham might be forester.[1]

William de Stutevill fined in £500 to have the custody of the county of Northumberland, as Sheriff, on the terms by which he held Yorkshire.

This same William de Stutevill fined CC marks to have the town of York in his hands, as Sheriff, yielding for it the ancient ferm, and paying no increment, as long as the King pleased to have it so.

In the seventh of John, A.D. 1205,—the time of Hubert Walter death, and the commencement of the great contest with Rome, on his successor,—William, Earl de Warenne, fined in one palfrey and one sore[2] hawk, that he might not be Justice of the Cinque Ports. This appointment, most honourable in itself, shews the confidence the King had in the integrity of the man. He was Chief Justiciary of the Jews' Exchequer at the time.

The men of the county of Lancaster fined in C marks, that Richard de Vernun might be their Sheriff.

Thomas de Muleton gave 500 marks and five palfreys, to have the county of Lincoln for seven years, yielding the ancient ferm, and the increment of CCC marks, added by Simon de Kyme, for the sheriffalty.

Fulk, son of Theobald, gave C and xx marks and iij palfreys, for the counties of Cambridge and Huntingdon as ferm for seven

---

[1] Madox, vol. i. p. 460.   [2] That is "soar" or hunting hawk

years, with the custody of Cambridge Castle, (as Sheriff,) rendering the usual ferm, and likewise C marks increment for every year.[1]

Robert de Turnham was Seneschall of Poictou, in the early part of the reign.

Thomas *Camerarius*, the "Clerk of our chamber," very often appears in the Tower writs as an important and confidential man of business.

Reginald de Cornhill was Sheriff of Kent, Middlesex, and London, on the breaking out of the Norman war. At the same time, Alan Young of Shoreham, Walter Scott, Vincent of Hastings, and Wimund of Winchelsea, were Barons of the Cinque Ports.

In the fifth year of John, A.D. 1203, Geoffrey Fitz-Peter de Stokes, Earl of Essex, and Chief Justiciary of England, was Sheriff of Hampshire.

William Plantagenet, the base-brother of the King, and son of fair Rosamond Clifford, was High Admiral of England, and one who rendered untold service to the Crown of England by destroying the French fleet at Swines, when Louis's army was on the heights of Boulogne waiting for transports for the invasion of England.

Martin Algais was Seneschall of Gascony and Perigord during the Norman war.

Hubert de Burgh, Earl of Kent, was Chief Justiciary immediately after the signing of Magna Charta, on June 15, 1215. Perhaps he succeeded Geoffrey Fitz-Peter in office on his death, A.D. 1214.

Hubert de Burgh could only have been in this office a short time, for at the time of the King's death, Peter de Rupibus held the office, along with the Chancellorship.

Brother Alan, Preceptor of the College of the Temple, A.D. 1205.

Geoffrey Plantagenet, brother of William, the High Admiral, was Archbishop of York, by purchase from Richard I.

---

[1] Madox, vol. i. p. 461.

He bought the sheriffalty of Yorkshire at the same time, and perhaps in one lot, of his base-brother, Richard I., who sold everything, repudiated the sale, kept the purchase-money, and then re-sold the sold commodity!

Reginald de Cornhill was the Government city banker of the reign of John, though the Master and Brothers of the Temple, near the Fleet Bridge, were the great European money-exchangers in England at the time. They were emphatically the Rothschilds and Barings of their day. The Master of this great money-exchanging fraternity, Amuerie, stood amongst the Barons of Runnemede, and on the King's side, on the 15th day of June, A.D. 1215.

Robert Fitz-Neel and William de Rughedon (Rushton in Northamptonshire?) were "companions" of Hugo de Nevill, Justiciary of woods and forests.

Gerard de Canvill was made Sheriff of Lincolnshire by letters patent, "habendum quamdiu nobis placuerit"—the common language of all feudal appointments.

On the same terms William de Botterell was made Sheriff of Cornwall.

William Briwerr was made Sheriff of the county of Southampton.

William Briwerr was also made Sheriff of the counties of Somerset and Dorset.

Geoffrey de Nevill was made Sheriff of Wiltshire.

Richard de Muscengros was made Sheriff of Gloucestershire— during the King's pleasure—as usual; for all these feudal or baronial appointments, without any exception, were made *to be held* during the King's pleasure; for the "habendum et tenendum quamdiu ipse nobis bene servierit." This "*quamdiu nobis placuerit,*" appears to have been the very life's blood of feudalism; for all grants of position in nationalities rested upon it.

In the twelfth year of this reign, Engelard de Cigony, Sheriff of Gloucestershire, acted as a Justiciary-Itinerant, in that county.

In the seventh year of the reign, the several Sheriffs of England made the views of their accounts at the Exchequer in Easter Term. Memoranda thereof are entered in a schedule annexed to the Great Roll of the Pipe, remaining in the Tower of London.[1]

William de Vernun, Earl of Devon, had his third penny paid to him by the Sheriff from his county.

In the ninth year of this reign, Fulk Fitz-Warin found two-and-forty sureties for a debt which he owed to the Crown.

We have a suggestive contrast in this Writ to what monk and priest prate of the King's thoughtless prodigality in public business.

Henry, the son of Hugo de Nevill, (Justiciary of the woods and forests,) was disseised of his land, for not observing the terms set him for payment of his fine.

This Hugo was a confidential minister for hunting and hawking; but if his son could not remember the rent-day, he must lose his farm at once. No cowardly collusion here.

Godfrey de Craucumbe was Sheriff of Oxfordshire.

Peter de Schidimor was Sheriff of Dorset and Somerset.

In the second year of his reign, John seized the barony and regality of Geoffrey Plantagenet, Archbishop of York, for certain debts due to the Crown, and for other reasonable causes; and this he did by the judgment of his court.[2]

In the sixth year of King John, Laurence, son of Alienor, fined to the King in Lx marks and one palfrey, that he might have his inheritance, the reshery of the Exchequer at Westminster, with the appurtenances.[3]

The office of Marshall of the Exchequer was in the gift of the Earl Marshall of England. This officer was sometimes styled Clerk of the Marshalsey of the Exchequer.

In the fourth of John, Thomas de Wyndesore was Pesour Ponderator, or Weigher of the Exchequer. This office stood in rank as a sergeanty only.

---

[1] Madox's History of the Exchequer, vol. ii. chap. 23, p. 158.
[2] Chart. 2, J. M. 11, dors.   [3] Mag. Rot. 6 John.

In the fifth and sixth of this reign, William de Warenne, Earl Warenne, Geoffrey de Norwich, and Thomas de Nevill, were Barons of the Exchequer and Justiciaries of the Jews.[1]

In the seventh year of King John, the Barons of the Exchequer were—Geoffrey Fitz-Peter, Earl of Essex, Chief Justiciary of England; William de Warenne, Justiciary of the Jews; Thomas de Nevill, of the Jews' Commission, Guardian, and Geoffrey de Norwich, " Custos Judæorum."

William, Earl Marshall.

Randulph, Earl of Chester.

William, Earl of Salisbury.

William, Earl of Arundel.

William Briwerr, the Treasurer. " Et alii Baronis."

In the eighth year of John, the Barons of the Exchequer were— John Gray, Bishop of Norwich; Geoffrey Fitz-Peter, Earl of Essex, Chief Justiciary; Robert Fitz-Roger (de Laci,) Simon de Pateshull.

In the tenth year of King John, the Barons of the Exchequer were—William Briwerr, the Treasurer; William, Archdeacon of Huntingdon; Gerard de Canvill, William de Bovenes, and other barons, the Chancellor.

In the thirteenth year of John, Saher de Quinci, Earl of Winchester; William, "Domini Regis Thesaurius;" Richard de Marisco, Deputy Chancellor for Walter Gray; William, Archdeacon of Huntingdon, and other barons.

In the fourteenth year of King John, the Barons of the Exchequer were—Geoffrey Fitz-Peter, " Justiciarius Regis;" Saher de Quinci, Earl of Winchester; William Briwerr, Treasurer; " *Magister*," Richard de Marisco; Peter de Rupibus, Bishop of Winchester.

Geoffrey de Marisco was Justiciary of Ireland in the latter years of the reign.

---

[1] Mag. Rot. 6 J., Rot. 8 b., Post Surreiam. Madox, vol. ii. chap. xxv. p. 315.

On the breaking out of the quarrel between King John and Pope Innocent III., the first step taken by the King was to make Roger de Laci Sheriff of Yorkshire and Lancashire. He was Sheriff of Lancashire when he died, A.D. 1209.

When I see the modern lists of modern Sheriffs, I point to A.D. 1206. Look here! compare the lists of King John with them, and judge!

Ferling the huntsman, who had $7\frac{1}{2}$d. a day, was the Master of the stag-hounds of the court. Thomas le Porkerer, also, was a huntsman in another department—the wild-boar hounds. He also had $7\frac{1}{2}$d. a day.

The chief "Berner" or bear-hunter, more properly bear-baiter, as we understand the terms of the sports of the field, had $7\frac{1}{2}$d. a day.

Robin de Samford, the chief coachman, had 2d. a day. This 2d. a day was a common allowance for officials of the court, and an honourable one, too, when skilled workmen of the cities and boroughs had only one halfpenny a day. The wolf-hunters of the royal establishment of Henry II. are not once named as existing, though Government paid 5s. for every wolf destroyed.

It were wearying to enumerate similarly the officials and representatives of John in Normandy and the other English possessions. We pass them over.

We may now give a few illustrations of the discipline in which even the highest ministers of the Crown were held by the King, which will go far to prove that John was truly master of his own position, and will also shew his relations to his officials generally. Take the following as an example.

A.D. 1211, or the thirteenth year of John, Geoffrey Fitz-Peter, Earl of Essex, the Chief Justiciary of England, paid a fine of two good Norway hawks, in good condition, and two tercells, (but he had on that account an acquittance by a brief of the King,) for licence given to Walter le Madine for conveying one hundred pounds of cheese beyond the dominions of the King.[1] This Geoffrey Fitz-Peter was the first minister of the Crown; he was head of the Exchequer, and yet he could not export one hundred pounds of cheese without complying with the terms laid down in the national tariff. Does this accord with the monkish story of the thirteenth century on the reign of John?

A Writ, issued against another minister of the Crown, Hugo de Nevill, the Justiciary of the woods and forests, and as such a Baron of the Exchequer, shews that no fraud, connivance, or conspiracy existed between King John and his ministers against the rights and liberties of the people of England. John was fully master of his ministers.

Hugo de Nevill returned a reckoning of 6000 marks for having the forgiveness of the King, for two prisoners taken in the castle of Carrickfergus, who were in his custody, and escaped—to wit, Hubert Hose and Richard de Alta Ripa; and for other reasons assigned in his charter, which was freed upon the Exchequer to be placed in the Treasury. The terms of payment being at the Feast of Saint Ylary, in the fourteenth year of the reign, £500; and at the Feast of Pascal Lamb next following, £500; and at the Feast of Saint John, in the fifteenth year of the reign, £500; and at the Feast of Saint Michael, £500; and in the following year, 2000 marks; and in the third year as much, at the same terms of payment. "And by this fine all his shall be acquitted, as well clergy as laicks; and he, Hugo and his heirs, for ever shall be acquitted from all reckonings and inquisitions and complaints and exactions which appertain to the forest, from the time when first he had (the department of) the woods and forests, even to the Feast of All Saints, in the year of the reign xiiij. And as, moreover, they may be acquitted, as well himself as his, for all receipts which they have received from the bishopric of Salisbury, whilst in the custody of the said Hugo, on which account he has

---

[1] Mag. Rot. 13 John, Rot. 6 b. Essex and Hertfordshire.

not answered, over and above what he may have paid to the Bishop."[1]

William, Earl Warenne, Earl of Surrey, was Chief Justiciary of the Jews, and was a very respectable, amiable man, but not equal to the exigencies of the time; he wanted nerve. The following writ points to a wavering, or a quailing before the power of France:—

"The Earl de Warenn hath sworn at the hand of the King, that he will stand in his council, and in the council of Geoffrey Fitz-Peter, Earl of Essex, and the Earl of Arundel, and others whom he might wish to call to that council: beyond the manor of Roynges, on that account, we have moreover given to him seisin of Doon Bardulph."[2]

The Earl de Warenne held his baronage by the manor of Roynges; but, in addition to this, he is to have Doon Bardulph, on his declaration of homage for the same. He is to stand by the King in his council, and in the council of the Chief Justiciary, the Earl of Essex, and of the Earl of Arundel, and others whom the King might wish to call to that council.

We have seen that King John took his coronation oath, on coming to the throne, May 27th, 1199, when the coronation gathering was turned into a great national council of the baronage of England, for the despatch of urgent business, at which prelates, earls, barons, and a multitude of other nobles (*subinfeudatories*) attended.

The second national council was held at Lincoln on November 22d, A.D. 1200, to which were summoned all the nobility, clerical as well as lay, of England and Scotland, but adjourned,—when William, King of Scotland, did homage, January 2d, A.D. 1201. A "colloquium" was held at Oxford, January 2d, 1204, when the Archbishop of Canterbury, bishops and abbots, and "magnates regni," were present.

---

[1] Magnus Rotulus, 14 J., Rot. 16, b. tit. The residue of the composition of Hugo de Nevill.
[2] Rotuli de Liberate, p. 92.

April 25th.—A "common council of barons" was held at Winchester.

A.D. 1205, May 15th.—A general assembly was held in London, consisting of "magnates terræ," archbishops, bishops, earls, barons, "omnesque fideles Angliæ."

A.D. 1207, Jan. 8th.—A council met in London, and, by prorogation, at Oxford, on Feb. 9th, at which were present the prelates of the Church, and the "magnates regni," bishops, abbots, priors, earls, barons, and other great men.

In May a convocation of the clergy assembled at St Albans.

Dec. 25th.—A "curiæ" was held in Winchester, "præsentibus magnatibus terræ."

A.D. 1208.—A National Council met in London, "Præsidente Archiepiscopo cum toto secta laicali."

A.D. 1210, Dec. 25.—A "curiæ" was held at Windsor, "præsentibus omnibus Angliæ magnatibus."

A.D. 1211, September.—A convention of prelates was held in London.

A.D. 1212, Dec. 25th.—A "curiæ" was held at York, "præsentibus comitibus et baronibus regni."

A.D. 1213, May 13th.—A convention was held at Dover. The King, and many earls and barons, and Pandulph, the Pope's legate, were present.

At this convention the King agreed to hold his kingdom in vassalage from the Pope, and to pay a yearly tribute of one thousand marks, (£25,000 in our money.)

This was done "communi consilio baronum."

July 20th.—A convention met at Winchester.

Other cliques and coteries assembled in church and monastery for seditious purposes; but as the "baronage" of England was broken *by the great council at Dover*, it needeth not that we recount them.

Moreover, the discussion of them belongs to the sequel.

According to Matthew Paris, John Gray, Bishop of Norwich,

was chaplain to the king, and President of the Council, when Hubert Walter died, A.D. 1205. When John Gray was appointed to the viceroyalty of Ireland, A.D. 1211, he was also, at the same time, made Chief Justiciary of Ireland.

William de Stutevill was, in the first year of the reign, appointed to the *"charge"* of Northumberland and Cumberland. During the whole reign there does not appear to have been any Earl of Northumberland or Earl of Cumberland. As William de Stutevill was a Baron of the Exchequer, could he have been appointed as Justiciary of the Border counties? A man in his position would scarcely have been appointed in this *"vague"* manner to such a trust, as Vice-count or Sheriff.

Let your accepter of the historical John as opposed to the actual John meditate upon the roll of names submitted in this chapter. How does the charge of employing "low-born" men, "low-mannered," "vile," "weak," &c., &c., vanish in the light of the men who really filled the "high places" in his reign. If we measure the masterdom of Elizabeth and Cromwell by the names who gathered in willing allegiance around them, why refuse the same verdict in the case of John? Instead of the "gossip" and malignant "evil-speaking" of monkish "chroniclers" and priestly slanderers, let your "modern HISTORIANS" (so-called) produce the names of weight and worth that were not found at the court of the actual John. We make bold to say that, unless suborned by the deflecting claims of another sovereignty—that of the Pope—all the brain and worth of England recognised John as a MAN in the highest sense of the abused word; for many "men," "modern historians," and the like, are old women.

CHAPTER V.

DIFFICULTIES IN NORMANDY AND DEATH OF ARTHUR.

DOMESTIC troubles were not all that gathered around the throne of John, even thus early. We have seen that he became King by designation of his brother Richard—that he was unanimously "*elected*"—that proclamation was made by the Archbishop of Canterbury, who was also Chancellor, as the voice of the "Great Council"—and that the Great Council spake for the nation—"*ab universitate regni.*" But intrigue was abroad. His nephew, Arthur, found one ready to urge his claims upon the succession. Married—while a mere boy—to Mary, daughter of Philip, King of France, his father-in-law, wily and lustful of power, sought, if not to secure England to Arthur, at least to recover for his own family the English possessions in France, which amounted at this time to one-fifth of the whole kingdom.

Philip, cognisant of the impetuosity and vigour of John—as all his contemporaries, where we can interrogate them, seem to have been,—a very striking commentary on your modern lavishment of "feeble," "unpatriotic," "pusillanimous," and the like, upon his memory!—went about his project dexterously. He essayed to obtain by flattery what he well knew never would be surrendered to bravado.

He invited John to the French court as an honoured guest. The invitation was accepted. Roger de Wendover, the chronicler, informs us, that on November the 21st, A.D. 1200, the English King held an assembly at Lincoln, at which William, King of

Scots, attended, with all the clergy and laity of both kingdoms, on which occasion Saint Hugh was buried on the 24th with solemn pomp, the two kings being pall-bearers; after which the King of England, along with his queen, repaired to Guildford, where they kept their Christmas, and distributed festive garments amongst the guests of the court.

April 30th, 1201, the King was at Tewkesbury, where he issued a proclamation for all his earls, barons, vavasours, and freeholders, who owed him military allegiance and service, to join him at Portsmouth, where he intended to keep the festival of Whitsuntide of 1201.

On the appointed day of meeting, many of the nobles obtained permission to remain in England, on paying to the King as a fine two marks of silver for each 'scutcheon.

On Monday, May 14th, 1201, the King and Queen embarked, and, after a stormy voyage, reached Normandy, where they remained nearly thirty-one months. This sojourn in Normandy for this long period, and while war was fiercely raging between England and France, does not indicate the coward on the part of King John—eh?

Shortly after the arrival of the King of England, the two Kings of England and France held a conference near to the Isle of Andelys, the result of which was a truce of peace. As one seal of it, it was mutually agreed that if either of them should violate the terms, the barons who were the sureties should be absolved from all fealty to their lord and master.

Hereupon John went on a visit with Philip to Paris, when, with politic courtesy, the French king gave up his royal palace to his English brother; himself taking up his residence in an inferior house elsewhere. Having been shewn every possible honour, John took his departure, and proceeded to Chinon.

Advancing to 1202, we find John keeping the festival of Christmas at Argentum, in Normandy, and that during the following Lent, another interview and conference took place between the two

Kings of France and England, near to the castle of Guletune, when Philip urged John—the vizard being now half-lifted or half-slipped off—to surrender to his nephew, Arthur, Count of Brittany, all his possessions in France, as vassal of the King of France—namely, Normandy, Tours, Anjou, and Poictou. The answer was swift and sharp—No!

Enraged, the French king made a sudden attack upon the castle of Butavant, in which he was successful, and razed it to the ground. Marching quickly thither, he took the town of Angi, with the castle of Linno and other fortresses. He met with a check at the castle of Radepunt, which he besieged for eight days, but had to abandon in confusion on the approach of John himself.

Turning to Gournage he pierced the embankment of the lake, and thereby flooded the town to such an extent that the garrison fled, and thus lost the town to John.

War was now commenced in terrible earnest between the two kingdoms and their dependencies. Anjou, Touraine, and Maine with Poictou, including thus nearly all Eleanor's dower, declared, under French influences, for Arthur. Normandy and Guienne adhered firmly to John. The queen-mother was a tower of strength to her son. History has few nobler spectacles to shew than this leonine-hearted woman defending her castle against the chivalry of France, with a head whitened by the snows of eighty winters.

Stimulated by the Pope, Philip introduced Arthur as an actor in the war. He sent him, with a military force of two hundred chosen knights, to take possession of the inheritance to which he made a legal claim as Duke of Brittany.

With this force siege was laid to Mirabeau, a fortified place near Poictiers, held by Eleanor, mother of King John. It was youth against age—a man, if man he is to be called, against a true and noble woman. The town was soon taken, when the octogenarian commanderess had to retreat to the keep of the castle, and there she defended herself as a lioness her cubs, until her son hastened to her rescue—she having despatched messengers to inform him of her perilous position.

Quick as lightning—for all the actual, as contrasted with your modern historical, John's movements were prompt and his decisions instant, a trait splendidly recognised by Shakespeare, as witness the motto on our title-page—John set out with a strong force, and, travelling night and day, accomplished the distance in an incredibly short space of time.

Their first knowledge of his movements was his own approach. The two little armies,—little comparatively,—closed in mortal conflict, and fighting foot to foot onward, the troops of both entered the castle, when a most sanguinary struggle took place on the esplanade. Victory declared itself for John. The surviving besiegers were taken prisoners. Dead or as prisoners, the whole roll of two hundred, with Arthur at their head, were accounted for. The chroniclers tell us that Arthur was taken to Falaise, and there executed in private. They furnish full histories of the manner and circumstances of the death, actions, and speeches on each side. Let the curious turn to Roger de Wendover, Matthew of Westminster, Walter of Coventry, with a host of others, as Boquet, Hemingford, Knighton, Peignot, and their copyists, down to David Hume;[1] but the whole is as mendacious, or veracious, as you will, as the speeches that adorn Tacitus. Sentimentalists pule and whimper over the "innocent youth!" Ay, but that youth had already been made a tool, and might, certainly would, be used to keep up a never-ending controversy.

King John needs no defender in this matter; but indeed it remains very uncertain how Arthur died or was put to death.[2]

---

[1] David Hume's History of England. It is extraordinary that the number of houses in several cities and towns stated by Hume, as extracted from Domesday, is incorrect in every instance. Henshall's History of the County of Kent, page viii.

[2] The History of Gervace, the Monk of Canterbury, informs us that John the King was suspected of slaying his nephew, Arthur, with his own hands. Collectanea Lelandi, 8vo, 1770, vol. i. p. 264.

A.D. 1400

Henry de Knighton [1] affirms that John caused him to be murdered by Peter de Malo Lacu, one of his esquires, to whom, as a reward, was given the heiress of the barony of Mulgrief to wife.

Leland, in his "Collectanea," says:—"Some say that Arthur, nephew of King John, died in prison at Rouen, and others that he was drowned on shipboard, or when passing from one ship to another while a prisoner, the plank having been placed insecurely on purpose by a sailor."[2] Roger de Wendover merely states that, on Arthur's being sent a prisoner to the "New Tower" at Rouen, he suddenly disappeared.[3] Ralph Brooke, York Herald's baronage, narrates that, being made prisoner at the castle of Merebel, in Normandy, he was conveyed to Rouen Castle, where, leaping from the wall with intent to escape, he was drowned in the ditch, A.D. 1202;[4] while David Hume narrates that John went in the night-time in a boat to Rouen, and that he invited Arthur to take a seat therein, and that he stabbed Arthur where he sat; and then, fastening a stone to the body, sank it in the Seine.[5]

He must be a no less foolhardy than uncritical student of history who will found a charge to blot the memory of John, on so conflicting and entangled a narrative, as these statements and counterstatements shew all the accounts and theories of the death of Arthur to be. And yet writers have been found to echo Knighton's audacious and outrageous designanation of "murder."

Beyond all question, Arthur was tried in private for high treason, and executed; and I hold this on the ground of the unimpeachable character of the Chancellor Hubert, and his foster-son, John Gray, to say nothing of William Marshall, Peter de Rupibus, and a score more connected with the court and its ministry at the time.

Let the *private execution* be accepted, on the strength of the character of the ministers of the Crown, and then it will be seen

---

[1] Vol. ii. folio, col. 2414.
[2] Leland's Collectanea, vol. ii. p. 534.
[3] Roger de Wendover's Chronicle, vol. ii. p. 205, 12mo edition.
[4] Folio, 1602, p. 80.
[5] Hume's History of England, vol. ii. chap. xi. p. 48.

that it was no mere private or personal feeling that dictated it, but stern necessity—to strike at Philip, and at the Pope through him; for, as every reader of history knows, Innocent III. had flung himself into the quarrel, on the side of Arthur.

Many of the other prisoners were names of renown. They included the Count de la Marche, the vice-counts of Limoges, Tours, and Lusignan. But none was led to scaffold or block. They were degraded with gyves at their wrists, and then taken to various prisons in England.

On tidings of the death of Arthur reaching Philip, he summoned John to appear before him, as his vassal, to answer for the "murder" of his nephew. With scorn for scorn, the King of England tossed back the insolent summons. Vassalage, as a formality of holding "lands and possessions" in France, was not to be elevated into jurisdiction over his acts as a monarch "at war." No token yet of that pusillanimity the slanderers of John would have us accept as his ground-character! Nor will it ever appear.

Philip proclaimed John to be a traitor to the crown of France, and, as such, deprived, by forfeiture to his superior lord, the King of France, of all his dominions in France. The proclamation was hardly made, when Philip proceeded to take possession of his new inheritance.

Rouen and many towns of Normandy were seized, and soon to these were added Maine, Touraine, Anjou, and Poictou.

It was a crisis to test the "stuff" of which John was made. The trial was all the greater, in that his English subjects, to whom he had a right to look, refused to aid him in these "foreign wars." It were mirthful, if it were not so mournful, to read the "improvement" (if the old Puritan sermon term may be allowed) made of this treasonous refusal.

Some impute great virtue to the English nobility, and interpret their lukewarmness to have been the detestation of the "murder" of Arthur! All the cowardice of the earls, barons, knights, vavasours, and freeholders, ay, and the prelates of England, during the whole reign of John, has sheltered itself behind the alleged heinousness of the "murder" (not execution) of the French King's boy son-in-law, and French educated vassal! Contemptible perversion of facts! Why malign John and defend Alfred? We have seen that the great Saxon passed four nephews, and one niece, in the succession to the throne of England; and every one knows that Edward the Elder, eldest son of Alfred, had to meet in the field Ethelwald, son of Ethelred, and this under the Danish flag. Elfleda, sister to the king, and daughter of Alfred, engaged the Danes with Ethelwald at their head, and Ethelwald was slain; but who ever heard of the "murderess" Elfreda? No! that is not the way to read history. The true solution of the pigeon-livered "refusal" lies here: Innocent III. was Pope, and the earls, barons, knights, prelates of England, save a few noble exceptions, were unpatriotic cowards, who dared not oppose the power of Italy, even when exerted against their own England. Fittingly does the old poet make John say—

> "My people, frighten'd with the roaring threat
> Of wrathful Bulles, to England daily sent,
> Their due alleageance to their Lord forget;
> Th' inglorious Peeres, as if the gouvernment
> Had been transferr'd from *John* to *Innocent*,
> Did shrinke from me, and would not by me stand,
> For th' impeacht priviledge of our free land." [1]

Events thickened. The queen-mother Eleanor, at the age of eighty years, defended the tower within the city of Mirabeau for her illustrious son. Philip was "in the field" with a large army before the castle of Angues, which he harassed by his engines placed around it, his *pœtrariæ* and *balustæ* being applied to the towers and walls for fifteen days. The garrison within the walls worked their levers for throwing darts, javelins, and arrows, with equal energy and ardour.

---

[1] A Mirour for Magistrates, "King John," p. 690.

It was during this memorable siege that the news of the capture of Arthur and his little army reached Philip.

The forces were at once withdrawn, the siege raised, the retiring troops, in vexation and spite, destroying by fire and sword the whole country,—even monasteries and churches falling before them in their retreat to Paris. Having reached his capital, the French king remained inactive during the year.

A.D. 1203. King John spent his Christmas at Caen, in Normandy, on which occasion many adventures took place between the two armies, Philip inflicting as much damage as he could; taking castles in the province, as Montfort and Ruyl, and marching at will across it. John seeing his provinces thus ravaged, set sail for avenging aid for England. He landed on Saint Nicholas's day at Portsmouth, after having been abroad again at least nineteen months. Immediately—and with that contradiction of modern history that all the real John's actions give—he set himself with energy and resoluteness to collecting supplies for the future campaign in France. For then, not invasions of England by France, but of France from our "inviolate island" was the "thing of dread." His whole soul was stirred within him. He appealed to the ignoble "nobles." They hung back. He charged the earls and barons of England with desertion of his cause, and righteously taunted them with the successes of Philip in Normandy through their defection. He was not a man to be put down. He would rule as well as "reign"—govern as well as fill the throne. If they would not go with him, their "substance" must. He levied a tax or fine of one-seventh on all their moveables. This impost he exacted "by law" through the writs of his ministers and their tax-collecting agents; his right hand being Geoffrey Fitz-Peter, his Chief Justiciary of England. The Church also was made to contribute in a like proportion, both conventual and parochial, and this through Hubert, Archbishop of Canterbury, and his assistants.

A.D. 1204. John kept his Christmas at Canterbury, Hubert

Walter, the Archbishop, entertaining the King as his guest. Thereafter the King and his barons repaired to Oxford for a conference or council, when supplies were voted for the war in Normandy. The vote was two marks and a half for each "'scutcheon," or £1, 13s. 4d.; the bishops and abbots representing the Church gave a pledge of a like sum, to be raised upon their "'scutcheons."

During all this trying period, upwards of a year, Philip was as busily employed with his forces in Normandy as ever King John could be. Now we find him trying persuasive promises of reward, and now threats of a terrible vengeance, with the stout-hearted Englishmen who held its towns and castles in brave fealty to the standard of the island. Throughout nearly the entire year, the castle of the Rock of Andely was besieged. The story of the siege reads like a romance. The wall was undermined; again and again breaches were made; but ever behind the breach stood a living wall of Englishmen, headed by the noble Roger de Laci, Constable of Chester, and one of the twenty-five barons of Randulph Blandeville, Earl of Chester. Sad to tell, the stock of provisions became completely exhausted, when he and his brave comrades mounted their horses and sallied from the castle.

The little "handful" of brave men was overpowered, and either killed or taken prisoners. Andely fell on the 6th of March 1204, when Roger de Laci was for his bravery held prisoner "on parole." I fear King John had very few Roger de Lacis in his dominions at this time.[1]

The 'heroes' had all been killed or confiscated out of England in the wars of the grandchildren of William the Conqueror, or

---

[1] Leland, in his Collectanea, vol. i. p. 293, quotes from the Book of Annals of John Bevyer the following: "And he (the King) restored to Roger de Laci, Constable of Chester, his castle of Pontefract; his son and heir first being received as a hostage." The branch of the Laci family located at Pontefract had got into trouble and disgrace, ending in confiscation of the barony of Pontefract Castle, by the part they took in the quarrels of the children and grandchildren of William the Conqueror; for in those family strifes all the adherents of the losing party were sure to suffer disgrace, with confiscation. The Lacis had been on the losing side, and so lost Pontefract.

drafted as Crouch-backs to Palestine, there to fall before the gates of Jerusalem at the hands of the infidel, for the sins of Richard I., committed against heaven and his father; and, with very few exceptions, there were nothing left among the "nobles" but traitors and cowards. Perhaps at no time was there a period in baseness equal to this in English history; for, on the one hand, there was manly intrepidity and firm resolve to free these realms from all foreign dictation and interference, temporal or spiritual, on the part of the King and his ministers; and, on the other, a priest-ridden, cowl-wearing, absolution-loving peerage, baronage, and free-tenancy. These wars in Normandy testify to this, and the whole baronage career of the eighteen years of John. It was the age of traitors; it was the age of cowards! for even MAGNA CHARTA itself was but a French conspiracy, as shall duly appear.

On the fall of the Rock-castle of Andely, and its right noble defender, Roger de Laci, being taken prisoner, all the holders of castles in the transmarine territories of John, together with the citizens and other subjects, sent messengers to England to inform their King of the precarious position in which Normandy was placed, and that the time for conditional surrender agreed upon with the King of France was nearly expired; for they had agreed to a surrender if not "delivered" by their King, and the hostages redeemed.

John was in the midst of his harassments with his barons, and had to return answer, that he could as yet give no assistance; but, kingly-natured, stout-hearted as he was, urged all to do the best they could to keep possession. It was sadly impossible. The whole of Normandy, Tours, Anjou, and Poictou, with all their cities and castles, excepting only the castles of Rochelle, Thomars, and Morz, fell under the dominion of Philip, A.D. 1204. King John kept his Christmas at Tewkesbury, but scarcely remained there above one day, so anxious was he in preparing for the Spring campaign in Normandy. His resources were now somewhat adequate, and, like a lion in the leash, he was eager to grapple with his enemy.

He proceeded to Portsmouth, where a large fleet was collected for carrying over his army to Normandy. The King found, on his arrival at Portsmouth, that his knights and men-at-arms professed to have exhausted all their resources, and that they refused to embark unless they received wages for their services. John was profoundly moved with this fresh desertion of him by his "feudatories." In sadly bitter and vehement words he reproached them, that they, "knights" of their "sovereign lord," should plead for the hire of mercenaries. Undeterred by this military defection—this feudal insubordination and cowardice at the bidding of the Pope's representative (as by and by will appear)—John embarked with a few of his own personal servants only, anticipating that he should shame the traitors into a sense of duty. Thus abandoned, he arrived at Jersey in three days. He there waited the arrival of his feudatories, the " glory of chivalry " (shame !) but waited in vain; for not one knight of them all followed. The King, filled with disappointment, returned in anger to England, and assembled some forces to punish these traitors and cowards; but the Archbishop of Canterbury, the French-fealtied Archbishop, (for the noble Hubert had died in the interval,) Stephen Langton, pressed upon him to let the defection, if defection it were, pass. Beyond all gainsaying, the Archbishop was the instigator of the whole miserable thing. Shame to tell, as Roger de Wendover informs us, barons and prelates alike refused to "accompany him," preferring to pay the fine. It was nothing to them that a crown-jewel, such as Normandy, was being filched from England. They had other allegiance far—to Philip himself, and to Philip's iron-willed master, Pope Innocent III. So far well was it, that the fines of the earls, barons, knights, and religious men amounted to a very considerable sum. John, not easily to be driven from his purpose, persevered in his avenging plans, when the Archbishop assumed more than persuasion, more than dissuasion, and from entreaties hinted threats.

Again, at Whitsuntide, in the year A.D. 1206, King John assembled another large army at Portsmouth, and, taking ship on the 1st of June, (according to the Itinerary,) landed on the 8th of the same month at Rochelle; when, being well received by the inhabitants, who promised supplies of money and assistance, he marched forward with more confidence, and subdued a great portion of the country.

After a while he arrived before the castle of Montauban, in which his warlike enemies were shut up, to which he laid siege, and took, after fifteen days of continued assaults, from petrariæ, balistas, and slings, at which warfare the English soldiers were quite at home, for they scaled the walls and exchanged blows on the ramparts with their enemies. According to Roger de Wendover, the castle was taken on the day of Saint Peter ad Vincula, (Tuesday, August 1, 1206.)

This fortress was exceedingly strong—so strong that Charlemagne could not subdue it after a seven years' siege. King John's sojourn in Normandy on this occasion extended over a period of six months.

For six years after the above sojourn John never visited France, he being fully occupied in England in repelling the treasons of Stephen Langton and his tools, the agents of the French King.

No sooner were the documents for the surrender of England to the Pope duly signed, and mass duly said—of all which more anon—than John repaired, *immediately repaired*, to Portsmouth,[1] where his "knights and army were expected to be in readiness to cross to Poictou," the charge of the kingdom, in the meantime, being given to Geoffrey Fitz-Peter, his Chief Justiciary, and Peter de Rupibus, Bishop of Winchester, the Treasurer of Poictou.

The King had no sooner arrived at Portsmouth than there

---

[1] Roger de Wendover, vol. ii. p. 274, A.D. 1213.

came to him "an immense number of knights," complaining that, during their long stay there, they had spent all their money, and that, therefore, unless they were supplied with money "*from the treasury*," they could not follow him. On this, in a noble rage, the King embarked with his few attendants only, and landed at Guernsey in a day or two; but had to return to Corfe Castle, according to the Itinerary, on Friday, August 9th, 1213. The barons and knights, the chivalry of England—they returned home, and thus defeated the expedition for that time.

John, nothing daunted by this defection of his barons and knights in August, set himself to work at raising troops by other means than the chivalric feeling of feudal land-tenures—I suppose, by bounties paid at the Exchequer, of which I have met with hundreds of instances in the Tower Records, with even the granting of feudal tenures on the national revenue, to be paid half-yearly, as to state pensioners. Writs upon the Exchequer were the main instruments in the hands of royalty for raising troops, when feudal land-tenures ceased to be binding on the honour of the old nobility.

By some means or other, beyond the influence of feudal land-tenures, a large army was again assembled at Portsmouth in the February following, A.D. 1214, with which the King set sail on the 9th for Rochelle, where he arrived on the 15th of the same month, when many barons of Poictou came and swore fealty to him.

In about three months John wrote to his Justiciaries in England, informing them of his great success in Normandy, and how he had taken the castle of Mervaut, belonging to Geoffrey de Lusignan, by force, after one assault, lasting from early morn to one o'clock at noon; that two days afterwards, on Whitsunday, he laid siege to another castle of Geoffrey's, called "Novent," in which Geoffry and his two sons were shut up; and how, after three days of working of the petrariæ, the Count de la March came to inform him that Geoffrey threw himself, with his two sons, his castle, and everything, on his mercy; that, at Parthenay, the Counts de la March and Augi came to him with the aforesaid Geoffrey de Lusignan, and did homage, and swore fealty to him.

On this occasion King John granted to the Count de la March the favour of his own daughter in marriage, in fulfilment of a former treaty with the Count's son. All this once more shews anything but *coward* in King John—eh!

About this time John led his army from Poictou into Lesser Britain, and there stayed three days and three nights; and when before Nantes, threatening to attack it, the knights and citizens came out to the bridge, and gave battle to the English army. John gained the victory, and took twenty knights prisoners, amongst whom stood the son and heir of Robert de Drus, uncle of the French King. This knight the King loaded with chains, and took away with him. After this, John marched his army to the castle of Rocheau Maine, and laid siege to it, but was obliged to retire before the French army, through the defection of the barons and knights of Poictou, who refused to meet the French army in a pitched battle. Immediately after this, the English army of Flanders entered Poictou, and devastated the country in a relentless manner, William, Earl of Salisbury, being at their head. The French King marched against them with all the forces he could collect of earls, barons, knights, and soldiers, horse and foot, with the commoners of the cities and towns. An engagement took place, and the English had the worst of it. A truce was thereupon signed between the two kings for five years, when John returned to England, after an absence of eight months, never more to visit France.

To England, Eleanor's dower, along with Normandy, was lost for ever, leaving only the Channel Islands, Jersey, Guernsey, Alderney, and Sark, substantial evidences of the original possessions.

In the whole of this disastrous conflict for a mother's dower, I have looked for symptoms of cowardice or irresolution in King

John, but I have looked in vain, although the time occupied by the dispute and conflict extended over fourteen years. What saith my reader? Is the real and actual John not a very different man and King from what history (so-called) has made him?

CHAPTER VI.

THE DEATH OF HUBERT WALTER, ARCHBISHOP OF CANTERBURY.

ON the 13th of July, A.D. 1205, Hubert Walter, Archbishop of Canterbury, died, to the irreparable loss both of the King and the kingdom. This great man, crusader with Richard I., statesman, priest, lawyer, engineer, and philosopher, was the real moving power of the state during the first seven years of the reign of John. He was foster-child of the Chief Justiciary of Henry II., Randulph de Glanville, the English lawyer; and he in turn brought up as his own son John Gray, the Bishop of Norwich, and successor as a statesman in the heart and confidence of his master, King John. It would be impossible in the few pages we can spare, to give any adequate narrative of the doings of this man in the early years of the reign of John. I hope another will one day tell his great life-story worthily and proportionately.

The disforesting of the Forest of Middlesex was, for the citizens of London, a very great work of his, as it enabled building land to be bought and sold outside the walls of the city. In his time the Cinque Ports first enjoyed their franchises. The city of London exchanged its bailiffs for Mayor and Sheriff.[1]

In the year 1200 the Bishop of Durham obtained a charter to hold fairs annually at Howden and Northallerton, in which we have the origin of those two great horse fairs held in the above towns at this day. In A.D. 1211 the citizens of London began to encompass their ancient city wall with a deep ditch, 200 feet wide.

---

[1] Harding's Chronicle, Collectanea, vol. iii. p. 430.

A charter was granted for holding a fair at Skipton at Whitsuntide; and, in the year 1200, another to Robert de Turnham, for an extra day, or third day, on the 26th of July, for the fair at Doncaster, the former fair being held on the vigil of St James the Apostle and on the following day. Under this minister King John coined sterling money for his subjects, he being the first king of England since the Norman conquest who had done this. It was through the influence of Hubert Walter, too, that an excise of wine was enacted, to keep the wine merchant to his just measure, and to preserve the customer from having his twelve quarts of wine measured out into fourteen or sixteen bottles, as is now the case in the wine trade.

The excise of bread also was enacted through his influence in 1200, and if another excise could be enacted for 1864, a great boon would be given to the public in the assurance of a full supply of wheaten flour, instead of pea-meal, bean-meal, plaster of Paris, or burnt bones!!!! For a specimen of Hubert Walter's acts and deeds, read the following :—

Concessimus.—" The King to all who desire to have burgages in the town of Liverpool greeting.—Know ye, that *we have granted* to all persons who have taken burgages at Liverpool, that they may have in the town of Liverpool, all the liberties and free customs enjoyed by any free burgh on the sea coast; and therefore we command you that ye may go thither securely, and in our peace, to take your burgages and dwell therein; and in testimony hereof, we transmit to you these our letters patent.—Witness Simon de Pateshull, at Winchester, on the 28th day of August, in the ninth year of our reign." [1]

May we not consider this letter patent to be the authority for the enfranchisement of the borough of Liverpool, in the ninth year of the reign of King John, A.D. 1207?

King John, through the support of this great man, and his

---

[1] Introduction to Rotuli Littcrarum Patentium folio, p. 6.

disciple and successor, John Gray, became the most enlightened and patriotic of England's kings. The death of this minister caused such disasters in the realm as have never been known since, and this through the firmness of the King, in electing a suitable successor, in John Gray, to the Archbishopric of Canterbury. John staked his peace of mind, yea, his very existence as a king, upon the appointment of a suitable successor to HUBERT WALTER, and lost; and received his reward, from an ungrateful people—the brand of cowardice. I have it not in my power to follow all the enlightened policy of Hubert Walter. He was a large-hearted, patriotic, noble man.

CHAPTER VII.

ELECTION OF A SUCCESSOR TO HUBERT WALTER, ARCHBISHOP OF CANTERBURY.

WE now approach the most crucial event of the reign, in estimating John's real character; the appointment of John de Gray, the disciple and foster-child, friend, and Minister of State, under the late Archbishop—to the Archbishopric of Canterbury. This was emphatically the King's own appointment, and one on which he determined to stake his crown, and, if need be, his life.

To shew the mood in which the King viewed the rising storm of priestly opposition, he at once made Roger de Laci, Constable of Chester, High Sheriff of Yorkshire and Lancashire. This occurred in the year 1206; and the following letters-patent, dated Nov. 3, 1208, shew that the appointment was not made by one who was "cowardly," "unstable," as your histories (so-called) maunder and babble:—

"The King to Roger (de Laci), Roger de Montbegon, Robert de Gresley, and William Butler," &c.—"We beg of you, to give us the assistance of your people in Lancashire, to make the fosses round our castle at Lancaster, and our thanks will be due unto you therefore, since we do not ask it by custom, but this time even of your favour. Witness ourself at Clarendon on the 3d day of November 1208."

Blockheads talk of cowardice and instability of character! The foster-son of the great lawyer, Randolph Glanville, is dead, and King John, John Gray, and Roger de Laci, are bent upon turning the world upside down upon the choice of his successor!

John Gray, or de Gray, had been consecrated Bishop of Norwich, A.D. 1200, or the second year of the reign. For the first six years of the reign, till Hubert died on the 13th of July A.D. 1205, he had been a "Minister" of State. Moreover, he was the uncle, preceptor, friend, and adviser of Walter Gray.

On Hubert's death being known, the King immediately sent an express to York, where John Gray was, on the King's business, commanding him to repair to Canterbury immediately, there to be installed into the vacant Archbishopric.

Gray obeyed the King's summons, and repaired to Canterbury, where he was elected Archbishop of Canterbury by the Benedictine monks, although they had, in the secrecy of the night, privately elected their Sub-Prior.

The suffragan bishops of the Church of Canterbury also claimed the right of election, when the dispute was referred by both parties to the Pope. The Pope decided in favour of the Prior and Convent of the Church of Canterbury, as to the right of election *for the future*, both parties being wrong in the *present instance*.[1]

After many law proceedings in production of witnesses and affidavits at the Court of Rome, the Pope, by the advice of his cardinals, decreed that neither monks nor bishops at Canterbury should have any share in the election of their Archbishop, but that the right of election should rest with the Pope alone.[2]

On annulling the above elections, the Pope went to work at once, and made Cardinal Stephen Langton, a Professor of Theology at the University of Paris, where he had resided for twenty-three years, Archbishop of Canterbury. The monks were ordered to elect this man, but held out against the order; till the threat of excommunication brought them to obedience to the Pope, when they completed the election of Stephen Langton, as ordered.[3]

No sooner was the French priest elected Archbishop of Canterbury, by order of Pope Innocent the Third, than letters were sent

---

[1] Roger de Wendover, A.D. 1206, vol. ii. p. 219.
[2] Ibid., p. 237.
[3] Ibid., p. 238.

from the Pope to King John, requesting him to receive with kindness the newly-elected Cardinal Archbishop.

When the King received these letters demanding this recognition of the French cardinal for his Archbishop of Canterbury, he was exceedingly enraged, and charged the monks of Canterbury with treachery, and cowardice in giving their votes in three elections.[1]

The king thereupon sent two " cruel and inhuman knights," with armed attendants, to expel the monks from Canterbury, or else to consign them to capital punishment. The order was obeyed at once by this armed party, who entered the monastery with drawn swords, and in the King's name, ordered the Prior and monks to leave England immediately, as traitors to the crown. This must be done at once, or they would instantly fire the monastery and adjoining offices. The threat had the desired effect upon the monks, who at once embarked for Flanders, where they were honourably entertained at the Abbey of St Bertinus, and other monasteries. This took place July 14, 1207.

As soon as the monks were gone, John sent messengers with letters to the Pope, complaining of the conduct of his Holiness in placing a French priest in Canterbury as Archbishop thereof, to the annulling of the previous election of his Minister, John Gray, and this too, without any notice having been given to himself, as King of England.

Pope Innocent replied with a good deal of priestly sophistry, but yet the usual determination of your priest in power—that the election of Stephen Langton must stand good to the exclusion of John Gray.

As King John could by no possibility submit to this dictation in so momentous a national matter as the election of the Archbishop of Canterbury, without his concurrence or knowledge; the Pope sent orders to William of London, Eustace of Ely, and

---

[1] Roger de Wendover, p. 240.

Mauger of Winchester, to go to the King about this election business, and try to persuade him to submit to the Pope's dictation in the matter, and threaten him with a national interdict if he should be found to be rebellious; and still more, to threaten John personally with a heavier infliction from priestly power if he still went on in his unsubmissive career.

The Bishops of London, Ely, and Winchester, as Pope's legates, went to King John, and entreated him to recall the banished Archbishop and the monks of Canterbury to their Church. What was King John's reply? He stopped the legates short in their discourse, and, mad with rage, broke forth in words of blasphemy against the Pope, and against his cardinals, swearing that if they or any other priests dared to lay his dominions under an interdict, he would immediately send all prelates, clerks, and ordained persons to the Pope, and confiscate all their property.

He peremptorily ordered the bishops to withdraw at once from his sight, if they wished to save themselves from bodily chastisement.

The bishops withdrew, and on Monday morning, in Passion week, laid a general interdict on the whole of England.

From that Monday morning, all church services ceased in England: the bodies of the dead were carried out of cities and towns, and buried in roads and ditches without prayers or the attendance of priests.[1] As soon as the interview closed, William of London, Eustace of Ely, Mauger of Winchester, Jocelyn of Bath, and Giles

---

[1] Can there be any doubt but that many of the remains of human beings constantly brought to light in England, are the representatives of the excommunicated dead, during those six years of John's reign? Only last year a number of bodies, properly and regularly laid, according to the prescribed direction of east and west, were found at Guildford in Surrey. Guildford was an important place A.D. 1207, and might be under the especial control of the Archbishop of the Convent of Canterbury, or his suffragan bishops, or the monks and Prior of the Benedictine order of Canterbury; if so, not a person dying at Guildford, between A.D. 1207, and A.D. 1213, would be allowed the honours of a Christian burial in consecrated ground. Much the worse they were of the impudent ban!

of Hereford, left England as quickly as they could, to avoid any accident from the King's violence.

King John, nothing daunted by this priestly assumption, but greatly moved at the insult received, sent orders to his sheriffs and their bailiffs and constables to remove all refractory priests from the kingdom and seize their possessions.[1]

The kingdom of England having suffered all the inconveniences of the interdict for two years without producing the slightest effect upon the King's mind, but that of a deepened resolve to have vengeance for the insult which he had received at the hands of the Pope, another turn must be given to the Italian screw, and John must be still further degraded by a personal excommunication.

Orders were given from Rome to the Bishops of London, Ely, and Hereford, to declare the King excommunicated by name, and solemnly to publish this sentence every Sunday and fast-day in all the conventual churches throughout England.[2]

According to Roger de Wendover, it appears that this sentence of excommunication was more threatened and talked about than executed, for that the monks dared not publicly to read the sentence in their monasteries at or before divine service; but that, shortly afterwards, all princes and others, high or low, who owed fealty to the English crown, were threatened with excommunication if they associated with the King at table, in council, or converse.

To fill up the measure of priestly assumption, the Pope, by the advice of his cardinals, bishops, and others, definitively decreed that John should be King of England no longer, and that his kingdom should be given to another;[3] and, in pursuance of this decree, wrote to Philip, King of the French, ordering him to expel the King of England from his throne, and take possession of his kingdom, and hold it as a French conquest and possession, for him and his heirs for ever.

---

[1] Roger de Wendover, vol. ii. p. 246. [2] Ibid., p. 250. [3] Ibid., p. 259.

Besides the above, the Pope sent letters over Europe inviting all nobles, knights, and soldiers of fortune to embark in this crusade against the King of England, under the leadership of the King of the French.

After this, the Pope sent Pandulph, a sub-deacon, with his Archbishop of Canterbury, and the bishops above named,[1] William of London, Eustace of Ely, Mauger of Worcester, Jocelyn of Bath, and Giles of Hereford, to France, to excite and preach up the invasion of England. The above act of publicly preaching up an invasion of England in France by the *Archbishop of Canterbury*, and five English bishops acting under him, brands the whole party as traitors to the crown of England.

We will not waste space here—but look after the *traitor Langton*, and see who were his tools in this great ecclesiastical drama. Here we have the traitors at their invasion work again; for, in January 1213, Stephen Langton, William of London, and Eustace of Ely held a council in France, at which they solemnly opened out to the King of the French, the bishops, clergy, and people, the decree which had been sent from Rome to England against the English King.

These clerical agents of Rome, in the name of the Pope, enjoined on the King of the French, as well as others, the duty of invading England, deposing John, the reigning sovereign, from his throne, and electing another king in his place.

The King of the French, accepting the invitation of the Archbishop of Canterbury for the invasion of England, immediately ordered all his subjects alike—dukes, counts, barons, knights, and attendants—to be equipped with horses and arms at Rouen for the invasion of England in the octaves of Easter. As soon as King John heard of the doings of the spurious Archbishop of Canterbury and the King of the French, he also set about military preparations to meet the threatened invasion of England.

---

[1] Roger de Wendover, vol. ii. p. 261.

He sent the following warrant to each of the bailiffs of the seaports—a warrant ill fitting with the historical John "coward," &c. &c. &c. :—

"*John, King of England, &c.*—We command you that, immediately on the receipt of these our letters, you go in person, together with the bailiffs of the ports of each of the harbours in your bailiwick, and make a careful list of all the ships there found capable of carrying six horses or more; and that, in our name, you order the masters as well as the owners of those ships, as they regard themselves, their ships, and all their property, to have them at Portsmouth at Mid Lent, well equipped with stores, tried seamen, and good soldiers, to enter into our service for our deliverance ; and that you then and there make a true and distinct list of how many ships you find in each port, whose they are, and how many horses each ship can carry ; and you will then inform us how many and what ships are not in their harbours on the Sunday after Ash Wednesday, as we had ordered ; and this shall be your warrant for the same.

"Witness myself at the New Temple, this third day of March."

Having addressed the bailiffs of the sea-ports, the King next addressed the sheriffs of the counties as follows :—

"*John, King of England, &c.*—Give warning by good agents to the earls, barons, knights, and all free and serving men, whoever they be, or by whatever tenure they hold, who ought to have, or may procure arms, who have made homage and sworn allegiance to us, that as they regard us, as well as themselves and all their own property, they be at Dover at the end of the coming Lent, equipped with horses and arms, and with all they can provide, to defend our person and their persons, and the Land of England; and let no one who can carry arms remain behind, under penalty of being branded with cowardice, and of being condemned to perpetual slavery ; and let each man follow his lord ; and let those who possess no land, and who can carry arms, come to take service with us as mercenaries.

"And send, moreover, all victualling conveyances, and all markets of your bailiwick to follow our army, so that no market may be held elsewhere in your bailiwick, and do you yourself attend at that place with your agents aforesaid.

"And be sure that we wish to know in what manner all come from your bailiwick, and who come, and who do not; and see that you come properly supplied with horses and arms, so that we may not be obliged to deal with you in person. And see that you have a roll, so as to inform us of those who remain."

At this time, John Gray, Bishop of Norwich, came to the King from Ireland, (where he was viceroy,) with five hundred knights and a body of horse-soldiers. When assembled on Barham Downs, near Dover, the army mustered sixty thousand men, all well armed.

With such an army King John could not meet his enemy, for his men had been tampered with by the priestly superstition of the day; but while waiting the invasion from France at Dover, two brothers of the Temple arrived at Dover from Pandulph, the subdeacon and familiar of the Pope, informing King John that Pandulph wished to have an interview with him, to propose a form of peace which might be acceptable to him. Pandulph was invited to attend the King at Dover, which invitation was readily accepted by Pandulph, who crossed the sea from France for the purpose.

At this meeting, Pandulph informed King John that the King of the French was ready, by force of arms, to take possession of his kingdom of England, by authority from the Pope; and that he would bring with him the English bishops, Stephen Langton and the others above named, with the clergy; and that he would replace them by force in their bishoprics, monasteries, and parishes; and that he would, in the place of the English monarch, receive the fealties and homages due to the crown from these feudatories.

Pandulph, moreover, informed the King, that if he would submit himself to the Roman Catholic Church, and the Pope, the head of that Church, he should have his kingdom restored to him.[1]

Such was the proposal made by the Pope, backed by all the tremendous imagined sanctions of an authority that was credited as controlling not merely the destinies of the present world, but also of the shadowy realms beyond. Personally, John had no craven dread of either the head or the tail (if we may adopt a Bible figure.) To him the thunders of the Vatican sheathed no lightnings. It was different with the Nation, then and onward for centuries. To *it* the priest-king at Rome was the vicegerent of Almighty God. Blessing from him fetched down blessing, and ban, Divine ban. There was awful reality in the seemingly omniscient and omnipresent system. Sacredness hedged the meanest representative of it: the tiara sank the proudest crown, the crozier the sceptre.

Then behind all this was France and its king hungering for possession of the island-kingdom.

It was a hard problem that was thus submitted for solution to John, and under the most trying circumstances, seeing that his own ignoble nobles deserted him, and played into the hands of his enemies, even into the hands of Philip. War demands men and well-nigh infinite resources. Poor, meagre, traitorously inadequate had been the response to the gallant demands of the gallant King of England. He was over-matched, deserted, left alone. What was to be done? John was swift in decision as in action, and far-seeing in both. Might he not disappoint the King of France of his prey, and, at same time, secure the nationality of his loved England? To yield to circumstances, so as to mould these to a grand ultimate gain, is the mark of a statesman-mind. John was a statesman, and he resolved accordingly. He would acquiesce in the Papal proposals and terms; he would make the

---

[1] Roger de Wendover, vol. ii. p. 264.

formal transfer of his kingdom to the Pope. We say "formal;" for while the transference of the deeds to Rome, the Pope's unvarying language thereafter, and the payment of the "rent" down through fully a century and a half, without effectual dispute or intermission by the Kings of England, showed it was a grave reality, nevertheless the actual Nationality remained under the sceptre of the King. The substance remained, though the shadow went; but with the shadow also went the boasted claims of the nobility, together with the other guerdons of feudality. All this John discerned,—discerned that the surrender of his kingdom to the Pope as "superior" would put a weapon into his hands of which his Nobles should feel the weight, God helping him. As no longer chief of the Fee, he was only the tenant-in-chief of the realm. Who, then, and what, were the Peerage?

This sinking of his own opinions and feelings—this astute stooping to irresistible circumstances—this large grasping of future issues to be evolved from apparent defeat—mark out King John as a patriot, and as not a reigner merely, but a governer. He admitted the supernal claim (diabolical?) of the Pope, and thereby to all time saved THE NATIONALITY OF ENGLAND, as will appear in the sequel.

We have now to submit the documents relating to this memorable incident of a memorable life and period :—

On the 13th day of May, A.D. 1213, which was the Monday next preceding Ascension Day, the King and Pandulph, with the earls, barons, and a large concourse of people, met at Dover, and there they unanimously agreed to the underwritten form of peace :—

"*John, King of England, to all to whom these presents shall come, greeting.*—By these our letters-patent, sealed with our seal, we wish it known, that in our presence and by our commands, these our four barons,—namely, William, Earl of Salisbury, our brother; Reginald, Count of Boulogne; William, Earl Warenne; and William, Count of Ferrars,—have sworn on our soul that we will, in all good faith, keep the subscribed peace in all things. We therefore, in the first place, solemnly and absolutely swear, in the presence of the legate, to abide by the commands of our lord the Pope, in all the matters for which we have been excommunicated by him, and that we will observe strict peace and afford full security to those venerable men—

  Stephen, Archbishop of Canterbury,
  William, Bishop of London,
  Eustace, Bishop of Ely,
  Giles of Hereford,
  Jocelyn of Bath,
  Hubert of Lincoln,
  Prior and Monks of Canterbury,
  Robert Fitz-Walter, and
  Eustace de Vesci.

And also to the rest of the clergy and laity connected with this matter. We at the same time, in the presence of the same legate, publicly make oath that we will not injure them in property, or cause or permit them to be injured in person or property; and we will dismiss all our anger against them and will receive them into our favour, and observe this in all good faith; also, that we will not hinder the aforesaid archbishop and bishops, or cause or permit them to be hindered, from performing their duties in all freedom, and enjoying the full authority of their jurisdiction, as they ought to do. And for this we will grant our letters-patent, as well to our lord the Pope as to the said archbishop, and to each of the bishops, causing our bishops, earls, and barons, as many of them as the aforesaid archbishop and bishops shall select, to set forth by their oath and by letters-patent that they themselves will use their endeavours to see this peace and arrangement firmly kept. And if by any chance—which may God avert—we should, either by ourselves or by others, contravene this, they will then abide by the apostolic commands on behalf of the Church against the violaters of this peace and arrangement, and may we for ever lose the wardship of the vacant churches. And if by any chance we cannot induce them to agree to the last part of this oath, —namely, that if we contravene it, either by ourselves or others, they will abide by the apostolic commands on behalf of the Church against the violaters of this peace and arrangement,—we have for this by our letters-patent pledged with our lord the Pope and the Church of Rome all the right of patronage which we possess in the English churches. And we will transmit all these our letters-patent, which are granted for the security of the aforesaid prelates, to the archbishop and bishops, before they come to England. But should we require it, the aforesaid archbishop and bishops shall, saving the honour of God and the churches, give security on oath and in writing that they will not, either personally or by others, make any attempt against our person or crown, as long as we afford them the security above-mentioned, and keep the peace unbroken. We will also make full restitution of the confiscated property, and satisfy, for their losses, the clergy as well as laity who are concerned in this business, not only as regards their property, but also their rights, and we will protect their restored rights; the Archbishop and the Bishop of Lincoln we will indemnify from the time of their consecration, the rest from the commencement of this disagreement. And no agreement, promise, or grant shall be an impediment to these indemnifications for loss, or the restoration of the confiscated property of the dead as well as the living. Nor will we retain anything under pretence of service due to us, but afterwards a proper recompense shall be given for service done to us. And we will forthwith release, dismiss, and restore to their rights, all the clergy whom we are holding under restraint, as well as any of the laity who are detained in custody on account of this business.

"And immediately on the arrival of a fit person to absolve us, we will, in part restoration of the confiscated property, deliver to messengers deputed by the said archbishop, bishops, and monks of

Canterbury, the sum of eight thousand pounds lawful sterling money, for discharging what is due and for necessary expenses, to be carried to them without let or hindrance on our part, that they may be honourably recalled and returned to England as soon as possible, namely, to

Stephen, Archbishop of Canterbury,	£2500
William, Bishop of London,	750
Eustace of Ely,	750
Jocelyn of Bath,	750
Hubert of Lincoln,	750
Prior and Monks of Canterbury,	1000

And as soon as we know that this peace is confirmed we will assign, without delay, to the archbishop and bishops, to the clergy, and to each and all of the churches, by the hands of their messengers or agents, all the movable property, with free management of the same, and dismiss them peaceably.

"And we will also publicly revoke the sentence of outlawry which we have pronounced against the ecclesiastics, declaring by these our letters-patent, to be delivered to the Archbishop, that it in no wise pertains to us, and that we will never again pronounce that sentence against the ecclesiastics: we moreover revoke the sentence of outlawry pronounced against the laity concerned in this matter, and restore all that we have received from ecclesiastics since the interdict, except the custom of the kingdom and the liberty of the Church.

"But, if any question shall arise about the losses and confiscations, or the amount of computation of them, it shall be determined by the legate or delegate of our lord the Pope, after hearing evidence on the matter; and after all this is duly arranged, the sentence of interdict shall be withdrawn.

"As to the other points, if any doubts, worthy of being entertained, arise, if they are not set at rest by the legate or delegate of our lord the Pope, they shall be referred to the Pope himself, and whatever he determines shall be abided by.

"Witness myself at Dover, this 13th day of May, in the fourteenth year of our reign."[1]

Two days after signing the above charter for the restitution of confiscated property by King John, a meeting took place at the house of the Knights-Templars at Dover, on the eve of Ascension Day, between the English king, Pandulph the legate, and the nobles of the kingdom.

At this meeting, *according to a decree pronounced at Rome*, King John resigned his crown, with the kingdoms of England and Ireland, into the hands of the Pope, for him and his successors for ever; and the act was confirmed by the following charter:—

"*John, by the grace of God King of England, &c., to all the faithful servants of Christ who shall behold this charter, health in the Lord.*—We wish it by this our charter, signed with our seal, to be known to you, that we, having in many things offended God and our Mother the Holy Church, and being in great need of the Divine mercy for our sins, and not having wherewithal to make a worthy offering as an atonement to God, and to pay the just demands of the Church, unless we humiliate ourselves before Him who humiliated Himself for us even to death; we, impelled by the inspiration of the Holy Spirit, and not by force or from fear of the interdict, but of our own free will and consent, and by the general advice of our barons, assign and grant to God and His holy apostles Peter and Paul, and to the Holy Church of Rome our Mother, and to our lord Pope Innocent and his Catholic successors, the whole kingdom of England and the whole kingdom of Ireland, with all their rights and appurtenances, in remission of the sins of us and our whole race, as well for those living as for the dead: and henceforth we retain and hold those countries of the Church of Rome as vicegerent, and this we declare in the presence of the learned man Pandulph, sub-deacon and familiar of our lord the Pope.

---

[1] Roger de Wendover, vol. ii. p. 265.

"And we have made our homage and sworn allegiance to our lord the Pope and his Catholic successors, and the Church of Rome, in manner hereunder written; and we will make our homage and allegiance for the same in presence of our lord the Pope himself, if we are able to go before him; and we bind our successors and heirs by our wife for ever, in like manner, to do homage and render allegiance, without opposition, to the supreme Pontiff, for the time being, and the Church of Rome.

"And, in token of this lasting bond and grant, we will and determine that, from our own income, and from our special revenues arising from the aforesaid kingdoms, the Church of Rome shall, for all service and custom which we owe to them, saving always the St Peter's pence, receive annually a thousand marks sterling money,—that is to say, five hundred marks at Michaelmas, and five hundred at Easter: that is, seven hundred for the kingdom of England, and three hundred for Ireland; saving to us and our heirs all our rights, privileges, and royal customs. And as we wish to ratify and confirm all that has been above written, we bind ourselves and our successors not to contravene it; and if we, or any one of our successors, shall dare to oppose this, let him, whoever he be, be deprived of his right in the kingdom.

"And let this charter of our bond and grant remain confirmed for ever.

"Witness myself at the house of the Knights of the Temple, near Dover, in the presence of Henry, Archbishop of Dublin; John, Bishop of Norwich; Geoffrey Fitz-Peter; William, Earl of Salisbury; William, Earl of Pembroke; Reginald, Count of Boulogne; William, Earl Warenne; Sayer, Earl of Winton; William, Earl of Arundel; William, Earl of Ferrars; William Briuere; Peter Fitz-Herbert; and Warin Fitz-Gerald, this fifteenth day of May, in the fourteenth year of our reign."[1]

---

[1] Roger de Wendover, vol. ii. pp. 268-9.

The above charter, fairly written out, was given to Pandulph to be taken to the Pope; after which the King of England did homage to Innocent III., represented by his legate.

"I, John, by the grace of God, King of England and Lord of Ireland, will, from this time, as formerly, be faithful to God, St Peter, the Church of Rome, and to my liege lord Pope Innocent and his Catholic successors. I will not act, speak, consent to, or advise anything by which they may lose life or limb, or be exposed to caption by treachery. I will prevent damage to them if I am aware of it; and if in my power, will repair it; or else I will inform them as soon as in my power so to do, or will tell it to such a person as I believe will be sure to inform them of it. Any purpose which they may entrust to me themselves, or by their messengers or letters, I will keep secret, and if I know of it, will not disclose it to any one to their injury. I will assist in holding and defending the inheritance of St Peter, and particularly the kingdoms of England and Ireland, against all men, to the utmost of my power. So may God and the holy gospel help me. Amen."[1]

On the completion of the matter, Pandulph immediately crossed the sea for France, taking with him the above charters, and £8000 of sterling money, for Langton, the Archbishop of Canterbury; William of London; Eustace of Ely; Giles of Hereford; Jocelyn of Bath; and Hubert of Lincoln; the Prior and Monks of Canterbury; Robert Fitz-Walter, and Eustace de Vesci, and other traitors employed in France in urging forward the French invasion.

As peace was guaranteed to all involved in the conspiracy— for such it was—Pandulph strongly advised the party to return to England, and there receive the rest of their indemnity money.[2]

After Langton and his comrades in treason had been disposed of, Pandulph next turned his attention to the French king, whom

---

[1] Roger de Wendover, vol. ii. p. 270.   [2] Ibid., p. 271.

he tried to persuade to give up his intentions of invading England, and to return home in peace; for that an attack upon England would be an attack upon the Catholic Church of Rome, and Pope Innocent III. himself.

What could the French king say to this? He had been invited by the Archbishop of Canterbury, with other bishops, at the Pope's request, to invade England; and now, when his vast fleet was collected in the Seine for the conveyance of that army to England, the Pope sends him word that England had been given to the Church of Rome—was sacred property—and that therefore the French king must not touch it.

The French king, enraged beyond measure, complained of the treatment received from the Pope, and declared that he would not have acceded to the Pope's request had it not been for the disaster which his fleet had met with at Swine, in Flanders, where it had been followed by the more powerful English fleet, under the command of the English admiral, William Plantagenet, and for the most part sunk, burnt, or taken,—a circumstance which completely destroyed the French power at sea, and this at a moment when, before all others, the French fleet was most needed.

No sooner had John heard of the complete annihilation of the French fleet at Swine, without any loss whatever to his own more powerful fleet, than he disbanded his army on Barham Downs, near Dover, and repaired to Portsmouth, where he had ordered a large army to assemble, for carrying on the war operations in Poicton and Flanders, now that England was secure, for some time at least, from any invasion from France.

When John arrived at Porstmouth, full of high expectation, what did he find?—the English barons refusing to follow him till he was absolved from the sentence of excommunication.[1]

To surmount this difficulty the King sent the warrants of

---

[1] Roger de Wendover, vol. ii. p. 273.

twenty-four earls and barons to the aforenamed archbishop and his bishops, guaranteeing them security on their return, and indemnity for their losses. On this these men, with their accomplices, returned to Dover, when John was absolved with great pomp at Winchester on July 16th, 1214.

Now, when this was done, and John was once more at Portsmouth, ready to cross to Poictou, what again happened? His knights complained that they had no money, and unless he paid them as mercenaries, they could not follow him. John, in a rage, took a fishing smack, and set sail by himself. We hear of the cowardice of King John *ad nauseam*, but other parties in the kingdom shewed more of that than ever was shewn by him. More of all this archbishopric contest and pope-triumphing for the moment, by and by.

CHAPTER VIII.

CHARTER "WORRY"—LANGTON AGAIN.

No sooner had the feudatories of the crown refused to obey the King, than he at once took measures for correcting the refractory; upon which the Archbishop Langton went to John at Northampton, and told him that it would vitiate the oath he had just taken if he attempted to carry war against any one without the concurrence of the Pope. The King, indignant enough at this traitor's interference in a matter of feudal tenure and fealty to the crown, persisted in his design.

On the following day he proceeded towards Nottingham, with the full determination of punishing his traitorous feudatories. The Archbishop still followed him, and, more boldly than the day before, declared that, unless he desisted from his undertaking, he would anathematise all who waged war before being absolved from an interdict.

The Archbishop did not leave the King till he had diverted him from his purpose by priestly threats.[1]

On the 25th day of August, Stephen Langton and his confederates met others at St Paul's Churchyard, a great place for national gatherings, and there professed to explain the advantages of a return to the laws of Edward the Confessor,[2] instead of the improved laws of the Norman kings, more especially the enlightened improvements from France by that great sove-

---

[1] Roger de Wendover, vol. ii. p. 275.   [2] Ibid., p. 276.

reign in legal innovations, Henry II. We cannot stop here to compare laws, but at this time much noise was made on the return to the Confessor's code. It might proceed from ignorance, or it might be something worse. At this meeting a charter of Henry I. was produced as a great and wonderful discovery, and, of course, the most was made of it, for its enlightenment, in contrast with any charter of Henry II. We take for granted that Henry I.'s charter was the common coronation oath of all our kings, Saxon or Norman. All these kings took coronation oaths, to observe strictly all the laws of the realm, and these laws were more or less recapitulated according to the feelings of the ministers of the crown at the time, and the taste of the age. John took oaths enough in Westminster Abbey when crowned by Hubert Walter. There was no necessity to seek out old charters from muniment chests. No; John's oath or charter was as full and complete as Henry I.'s could be. Certainly; but Langton wanted pretext to serve the King of France, and insult not only King John, but his father, Henry II., the most enlightened of England's kings. About the same time, Langton and his bishops, with one or two lay members well known, held a meeting at St Edmund's, in Suffolk, much of the same nature as the London meeting, to wonder over the recent discovery in the chest of the monastery, of the charter of Henry I., and to consider how they could add insult to injury, by making John swear to this charter, in addition to all former swearings at his coronation. They all agreed—at least so Roger de Wendover narrates in his "Flowers of History" —'that if the King would not again swear this charter, *they would withdraw from their allegiance to him, and make war on him, till he should, by a charter under his own seal, confirm to them everything they required.*' Here we have the same French party at work again, under Stephen Langton, with their threat of withdrawal of *allegiance*, and *making war* upon the King. They went further than this; they decided to provide themselves with horses and arms in order to compel the King to satisfy their demands.[1]

A.D. 1214–15, King John held his court at Worcester at Christmas, from which he repaired to the New Temple, London. Thither Stephen Langton, his bishops, and, probably, Robert Fitz-Walter and Eustace de Vesci, his party, went, in military array, to demand the liberties and laws of Edward the Confessor, and other liberties granted to the nation and Church of England, by Henry I. They asserted that the King had broken the oath taken at Winchester, at the time of his absolution, and also, that he had promised to restore the ancient laws and liberties of our Saxon ancestry; and that by his oath he was bound to observe them. The King, seeing the party prepared for battle, feared an attack from them, and so asked for a truce till the end of Easter, that he might be able to satisfy them, as well as the dignity of the crown. In the meantime, to escape priestly vengeance, the King assumed the cross of our Lord, hoping, by these means, to be saved from the knife of the assassin.

In Easter week the same nobles assembled at Stamford, with horses and arms, and at their head stood Robert Fitz-Walter and Eustace de Vesci; with Sayer, Earl of Winchester, among the party. The chronicler boasts of their numbers, and closes the account with this:—that "they were supported by the concurrence of Stephen, Archbishop of Canterbury, who was at their head."[2] Coupling this assemblage, and the Fleet-street muster, at the gates of the Temple, with the sojourn and seditious movements in France for at least five years, it would not be out of the bounds of Christian charity to affirm that Stephen Langton was a traitor to the King of England and his crown; and that Robert Fitz-Walter and Eustace de Vesci, his tools in sedition, were traitors likewise.

---

[1] Roger de Wendover, vol. ii. p. 303.   [2] Ibid., p. 306.

F

At the time of this outbreak the King was at Oxford waiting their arrival. The parties met, and the barons demanded a restoration of the old laws and customs of the kingdom, which were contained in the code of Edward the Confessor, and the charter of Henry I. The King, enraged at their assumption, laughed at their ignorance, and stated that "*their demands were vain and visionary, and were unsupported by any plea of reason whatever.*"

No king ever spoke truer words than these,—their demands were emphatically vain and visionary; and John knew it—knew it from his great Minister and Chancellor, HUBERT WALTER. John knew that the great legal improvements of the law-courts by his father, Henry II., were worth all the codes of all the kingdoms of the Saxon heptarchy put together.

We have translated all the Saxon laws, and, on that translation before us, *we affirm* that the code of Edward the Confessor could not be compared with the improvements in the law, and law practice, with *Circuit of Assize* of Henry II.

The next step taken by these traitors—for such they were—was to place Robert Fitz-Walter at their head, with the rank of Field-Marshal,—" MARSHAL OF THE ARMY OF GOD AND THE HOLY CHURCH;" and then they marched towards Northampton. On arriving at Northampton, they at once laid siege to the castle; but making no way in fifteen days, they proceeded to Bedford. When the army arrived at Bedford, William de Beauchamp, who held the castle for the King in feudation, received them with open arms. Messengers came from London inviting them to repair there at once, if they wished to be admitted into the city.

No sooner had this invitation arrived from the disaffected in London, than the barons moved to Ware, in Hertfordshire, about twenty-one miles from London; and in the night—for they marched the whole night—they proceeded to London, which city they entered early in the morning of Sunday, whilst the citizens were at their places of worship; and this they did to avoid tumult, as the

King John of England.

King's cause was popular with the great mass of the citizens. We may be permitted to state that John's cause was popular with all citizens and burgesses of all cities and boroughs. Why? Because it was the cause of Progress and Reform in its day, and, moreover, it was English; while the cause of Langton and Fitz-Walter was French, Papal, Priestly, Superstitious, and Retrogressive.[1]

The first step taken by the barons, when in undisputed possession of the city, was to take charge of the gates; then they took security from the citizens, for they were not at ease there.[2]

---

[1] Stephen Langton's cause was well understood by the middle classes, whether barons of the Cinque-Ports or London; or mere citizens, free tenants of the crown, of York, Bristol, or Norwich; or burgesses, free tenants of the crown also, of all boroughs, holding tenements by burgage tenures. All these thoroughly understood the dispute, and ranged themselves on the side of the King. If there were no cause for fear, why did the barons march from Ware to London in the night, and enter the city by daylight on Sunday morning, when the citizens were engaged in prayer? And when possessed of London by stealth in this way, why did the barons leave William d'Albini besieged for three months together in Rochester Castle, without their daring to leave London to render assistance to him in his extremity? Why did they abide in continuous inaction in London for the six months thereafter?

[2] Roger de Wendover, vol. ii. 307

CHAPTER IX.

MAGNA CHARTA TREASON—INVASION BY LOUIS.

THE city of London being now in the hands of the barons, they carried all with a high hand in town and country against the King. This led John to send his old friend and adviser, William Marshall, Earl of Pembroke to them, for an explanation of their wishes, with a declaration that the Charter of Liberties should be granted to them on any day that they would appoint to receive it.

The 15th day of June was fixed upon for this important business, and the place of meeting was also named, Runnemead, a large meadow lying between Staines and Windsor.[1]

As the Chroniclers give full particulars of all parties present, and the sides on which they were ranged, we may be allowed to sort them a little, seeing the greatest confusion prevails in the lists of both sides.

On the side of the barons there stood—

Stephen Langton, Archbishop of Canterbury.
William, Bishop of London.
Jocelyn of Bath.
Hubert of Lincoln.
Robert Fitz-Walter.

---

[1] In all these movements great confusion is made in classifying the names of the parties, and evidently from design, Stephen Langton being placed upon the same bench with Peter de Rupibus, or Walter Gray, or Randulph Blandeville. There is evident craft on the part of the Chronicler to *hide* *Stephen Langton* in the crowd of respectability. He is thrown in the same paragraph among the king's friends constantly, in order to disguise and mislead.

Saher, Earl of Winchester.
G. de Mandeville.
R., Earl of Clare.
Henry, Earl of Hereford.
Richard de Percy.
Eustace de Vesci.
John, Constable of Chester.
William de Mowbray.
Robert de Ross.
Roger, Earl Bigod.
Robert de Vere.
William Mallet, and others.

The King claimed as his friends—
Pandulph, the Legate.
Almeric, Master of the Knight-Templars in England.
William, Earl Marshal.
William Plantagenet, the Admiral.
William, Earl Warenne.
William de Fortibus, Earl of Albemarle.
Henry, Bishop of Dublin.
Peter de Rupibus, Bishop of Winchester.
Walter Gray, Bishop of Worcester.
William de Cornhill, Bishop of Coventry.
Hugo de Neville, Chief-Forester.
Hubert de Burgh, Seneschal of Poictou; with a number of others whose names are not given.

It may be asked with some impatience,—Where was Roger de Laci? He died A.D. 1209. Where was the crusading Bishop of Norwich, John Gray? He had been dead six months. Where was Geoffrey Fitz-Peter, the Chief-Justiciary? He had been dead twelve months. Last, but not least,—Where was Randulph Blandeville, Earl of Chester? Anywhere but at Runnemead; he was too proud to meet Langton and De Vesci at any parley.

As agreed upon, the King and nobles came to the appointed conference, where each party stood widely parted from the other; when a long discussion followed on peace and the (so-called) liberties demanded.

Certain laws and liberties were agreed to by the King, and confirmed by Charter; a Charter that, from its importance and mode of being obtained, has always been named

Magna Charta.

It must take its place in every history of John, and we give it for after-comment. Before turning to it we remark generally, that this vaunted 'Charter' has been more talked about and extolled, than either read or understood. It has come to be accepted as *the* thing whereby to bring down "thunders of applause" equally, by the democracy agitating for rights real or imaginary, and by the aspirant for a seat in the House. It were mirthful, if it were not mournful, to trace up the process of fraudulent gaining of the "public ear" by such sham watchwords as are current. With the *minimum* of historic work they have the *maximum* of historic acceptance. The multitude gape, and swallow, and applaud to the echo, what they really are as ignorant of as those who "spout" to them are. It is time, surely, to unconsecrate this one historical lie,—to lay bare the venal 'patriotism,' the needy "zeal," the traitorous and self-seeking desertion, of a true man and king,—the priestly arrogance and priestly dogmatism; and above all, and pervading all, the masked and false designs and motives of the contrivers of this (so called) "Magna Charta"—"sheet-anchor of English liberty!" &c., &c., &c.

In the sequel we shall see that if Stephen Langton and his fellow-conspirators were patriots, then Jack Cade and Wat Tyler deserve not the infamy of Robert Southey's praise, but statues of marble in the corridor of Westminster. As for the "Charter" itself, it was vitiated from its inception to its close—worthless, save as the parchment was good.

For the present, here is the Original, and a Translation on opposite pages, that all may read. Turn the leaf and judge, Reader, for thyself.

---

[1] We give the "Magna Charta" from the text of Richard Thomson, Esq., together with his idiomatic and accurate rendering; and follow his arrangement of placing the Latin and English on opposite pages. See his "Historical Essay on the Magna Charta of King John," 1 vol., 8vo, 1829,—a laborious as well as beautiful book, though we differ *toto cœlo* from many of his conclusions and opinions.—See the *facsimile* of the Charter in pocket of our volume.—C.

MAGNA CHARTA,

SEU

Charta de Libertatibus Regis Johannis,

Concessus Die Junii Quinto Decimo, A.D. 1215,

IN ANNO REGNI SEPTIMO DECIMO.

IN ARCHIVIS ECCLESIÆ CATHEDRALIS LINCOLNIENSIS ASSERVATA.

JOHANNES Dei Gratia, Rex Angliæ, Dominus Hiberniæ, Dux Normanniæ et Aquitaniæ, Comes Andegaviæ, Archiepiscopis, Episcopis, Abbatibus, Comitibus, Baronibus, Justiciariis, Forestariis, Vicecomitibus, Præpositis, Ministris, et omnibus Ballivis, et fidelibus suis,—Salutem. Sciatis Nos, intuitu Dei, et pro salute animæ nostræ, et omnium antecessorum, et hæredum nostrorum, ad honorem Dei, et exaltationem Sanctæ Ecclesiæ, et emendationem Regni nostri, per consilium venerabilium patrum nostrorum Stephani Cantuariensis Archiepiscopi, Totius Angliæ Primatis et Sanctæ Romanæ Ecclesiæ Cardinalis; Henrici Dubliniensis Archiepiscopi, Willielmi Londoniensis, Petri Wintoniensis, Joscelini Bathoniensis et Glastoniensis, Hugonis Lincolniensis, Walteri Wigorniensis, Willielmi Coventrensis, et Benedicti Roffensis, Episcoporum; Magistri Pandulfi Domini Papæ Subdiaconi et familiaris, Fratris Eimerici, Magistri Militiæ Templi in Anglia, et nobilium virorum Willielmi Marescalli Comitis Pembrochiæ, Willielmi Comitis Sarisburiæ, Willielmi Comitis Warreniæ, Willielmi Comitis Arundelliæ, Alani de Galweia Constabularii Scotiæ, Warini filii Geroldi, Huberti de Burgo Senescalli Pictaviæ, Petri filii Hereberti Hugonis de Nevillæ, Matthei filii Hereberti,

MAGNA CHARTA,

OR

The Great Charter of King John,

Granted June 15th, A.D. 1215,

IN THE SEVENTEENTH YEAR OF HIS REIGN.

TRANSLATED FROM THE ORIGINAL PRESERVED IN THE ARCHIVES OF LINCOLN CATHEDRAL.

JOHN, by the Grace of God, King of England, Lord of Ireland, Duke of Normandy and Aquitaine, and Earl of Anjou, to his Archbishops, Bishops, Abbots, Earls, Barons, Justiciaries, Foresters, Sheriffs, Governors, Officers, and to all Bailiffs, and his faithful subjects,—Greeting. Know ye, that We, in the presence of God, and for the salvation of our own soul, and of the souls of all our ancestors, and of our heirs, to the honour of God, and the exaltation of the Holy Church and amendment of our Kingdom, by the counsel of our venerable fathers, Stephen, Archbishop of Canterbury, Primate of all England, and Cardinal of the Holy Roman Church, Henry Archbishop of Dublin, William of London, Peter of Winchester, Joceline of Bath and Glastonbury, Hugh of Lincoln, Walter of Worcester, William of Coventry, and Benedict of Rochester, Bishops; Master Pandulph our Lord the Pope's Sub-deacon and familiar, Brother Almeric, Master of the Knights-Templars in England, and of these noble persons, William Mareschal Earl of Pembroke, William Earl of Salisbury, William Earl Warenne, William Earl of Arundel, Alan de Galloway Constable of Scotland, Warin Fitz-Gerald, Hubert de Burgh Seneschal of Poictou, Peter Fitz-Herbert, Hugo de Neville, Matthew Fitz-Her-

Thomæ Basset, Alani Basset, Philippi de Albiniaco, Roberti de Roppelay, Johannis Marescalli, Johannis filii Hugonis, et aliorum fidelium nostrorum; In primis concessisse Deo, et hac presenti Charta nostra confirmasse pro nobis et hæredibus nostris in perpetuum :—(I.) Quod Anglicana Ecclesia libera sit, et habeat jura sua integra et libertates suas illæsas, et ita volumus observari, quod apparet ex eo quod libertatem electionum, que maxima, et magis necessaria reputatur Ecclesiæ Anglicanæ, mera et spontanea voluntate, ante discordiam inter nos et Barones nostros motam, concessimus, et charta nostra confirmavimus, et eam obtinuimus a Domini Papa Innocentio Tertio confirmari : quam et nos observavimus, et ab hæredibus nostris in perpetuum bona fide volumus observari. Concessimus etiam omnibus liberis hominibus regni nostri, pro nobis et hæredibus nostris in perpetuum, omnes libertates subscriptas, habendas et tenandas eis et hæredibus suis de nobis et hæredibus nostris.—(II. 1.) Si quis Comitum vel Baronum nostrorum, sive aliorum tenentium de nobis in capite per servitium militare, mortuus fuerit, et cum decesserit hæres suus plene ætatis fuerit, et relevium debeat, habeat hæreditatem suam per antiquum relevium ; scilicet, hæres vel hæredes Comitis, de Baronia Comitis integra, per centum libras : hæres vel hæredes Baronis, de Baronia integra, per centum libras : hæres vel hæredes Militis, de Feodo Militis integro, per centum solidos, ad plus : et qui minus debuerit, minus det, secundum antiquam consuetudinem feodorum.—(III. 2.) Si autem hæres alicujus talium fuerit infra ætatem, et fuerit in custodia cum ad ætatem pervenerit, habeat hæreditatem suam sine relevio et sine fine.—(IV. 3.) Custos terræ hujusmodi hæredis qui infra ætatem fuerit, non capiat de terra hæredis nisi rationabiles exitus, et rationabiles consuetudines, et rationabilia servitia et hoc sine destructione et vasto hominum vel rerum. Et si nos commiserimus custodiam alicujus talis terræ Vicecomiti, vel alicui alii qui de exitibus illius nobis respondere debeat, et ille destructionem de custodia fecerit vel vastum, nos ab illo capiemus emendam, et

bert, Thomas Basset, Alan Basset, Philip de Albini, Robert de Roppel, John Mareschal, John Fitz-Hugh, and others our liegemen; have in the First place granted to God, and by this our present Charter, have confirmed, for us and our heirs for ever:— (I.) That the English Church shall be free, and shall have her whole rights and her liberties inviolable; and we will this to be observed in such a manner, that it may appear from thence, that the freedom of elections, which was reputed most requisite to the English Church, which we granted, and by our Charter confirmed, and obtained the Confirmation of the same, from our Lord Pope Innocent the Third, before the rupture between us and our Barons, was of our own free will: which Charter we shall observe, and we will it to be observed with good faith, by our heirs for ever.—(II.) We have also granted to all the Freemen of our Kingdom, for us and our heirs for ever, all the underwritten Liberties, to be enjoyed and held by them and by their heirs, from us and from our heirs. —(II. 1.) If any of our Earls or Barons, or others who hold of us in chief by military service, shall die, and at his death his heir shall be of full age, and shall owe a relief, he shall have his inheritance by the ancient relief; that is to say, the heir or heirs of an Earl, a whole Earl's Barony for one hundred pounds; the heir or heirs of a Baron for a whole Barony, by one hundred pounds; the heirs of a Knight, for a whole Knight's Fee, by one hundred shillings at most: and he who owes less, shall give less, according to the ancient custom of fees.—(III. 2.) But if the heir of any such be under age, and in wardship, when he comes to age he shall have his inheritance without relief and without fine.—(IV. 3.) The warden of the land of such heir who shall be under age, shall not take from the lands of the heir any but reasonable issues, and reasonable customs, and reasonable services, and that without destruction and waste of the men or goods, and if we commit the custody of any such lands to a Sheriff, or any other person who is bound to us for the issues of them, and he shall make destruction or waste upon the ward-lands we will recover damages from him, and the

terra committatur duobus legalibus et discretis hominibus de feodo illo, qui de exitibus respondeant nobis, vel ei cui eos assignaverimus. Et si dederimus vel vendiderimus alicui custodiam alicujus talis terræ, et ille destructionem inde fecerit vel vastum, amittat ipsam custodiam; et tradatur duobus legalibus et discretis hominibus de feodo illo, qui similiter respondeant nobis sicut prædictum est.—(V.) Custos autem, quamdiu custodiam terræ habuerit, sustinet domos, parcos, vivaria, stagna, molendina, et cætera, ad terram illam pertenentia, de exitibus terræ ejusdem, (35.) et reddat hæredi cum ad plenam ætatem pervenerit, terram suam totam, instauratam de carrucis et waignigiis, secundum quod tempus waignigii exiget, et exitus terræ rationabiliter poterunt sustinere.—(VI. 3.) Hæredes maritentur absque disparagatione, ita quod antequam contrahatur matrimonium, ostendatur propinquis de consanguinitate ipsius hæredis.—(VII. 4.) Vidua, post mortem mariti, sui statim et sine difficultate, habeat maritagium et hæreditatem suam; nec aliquid det pro dote sua, vel pro maritagio suo, vel hæreditate sua, quam hæreditatem maritus suus et ipsa tenuerint die obitus ipsius mariti; et maneat in domo mariti sui per quadraginta dies post mortem ipsius, infra quos assignetur ei dos sua.—(VIII. 17.) Nulla vidua distringatur ad se maritandum dum voluerit vivere sine marito; ita tamen quod securitatem faciat quod se non maritabit, sine assensu nostro de nobis tenuerit, vel sine assensu domini sui de quo tenuerit, si de alio tenuerit.—(IX. 5.) Nec nos nec Ballivi nostri, saisiemus terram aliquam nec redditum pro debito aliquo, quamdiu catalla debitoris sufficiunt ad debitum reddendum; nec plegii ipsius debitoris distringantur, quamdiu ipse capitalis debitor sufficit ad solutionem debiti; et si capitalis debitor defecerit in solutione debiti, non habens unde solvat, plegii respondeant de debito, et si voluerint, habeant terras et redditus debitoris, donec sit eis satisfactum de debito quod ante pro eo solverint, nisi

lands shall be committed to two lawful and discreet men of that fee, who shall answer for the issues to us, or to him to whom we have assigned them. And if we shall give or sell to any one the custody of any such lands, and he shall make destruction or waste upon them, he shall lose the custody; and it shall be committed to two lawful and discreet men of that fee, who shall answer to us in like manner as it is said before.—(V.) But the warden, as long as he hath the custody of the lands, shall keep up and maintain the houses, parks, warrens, ponds, mills, and other things belonging to them, out of their issues; (35.) and shall restore to the heir when he comes of full age, his whole estate, provided with ploughs and other implements of husbandry, according as the time of Wainage shall require, and the issues of the lands can reasonably afford.— (VI. 3.) Heirs shall be married without disparagement, so that before the marriage be contracted, it shall be notified to the relations of the heir by consanguinity.—(VII. 4.) A widow, after the death of her husband, shall immediately, and without difficulty have her marriage and her inheritance; nor shall she give any thing for her dower, or for her marriage, or for her inheritance, which her husband and she held at the day of his death: and she may remain in her husband's house forty days after his death, within which time her dower shall be assigned.—(VIII. 17.) No widow shall be distrained to marry herself, while she is willing to live without a husband; but yet she shall give security that she will not marry herself without our consent, if she hold of us, or without the consent of the lord of whom she does hold, if she hold of another.—(IX. 5.) Neither we nor our Bailiffs, will seize any land or rent for any debt, while the chattels of the debtor are sufficient for the payment of the debt; nor shall the sureties of the debtor be distrained, while the principal debtor is able to pay the debt; and if the principal debtor fail in payment of the debt, not having wherewith to discharge it, the sureties shall answer for the debt; and if they be willing, they shall have the lands and rents of the debtor, until satisfaction be made to them for the debt which

capitalis debitor monstraverit se esse quietum inde versus eosdem plegios.—(X. 34.) Si quis mutuo cæperit aliquid a Judeis, plus vel minus, et moriatur antequam debitum illud solvatur, debitum non usuret quamdiu hæres fuerit infra ætatem de quocumque teneat; et si debitum illud inciderit in manus nostras, nos non capiemus nisi catallum contentum in charta.—(XI. 35.) Et si quis moriatur et debitum debeat Judeis, uxor ejus habeat dotem suam, et nihil reddat de debito illo; et si liberi ipsius defuncti qui fuerint infra ætatem, remanserint, provideantur eis necessaria secundum tenementum quod fuerit defuncti, et de residuo solvatur debitum, salvo servitio dominorum. Simili modo fiat de debitis que debentur aliis quam Judeis.—(XII. 32.) Nullum scutagium vel auxilium ponatur in regno nostro, nisi per commune consilium regni nostri; nisi ad corpus nostrum redimendum, et primogenitum filium nostrum militem faciendum, et ad filiam nostrum primogenitam semel maritandam; et ad hæc non fiat nisi rationabile auxilium.—(XIII.) Simili modo fiat de auxiliis de civitate Londonii. Et Civitas Londonii habeat omnes antiquas libertates, et liberas consuetudines suas, tam per terras quam per aquas. Prætera volumus et concedimus quod omnes aliæ Civitates, et Burgi, et Villæ, et Portus, habeant omnes libertates et liberas consuetudines suas.—(XIV.) Et ad habendum commune consilium regni, de auxilio assidendo, aliter quam in tribus casibus prædictis, vel de Scutagio assidendo, summoneri faciemus Archiepiscopos, Episcopos, Abbates, Comites, et majores Barones, sigillatim, per literas nostras. Et præterea, faciemus summoneri in generali per Vicecomites et Ballivos nostros, omnes illos qui de nobis tenent in capite, ad certum diem, scilicet, ad terminum quadraginta dierum, ad minus, et ad certum locum; et in omnibus literis illius summonitionis causam summonitionis exprimemus; et sic facta summonitione, negotium ad diem assignatum procedat, secundum consilium illorum qui presentes fuerint, quamvis non omnes sum-

they had before paid for him, unless the principal debtor can shew himself acquitted thereof against the said sureties.—(X. 34.) If any one hath borrowed any thing from the Jews, more or less, and die before that debt be paid, the debt shall pay no interest so long as the heir shall be under age, of whomsoever he may hold; and if that debt shall fall into our hands, we will not take any thing except the chattel contained in the bond.—(XI. 35.) And if any one shall die indebted to the Jews, his wife shall have her dower and shall pay nothing of that debt; and if children of the deceased shall remain who are under age, necessaries shall be provided for them, according to the tenement which belonged to the deceased: and out of the residue the debt shall be paid, saving the rights of the lords (*of whom the lands are held.*) In like manner let it be with debts owing to others than Jews.—(XII. 32.) No scutage nor aid shall be imposed in our kingdom, unless by the common council of our kingdom; excepting to redeem our person, to make our eldest son a knight, and once to marry our eldest daughter, and not for these, unless a reasonable aid shall be demanded.—(XIII.) In like manner let it be concerning the aids of the City of London.— And the City of London shall have all its ancient liberties, and its free customs, as well by land as by water.—Furthermore, we will and grant that all other Cities, and Burghs, and Towns, and Ports, should have all their liberties and free customs.—(XIV.) And also to have the common council of the kingdom, to assess and aid, otherwise than in the three cases aforesaid: and for the assessing of scutages, we will cause to be summoned the Archbishops, Bishops, Abbots, Earls, and great Barons, individually, by our letters.—And besides, we will cause to be summoned in general by our Sheriffs and Bailiffs, all those who hold of us in chief, at a certain day, that is to say at the distance of forty days, (*before their meeting,*) at the least, and to a certain place; and in all the letters of summons, we will express the cause of the summons: and the summons being thus made, the business shall proceed on the day appointed, according to the counsel of those who shall be

moniti venerint.—(XV. 6.) Nos non concedemus de cætero, alicui, quod capiat auxilium de liberis hominibus suis, nisi ad corpus suum redimendum, et ad faciendum primogenitum filium suum militem, et ad primogenitam filiam suam semel maritandam; et ad hæc non fiat nisi rationabile axilium.—(XVI. 7.) Nullus distringatur ad faciendum majus servitium de Feodo Militis, nec de alio libero tenemento, quam inde debetur.—(XVII. 8.) Communia placita non sequantur curiam nostram, sed teneantur in aliquo certo loco.—(XVIII.) Recognitiones de Nova Dissaisina, de Morte Antecessoris, et de Ultima Presentatione, non capiantur nisi in suis comitatibus, et hoc modo:—Nos, vel si extra regnum fuerimus, Capitalis Justiciarius noster, mittemus duos Justiciarios per unumquemque comitatum per quatuor vices in anno, qui, cum quatuor militibus cujuslibet comitatus, electis per comitatum, capiant in comitatu, et in die et loco comitatus, assisas prædictas. —(XIX. 13.) Et si in die comitatus assisæ prædicte capi non possint, tot milites et liberæ tenentes remaneant de illis qui interfuerint comitatui die illo, per quos possint sufficienter judicia fieri, secundum quod negotium fuerit majus vel minus.—(XX. 9.) Liber homo non amercietur pro parvo delicto, nisi secundum modum delicti; et pro magno delicto, amercietur secundum magnitudinem delicti, salvo contenemento suo, et Mercator eodem modo, salva mercandisa sua, et villainus eodem modo amercietur, salvo waignaigio suo, si inciderint in misericordiam nostram; et nulla prædictarum misericordiarum ponatur, nisi per sacramentum proborum hominum de visneto.—(XXI.) Comites et Barones non amercientur nisi per Pares suos, et non nisi secundum modum delicti.—(XXII. 10.) Nullus Clericus amercietur de laico tenemento suo, nisi secundum modum aliorum prædictorum, et non secundum quantitatem beneficii sui ecclesiastici.—(XXIII. 11.) Nec villa nec homo distringatur facere pontes ad riparias, nisi qui

present, although all who had been summoned have not come.—
(XV. 6.) We will not give leave to any one, for the future, to take
an aid of his own free-men, except for redeeming his own body,
and for making his eldest son a knight, and for marrying once his
eldest daughter; and not that unless it be a reasonable aid.—
(XVI. 7.) None shall be distrained to do more service for a
Knight's-Fee, nor for any other free tenement, than what is due
from thence.—(XVII. 8.) Common Pleas shall not follow our
court, but shall be held in any certain place.—(XVIII.) Trials upon
the Writs of *Novel Disseisin*, of *Mort d'Ancestre* (death of the
ancestor), and *Darrien Presentment* (last presentation), shall not
be taken but in their proper counties, and in this manner:—We,
or our Chief Justiciary, if we are out of the kingdom, will send
two Justiciaries into each county, four times in the year, who, with
four knights of each county, chosen by the county, shall hold the
aforesaid assizes, within the county on the day, and at the place
appointed.—(XIX. 13.) And if the aforesaid assizes cannot be
taken on the day of the county-court, let as many knights and
freeholders, of those who were present at the county-court remain
behind, as shall be sufficient to do justice, according to the great or
less importance of the business.—(XX. 9.) A free-man shall not
be amerced for a small offence, but only according to the degree of
the offence; and for a great delinquency, according to the magni-
tude of the delinquency, saving his contenement: a Merchant
shall be amerced in the same manner, saving his merchandise, and
a villain shall be amerced after the same manner, saving to him
his Wainage, if he shall fall into our mercy; and none of the aforesaid amerciaments shall be assessed, but by the oath of honest men
of the vicinage.—(XXI.) Earls and Barons shall not be amerced
but by their Peers, and that only according to the degree of their
delinquency.—(XXII. 10.) No Clerk shall be amerced for his lay-
tenement, but according to the manner of the others as aforesaid,
and not according to the quantity of his ecclesiastical benefice.—
(XXIII. 11.) Neither a town nor any person shall be distrained to

ab antiquo, et de jure, facere debent.—(XXIV. 14.) Nullus Vicecomes, Constabularius, Coronatores, vel alii Ballivi nostri, teneant placita coronæ nostræ.—(XXV.) Omnes Comitatus et Hundredi, Trethingii, et Wapentachii, sint ad antiquas firmas, absque ullo incremento, exceptis Dominicis maneriis nostris.—(XXVI. 15.) Si aliquis tenens de nobis laicum feodum moriatur, et Vicecomes vel Ballivus noster, ostendat literas nostras patentes de summonitione nostra de debito quod defunctus nobis debuit, liceat Vicecomiti vel Ballivo nostro attachiare et inbreviare catalla defuncti inventa in laico feodo, ad valentiam illius debiti, per visum legalium hominum, ita tamen quod nihil inde amoveatur, donec persolvatur nobis debitum quod clarum fuit; et residuum relinquator executoribus ad faciendum testamentum defuncti et si nihil nobis debeatur ab ipso, omnia catalla cedant defuncto, salvis uxore ipsius et pueris rationabilibus partibus suis.—(XXVII. 16.) Si aliquis liber homo intestatus decesserit, catalla sua per manus propinquorum parentum et amicorum suorum, per visum Ecclesiæ distribuantur; salvis unicuique debitis quæ defunctis ei debebat. —(XXVIII. 18.) Nullus Constabularius vel alius Ballivus noster, capiat blada vel alia catalla alicujus, nisi statim inde reddat denarios, aut respectum inde habere possit de voluntate venditoris. —(XXIX. 19.) Nullus Constabularius distringat aliquem Militem ad dandum denarios pro custodia castri, si facere voluerit custodiam illam in propria persona sua, vel per alium probum hominem, si ipse eam facere non possit propter rationabilem causam: et si nos duxerimus vel miserimus eum in exercitu, erit quietus de custodia secundum quantitatem temporis quo, per nos, fuerit in exercitu.—(XXX. 20.) Nullus Vicecomes vel Ballivus noster, vel aliquis alius, capiat equos vel carettas alicujus liberi hominis pro carragio faciendo, nisi de voluntate ipsius liberi hominis.—(XXXI. 21.) Nec nos, nec Ballivi nostri, capiemus alienum boscum ad castra vel alia agenda nostra, nisi per voluntatem ipsius cujus boscus ille fuerit.—(XXXII. 22.) Nos non

build bridges or embankments, excepting those which anciently, and of right, are bound to do it.—(XXIV. 14.) No Sheriff, Constable, Coroners, nor other of our Bailiffs, shall hold pleas of our crown. —(XXV.) All Counties, and Hundreds, Trethings, and Wapentakes, shall be at the ancient rent, without any increase, excepting in our Demesne-manors.—(XXVI. 15.) If any one holding of us a lay-fee dies, and the Sheriff or our Bailiff, shall shew our letters-patent of summons concerning the debt which the defunct owed to us, it shall be lawful for the Sheriff or our Bailiff to attach and register the chattels of the defunct found on that lay-fee, to the amount of that debt, by the view of lawful men, so that nothing shall be removed from thence until our debt be paid to us; and the rest shall be left to the executors to fulfil the will of the defunct; and if nothing be owing to us by him, all the chattels shall fall to the defunct, saving to his wife and children their reasonable shares.—(XXVII. 16.) If any free-man shall die intestate, his chattels shall be distributed by the hands of his nearest relations and friends, by the view of the Church, saving to every one the debts which the defunct owed.—(XXVIII. 18.) No Constable nor other Bailiff of ours shall take the corn or other goods of any one, without instantly paying money for them, unless he can obtain respite from the free will of the seller.—(XXIX. 19.) No Constable (*Governor of a Castle*) shall distrain any Knight to give money for castle-guard, if he be willing to perform it in his own person, or by another able man, if he cannot perform it himself, for a reasonable cause: and if we have carried or sent him into the army, he shall be excused from castle-guard, according to the time that he shall be in the army by our command.—(XXX. 20.) No Sheriff nor Bailiff of ours, nor any other person, shall take the horses or carts of any free-man, for the purpose of carriage, without the consent of the said free-man.—(XXXI. 21.) Neither we, nor our Bailiffs, will take another man's wood, for our castles or other uses, unless by the consent of him to whom the wood belongs.—(XXXII. 22.) We will not retain the lands of those who

tenebimus terras illorum qui convicti fuerint de felonia, nisi per unum annum et unum diem; et tunc reddantur terræ dominis feodorum.—(XXXIII. 23.) Omnes Kidelli de cætero deponantur penitus de Thamesia et de Medeway, et per totam Angliam, nisi per costeram maris.—(XXXIV. 24.) Breve quod vocatur Præcipe, de cætero non fiat alicui de aliquo tenemento, unde liber homo possit amittere curiam suam.—(XXXV. 12.) Una mensura vini sit per totum regnum nostrum, et una mensura cervisiæ, et una mensura bladi, scilicet quartarium Londonii; et una latitudo pannorum tinctorum, et russettorum, et halbergettorum, scilicet, duæ ulnæ infra listas. De ponderibus autem sit ut de mensuris. —(XXXVI. 26.) Nihil detur vel capiatur de cætero pro Brevi Inquisitionis de vita vel membris; set gratis concedatur et non negatur.—(XXXVII. 27.) Si aliquis teneat de nobis per Feodi-Firmam, vel per Socagium, vel per Burgagium; et de alio terram teneat per Servitium Militare, nos non habebimus custodiam hæredis nec terræ suæ est de feodo alterius, occasione illius Feodi-Firmæ, vel Socagii, vel Burgagii; nec habebimus custodiam illius Feodi-Firmæ, vel Socagii, vel Burgagii, nisi ipsi Feodi-Firma debeat Servitium Militare. Nos non habebimus custodiam hæredis vel terræ alicujus, quam tenet de alio per Servitium Militare, occasione Parve Serjanterie quam tenet de nobis per servitium reddendi nobis cultellos, vel sagittas, vel hujusmodi.— (XXXVIII. 28.) Nullus Ballivus ponat de cætero aliquem ad legem, simplici loquela sua, sine testibus fidelibus ad hoc inductis. —(XXXIX. 29.) Nullus liber homo capiatur, vel imprisonetur, aut dissaisiatur, aut utlagetur, aut exuletur, aut aliquo modo destruatur; nec super eum ibimus, nec super eum mittemus, nisi per legale judicium parium suorum, vel per legem terræ.—(XL. 30). Nulli vendemus, nulli negabimus, aut differimus, rectum aut justitiam.—(XLI. 31.) Omnes Mercatores habeant salvum et securum exire ab Anglia, et venire in Angliam, morari et ire per Angliam, tam per terram quam per aquam, ad emendum et vendendum,

have been convicted of felony, excepting for one year and one day, and then they shall be given up to the lord of the fee.—(XXXIII. 23.) All kydells (*wears*) for the future shall be quite removed out of the Thames, and the Medway, and through all England, excepting upon the sea-coast.—(XXXIV. 24.) The writ which is called *Præcipe*, for the future shall not be granted to any one of any tenement, by which a free-man may lose his court.—(XXXV. 12.) There shall be one measure of wine throughout all our kingdom, and one measure of ale, and one measure of corn, namely, the quarter of London; and one breadth of dyed cloth, and of russets, and of halberjects, namely, two ells within the lists. Also it shall be the same with weights as with measures.—(XXXVI. 26.) Nothing shall be given or taken for the future for the Writ of Inquisition of life or limb; but it shall be given without charge, and not denied.—(XXXVII. 27.) If any hold of us by Fee-Farm, or Socage, or Burgage, and hold land of another by Military Service, we will not have the custody of the heir, nor of his lands, which are of the fee of another, on account of that Fee-Farm, or Socage, or Burgage; nor will we have the custody of the Fee-Farm, Socage, or Burgage, unless the Fee-Farm owe Military Service. We will not have the custody of the heir, nor of the lands of any one, which he holds of another by Military Service, on account of any Petty-Sergeantry which he holds of us by the service of giving us daggers, or arrows, or the like.—(XXXVIII. 28.) No Bailiff, for the future, shall put any man to his law, upon his own simple affirmation, without credible witnesses produced for that purpose. —(XXXIX. 29.) No free-man shall be seized, or imprisoned, or dispossessed, or outlawed, or in any way destroyed; nor will we condemn him, nor will we commit him to prison, excepting by the legal judgment of his peers, or by the laws of the land.—(XL. 30.) To none will we sell, to none will we deny, to none will we delay right or justice.—(XLI. 31.) All Merchants shall have safety and security in coming into England, and going out of England, and in staying and in travelling through England, as well by land as

sine omnibus malis toltis, per antiquas et rectas consuetudines; præterquam in tempore guerræ, et si sint de terra contra nos guerrina : et si tales inveniantur in terra nostra in principio guerræ, attachientur sine dampno corporum et rerum, donec sciatur a nobis, vel Capitali Justiciario nostro, quomodo Mercatores terræ nostræ tractentur, qui tunc invenientur in terra contra nos guerrina ; et si nostri salvi sint ibi, alii salvi sint in terra nostra.—(XLII. 33.) Liceat unicuique de cætero, exire de regno nostro, et redire salvo et secure per terram et per aquam, salva fide nostra, nisi tempore guerræ, per aliquod breve tempus, propter communem utilitatem regni : exceptis inprisonatis et utlagatis, secundum legem regni ; et gentæ de terra contra nos guerrina, et Mercatoribus de quibus fiat sicut prædictum est.—(XLIII. 36.) Si quis tenuerit de aliqua escaeta, sicut de Honore de Wallingeford ; Notingehamiæ, Bononii, Lancastriæ, vel de aliis escaetis quæ sunt in manu nostra, et sunt Baroniæ, et obierit, hæres ejus non det aliud relevium, nec faciat aliud nobis servitium quam faceret Baroni, si Baronia illa esset in manu Baronis ; et nos eodem modo eam tenebimus quo Baro eam tenuit.—(XLIV. 39.) Homines qui manent extra forestam, non veniant, de cætero, coram Justiciariis nostris de Foresta, per communes summonitiones ; nisi sint in placito, vel plegii alicujus, vel aliquorum qui attachiati sint pro Foresta.—(XLV. 42.) Nos non faciemus Justiciarios, Constabularios, Vicecomites, vel Ballivos, nisi de talibus qui sciant legem regni, et eam bene velint observare.—(XLVI. 43.) Omnes Barones qui fundaverunt Abbatias, unde habent cartas Regum Angliæ, vel antiquam tenuram, habeant earum custodiam cum vacaverint, sicut habere debent.—(XLVII. 47.) Omnes Forestæ quæ afforestate sunt tempore nostro, statim deafforestentur ; et ita fiat de Ripariis quæ per nos tempore nostro posite sunt in defenso.—(XLVIII. 39.) Omnes malæ consuetudines de Forestis

by water, to buy and sell, without any unjust exactions, according to ancient and right customs, excepting in the time of war, and if they be of a country at war against us: and if such are found in our land at the beginning of a war, they shall be apprehended without injury of their bodies and goods, until it be known to us, or to our Chief Justiciary, how the Merchants of our country are treated who are found in the country at war against us; and if ours be in safety there, the others shall be in safety in our land.—(XLII. 33.) It shall be lawful to any person, for the future, to go out of our kingdom, and to return, safely and securely, by land or by water, saving his allegiance to us, unless it be in time of war, for some short space, for the common good of the kingdom: excepting prisoners and outlaws, according to the laws of the land, and of the people of the nation at war against us, and Merchants who shall be treated as it is said above.—(XLIII. 36.) If any hold of any escheat, as of the Honour of Wallingford, Nottingham, Boulogne, Lancaster, or of other escheats which are in our hand, and are Baronies, and shall die, his heir shall not give any other relief, nor do any other service to us, than he should have done to the Baron, if that Barony had been in the hands of the Baron; and we will hold it in the same manner that the Baron held it.—(XLIV. 39.) Men who dwell without the Forest, shall not come, for the future, before our Justiciaries of the Forest on a common summons; unless they be parties in a plea, or sureties for some person or persons who are attached for the Forest.—(XLV. 42.) We will not make Justiciaries, Constables, Sheriffs, or Bailiffs, excepting of such as know the laws of the land, and are well disposed to observe them.—(XLVI. 43.) All Barons who have founded Abbies, which they hold by charters from the Kings of England, or by ancient tenure, shall have the custody of them when they become vacant, as they ought to have.—(XLVII. 47.) All Forests which have been made in our time, shall be immediately disforested, and it shall be so done with Water-banks, which have been taken or fenced in by us during our reign.—(XLVIII. 39.) All evil cus-

et Warrennis, et de Forestariis et Warrennariis, Vicecomitibus et eorum ministris, Ripariis et earum custotibus, statim inquirantur in quolibet comitatu, per duodecim Milites juratos de eodem comitatu, qui debent eligi per probos homines ejusdem comitatus, et infra quadraginta dies post inquisitionem factam, penitus, ita quod nunquam revocentur, deleantur per eosdem, ita quod nos hoc prius sciamus vel Justiciarius noster, si in Anglia non fuerimus.— (XLIX. 38.) Omnes obsides et cartas statim reddemus quæ liberate fuerunt nobis ab Anglicis in securitatem pacis, vel fidelis servitii.—(L. 40.) Nos amovebimus penitus de balliis parentes Gerardi de Atyes, quod de cætero nullam habeant balliam in Anglia; Engelardum de Cygonii, Andream, Petrum, et Gyonem de Cancelli, Gyonem de Cygonii, Galfridum de Martini, et fratres ejus, Philippum Marci, et fratres ejus, et Galfridum nepotem ejus, et totam sequelam eorumdem.—(LI. 41.) Et statim post pacis reformationem, amovebimus de regno omnes alienigenas milites, balistarios, servientes stipendarios, qui venerint cum equis et armis ad nocumentum regni.—(LII. 25.) Si quis fuerit dissaisitus vel elongatus per nos, sine legali judicio parium suorum, de terris castallis, libertatibus, vel jure suo, statim ea ei restituemus; et si contentio super hoc orta fuerit, tunc inde fiat per judicium viginti quinque Baronum, de quibus fit mentio inferius in securitate pacis. De omnibus autem illis de quibus aliquis dissaisitus fuerit, vel elongatus, sine legali judicio parium suorum, per Henricum Regem patrem nostrum, vel per Richardum Regem fratrem nostrum, quæ in manu nostra habemus, vel quæ alii tenent quæ nos oporteat warantizare, respectum habebimus usque ad communem terminum Crucæ Signatorum: exceptis illis de quibus placitum motum fuit, vel inquisitio facta per præceptum nostrum, ante susceptionem Crucis nostræ; cum autem redierimus de peregrinatione nostra, vel si forte remanserimus a peregrinatione nostra statim inde plenam justitiam exhibebimus.—(LIII.) Eundem autem re-

toms of Forests and Warrens, and of Foresters and Warreners, Sheriffs and their officers, Water-banks and their keepers, shall immediately be inquired into by twelve Knights of the same county, upon oath, who shall be elected by good men of the same county; and within forty days after the inquisition is made, they shall be altogether destroyed by them never to be restored; provided that this be notified to us before it be done, or to our Justiciary, if we be not in England.—(XLIX. 38.) We will immediately restore all hostages and charters, which have been delivered to us by the English, in security of the peace and of their faithful service.—(L. 40.) We will remove from their bailiwicks the relations of Gerard de Athyes, so that, for the future, they shall have no bailiwick in England; Engelard de Cygony, Andrew, Peter, and Gyone de Chancell, Gyone de Cygony, Geoffrey de Martin, and his brothers, Philip Mark, and his brothers, and Geoffrey his nephew, and all their followers.—(LI. 41.) And immediately after the conclusion of the peace, we will remove out of the kingdom all foreign knights, cross-bow-men, and stipendiary soldiers, who have come with horses and arms to the molestation of the kingdom.—(LII. 25.) If any have been disseised or dispossessed by us, without a legal verdict of their peers, of their lands, castles, liberties, or rights, we will immediately restore these things to them; and if any dispute shall arise on this head, then it shall be determined by the verdict of the twenty-five Barons, of whom mention is made below, for the security of the peace.—Concerning all those things of which any one hath been disseised or dispossessed, without the legal verdict of his peers by King Henry our father, or King Richard our brother, which we have in our hand, or others hold with our warrants, we shall have respite, until the common term of the Croisaders, excepting those concerning which a plea had been moved, or an inquisition taken, by our precept, before our taking the Cross; but as soon as we shall return from our expedition, or if, by chance, we should not go upon our expedition, we will immediately do complete justice therein.—(LIII.) The same respite will

spectum habebimus, et eodem modo de justitia exhibenda, de forestis deafforestandis, vel remansuris forestis quas Henricus pater noster, vel Ricardus frater noster afforestaverunt; et de custodiis terrarum quæ sunt de alieno feodo, cujusmodi custodias hucusque habuimus, occasione feodi quod aliquis de nobis tenuit per Servitium Militare; et de Abbatiis quæ fundate fuerint in feodo alterius quam nostro, in quibus dominus feodi dixerit se jus habere; et cum redierimus vel si remanserimus a peregrinatione nostra, super hiis conquerentibus pleplenam justitiam statim exhibebimus, —(LIV.) Nullus capiatur nec inprisonetur propter appellum feminæ de morte alterius, quam viri sui.—(LV. 37.) Omnes fines qui injuste, et contra legem terræ facti, sunt nobiscum, et omnia amerciamenta facta injuste, et contra legem terræ, omnino condonentur, vel fiat inde per judicium viginti quinque Baronum de quibus fit mentio inferius in securitate pacis, vel per judicium majoris partis eorumdem, una cum prædicto Stephano, Cantuariensis Archiepiscopo, si interesse poterit, et aliis quos secum ad hoc vocare voluerit: et si interesse non poterit, nihilominus procedat negotium sine eo; ita quod si aliquis, vel aliqui, de prædictis viginti quinque Baronibus, fuerint in simili querela, amoveantur, quantum ad hoc judicium, et alii loco illorum per residuos de eisdem viginti quinque tantum ad hoc faciendum electi et jurati, substituantur.—(LVI. 44) Si nos dissaisivimus vel elongavimus Walenses de terris, vel libertatibus, vel rebus aliis, sine legali judicio parium suorum in Anglia, vel in Wallia, eis statim reddantur; et si contentio super hoc orta fuerit, tunc inde fiat in Marchia per judicium parium suorum: de tenementis Angliæ, secundum legem Angliæ; de tenementis Walliæ, secundum legem Walliæ; de tenementis Marchiæ, secundum legem Marchiæ.

we have, and the same justice shall be done, concerning the disforestation of the forests, or the forests which remain to be disforested, which Henry our father, or Richard our brother, had afforested; and *the same* concerning the wardship of lands which are in another's fee, but the wardship of which we have hitherto had, occasioned by any of our fees held by Military Service; and for Abbies founded in any other fee than our own, in which the Lord of the fee hath claimed a right; and when we shall have returned, or if we shall stay from our expedition, we shall immediately do complete justice in all these pleas.—(LIV.) No man shall be apprehended or imprisoned on the appeal of a woman, for the death of any other man than her husband.—(LV. 37.) All fines that have been made by us unjustly, or contrary to the laws of the land; and all amerciaments that have been imposed unjustly, or contrary to the laws of the land, shall be wholly remitted, or ordered by the verdict of the twenty-five Barons, of whom mention is made below, for the security of the peace, or by the verdict of the greater part of them, together with the aforesaid Stephen, Archbishop of Canterbury, if he can be present, and others whom he may think fit to bring with him : and if he cannot be present, the business shall proceed, notwithstanding, without him; but so, that if any one or more of the aforesaid twenty-five Barons have a similar plea, let them be removed from that particular trial, and others, elected and sworn by the residue of the same twenty-five, be substituted in their room, only for that trial. —(LVI. 44.) If we have disseised or dispossessed any Welshmen of their lands, or liberties, or other things, without a legal verdict of their peers, in England or in Wales, they shall be immediately restored to them; and if any dispute shall arise upon this head, then let it be determined in the Marches by the verdict of their peers: for a tenement of England, according to the law of England; for a tenement of Wales, according to the law of Wales; for a tenement of the Marches, according to the law of the Marches. The Welsh shall do the same to us and to our subjects.

Idem facient Walenses nobis et nostris.—(LVII.) De omnibus autem illis de quibus aliquis Walensium dissaisitus fuerit, vel elongatus, sine legali judicio parium suorum, per Henricum Regem patrem nostrum, vel Richardum Regem fratrem nostrum, quæ nos in manu nostra habemus, vel quæ alii tenent quæ nos oporteat warantizare, respectum habebimus usque ad communem terminum Crucæ Signatorum, illis exceptis, de quibus placitum motum fuit, vel inquisitio facta per præceptum nostrum, ante susceptionem crucis nostræ. Cum autem redierimus, vel si forte remanserimus a peregrinatione nostra, statim eis inde plenam justitiam, exhibebimus secundum leges Wallensium, et partes prædictas.—(LVIII. 45.) Nos reddemus filium Leuelini, statim, et omnes obsides de Wallia, et cartas quæ nobis liberate fuerunt in securitatem pacis. —(LIX. 46.) Nos faciemus Alexandro Regi Scottorum, de sororibus suis, et obsidibus reddendis, et libertatibus suis, et jure suo, secundum formam in qua faciemus aliis Baronibus nostris Angliæ, nisi aliter esse debeat per cartas quas habemus de Gulielmo patræ ipsius quondam Rege Scottorum ; et hoc erit per judicium parium suorum in curia nostra.—(LX. 48.) Omnes autem istas consuetudines prædictas, et libertates quas nos concessimus in regno nostro tenendas, quantum ad nos pertinet erga nostros, omnes de regno nostro, tam clerici quam laici observent, quantum ad se pertinet erga suos.—(LXI. 49.) Cum autem pro DEO et ad emendationem regni nostri, et ad melius sopiendum discordiam inter nos et Barones nostros ortam, hæc omnia prædicta concesserimus, volentes ea integra et firma stabilitate in perpetuum gaudere, facimus et concedemus eis securitatem subscriptam ; videlicet, quod Barones eligent viginti quinque Barones de regno, quos voluerint, qui debeant pro totis viribus suis, observare, tenere, et facere observari, pacem et libertates quas eis concessimus et hac presente carta nostra confirmavimus : ita, scilicet, quod si nos, vel Justiciarius noster, vel ballivi nostri, vel aliquis de ministris nos-

—(LVII.) Also concerning those things of which any Welshman hath been disseised or dispossessed without the legal verdict of his peers, by King Henry our father, or King Richard our brother, which we have in our hand, or others hold with our warrant, we shall have respite, until the common term of the Croisaders, excepting for those concerning which a plea had been moved, or an inquisition made, by our precept, before our taking the Cross. But as soon as we shall return from our expedition, or if, by chance, we should not go upon our expedition, we shall immediately do complete justice therein, according to the laws of Wales, and the parts aforesaid.—(LVIII. 45.) We will immediately deliver up the son of Llewelin, and all the hostages of Wales, and release them from their engagements which were made with us, for the security of the peace.—(LIX. 46.) We shall do to Alexander King of Scotland, concerning the restoration of his sisters and hostages, and his liberties and rights, according to the form in which we act to our other Barons of England, unless it ought to be otherwise by the charters which we have from his father William, the late King of Scotland; and this shall be by the verdict of his peers in our court.—(LX. 48.) Also all these customs and liberties aforesaid, which we have granted to be held in our kingdom, for so much of it as belongs to us, all our subjects, as well clergy as laity, shall observe towards their tenants as far as concerns them.—(LXI. 49.) But since we have granted all these things aforesaid, for GOD, and for the amendment of our kingdom, and for the better extinguishing the discord which has arisen between us and our Barons, we being desirous that these things should possess entire and unshaken stability for ever, give and grant to them the security underwritten; namely, that the Barons may elect twenty-five Barons of the kingdom, whom they please, who shall with their whole power, observe, keep, and cause to be observed, the peace and liberties which we have granted to them, and have confirmed by this our present charter, in this manner: that is to say, if we, or our Justiciary, or our bailiffs, or

tris, in aliquo erga aliquem deliquerimus, vel aliquem articulorum pacis aut securitatis transgressi fuerimus, et delictum ostensum fuerit quatuor Baronibus de prædictis viginti quinque Baronibus, illi quatuor Barones accedent ad nos, vel ad Justiciarium nostrum, si fuerimus extra regnum, proponentes nobis excessum, petent, ut excessum illum sine dilatione faciamus emendari. Et si nos excessum non emendaverimus, vel si fuerimus regnum, Justiciarius noster non emendaverit, infra tempus quadraginta dierum, computandum a tempore quo monstratum fuerit nobis, vel Justiciario nostro, si extra regnum fuerimus, prædicti quatuor Barones referant causam illam ad residuos de illis viginti quinque Baronibus, et illi, viginti quinque Barones, cum communa totius terræ, distringent et gravabunt nos modis omnibus quibus poterunt; scilicet, per captionem castrorum, terrarum, possessionem, et aliis modis quibus poterunt, donec fuerit emendatum secundum arbitrium eorum; salva persona nostra, et Reginæ nostræ, et liberorum nostrorum; et cum fuerit emendatum, intendent nobis sicut prius fecerunt. Et quicumque voluerit de terra, juret quod ad prædicta omnia exequenda, parebit mandatis prædictorum viginti quinque Baronum, et quod gravabit nos pro posse suo cum ipsis: et nos publice et libere damus licentiam jurandi cuilibet qui jurare voluerit, et nulli umquam jurare prohibebimus. Omnes autem illos de terra, qui per se et sponte sua noluerint jurare viginti quinque Baronibus, de distringendo et gravando nos cum eis, faciemus jurare eosdem de mandato nostro, sicut prædictum est. Et si aliquis de viginti quinque Baronibus decesserit, vel a terra recesserit, vel aliquo alio modo impeditus fuerit, quominus ista prædicta possent exequi, qui residui fuerint de prædictis viginti quinque Baronibus, eligant alium loco ipsius, pro arbitrio suo, qui simili modo erit juratus, quo et cæteri. In omnibus autem, quæ istis viginti quinque Baronibus committunter exequenda, si forte

any of our officers, shall have injured any one in any thing, or shall have violated any article of the peace or security, and the injury shall have been shewn to four of the aforesaid twenty-five Barons, the said four Barons shall come to us, or to our Justiciary if we be out of the kingdom, and making known to us the excess committed, petition that we cause that excess to be redressed without delay. And if we shall not have redressed the excess, or, if we have been out of the kingdom, our Justiciary shall not have redressed it within the term of forty days, computing from the time when it shall have been made known to us, or to our Justiciary if we have been out of the kingdom, the aforesaid four Barons, shall lay that cause before the residue of the twenty-five Barons; and they, the twenty-five Barons, with the community of the whole land, shall distress and harass us by all the ways in which they are able; that is to say, by the taking of our castles, lands, and possessions, and by *any* other means in their power, until the excess shall have been redressed, according to their verdict; saving *harmless* our person, and *the persons* of our Queen and children; and when it hath been redressed, they shall behave to us as they have done before. And whoever of our land pleaseth, may swear, that he will obey the commands of the aforesaid twenty-five Barons, in accomplishing all the things aforesaid, and that with them he will harass us to the utmost of his power: and we publicly and freely give leave to every one to swear who is willing to swear; and we will never forbid any to swear. But all those of our land, who, of themselves, and of their own accord, are unwilling to swear to the twenty-five Barons, to distress and harass us *together* with them, we will compel them by our command, to swear as aforesaid. And if any one of the twenty-five Barons shall die, or remove out of the land, or in any other way shall be prevented from executing the things above said, they who remain of the twenty-five Barons shall elect another in his place, according to their own pleasure, who shall be sworn in the same manner as the rest. In all those things which are appointed to be done by these twenty-five Barons, if it happen that all the

ipsi viginti quinque presentes fuerint, et inter se super re aliqua discordaverint, vel aliqui ex eis summoniti nolint, vel nequeant interesse, ratum habeatur et firmum, quod major pars eorum, qui presentes fuerint, providerit, vel præceperit; ac si omnes viginti quinque in hoc consensissent: et prædicti viginti quinque jurent quod omnia antedicta fideliter observabunt, et pro toto posse suo facient observari. Et nos nihil impetrabimus ab aliquo, per nos, nec per alium, per quod aliqua istarum concessionum et libertatum revocetur vel minuatur. Et si aliquid tale impetratum fuerit, irritum sit et inane; et numquam eo utemur, per nos, nec per alium.—(LXII.) Et omnes malas voluntates, indignationes, et rancores ortos, inter nos et homines nostros, clericos et laicos, a tempore discordiæ, plene omnibus remisimus et condonavimus. Præterea, omnes transgressiones factas occasione ejusdem discordiæ, a Pascha anno regni nostri sextodecimo, usque ad pacem reformatam, plene remisimus omnibus clericis et laicis, et quantum ad nos pertinet, plene condonavimus.—(49.) Et, insuper, fecimus eis fieri literas testimoniales patentes domini Stephani Cantuariensis Archiepiscopi, Domini Henrici Dubliniensis Archiepiscopi, et Episcoporum prædictorum, et Magistri Pandulphi, super securitate ista et concessionibus præfatis.—(LXIII.) Quare, volumus, et firmiter præcipimus, quod Anglicana Ecclesia libera sit; et quod homines in regno nostro habeant et teneant omnes præfatas libertates, jura, et concessiones, bene et in pace, libere et quiete, plene et integre, sibi et hæredibus suis, de nobis et hæredibus nostris, in omnibus rebus et locis, in perpetuum, sicut prædictum est. Juratum est autem, tam ex parte nostra, quam ex parte Baronum, quod hæc omnia supradicta bona fide, et sine malo ingenio servabuntur. Testibus supradictis, et multis aliis. Data per manum nostram, in Prato quod vocatur Runimede, inter Windeleshorum et Stanes, quintodecimo die Junii, anno regni nostri septimo decimo.

twenty-five have been present, and have differed in their opinions about any thing, or if some of them who had been summoned would not, or could not be present, that which the greater part of those who were present shall have provided and decreed, shall be held as firm and as valid as if all the twenty-five had agreed in it: and the aforesaid twenty-five shall swear, that they will faithfully observe, and, with all their power, cause to be observed, all the things mentioned above. And we will obtain nothing from any one, by ourselves, nor by another, by which any of these concessions and liberties may be revoked or diminished. And if any such thing shall have been obtained, let it be void and null: and we will never use it, neither by ourselves, nor by another—(LXII.) And we have fully remitted and pardoned to all men, all the ill-will, rancour, and resentments, which have arisen between us and our subjects, both clergy and laity, from the commencement of the discord. Moreover, we have fully remitted to all the clergy and laity, and, as far as belongs to us, have fully pardoned, all transgressions committed by occasion of the said discord, from Easter, in the sixteenth year of our reign, until the conclusion of the peace.—(49.) And, moreover, we have caused to be made to them testimonial letters-patent of the Lord Stephen, Archbishop of Canterbury, the Lord Henry, Archbishop of Dublin, and of the aforesaid Bishops, and of Master Pandulph, concerning this security, and the aforesaid concessions.—(LXIII.) Wherefore, our will is, and we firmly command, that the Church of England be free, and that the men in our kingdom have and hold the aforesaid liberties, rights, and concessions, well and in peace, freely and quietly, fully and entirely, to them and their heirs, of us and our heirs, in all things and places, for ever as is aforesaid. It is also sworn, both on our part, and on that of the Barons, that all the aforesaid shall be observed in good faith, and without any evil intention. Witnessed by the above, and many others.—Given by our hand in the Meadow which is called Runningmead, between Windsor and Staines, this 15th day of June, in the 17th year of our reign.

The King accepted this 'Charter.' But now let us see the kind of men who framed it—let us uncover their motives and doings—let us rub off the whitewash of these 'stenching sepulchres.'

No sooner had the great Charter been duly ratified, than the assembled barons appointed twenty-five of their number to act as a committee and bond of safety for themselves, in seeing that the King duly observed the provisions of this great Charter. This was done before the dismissal of the barons from the scene of conference.

As soon as John had time to breathe, after the farce had been thoroughly gone through, he sent his letters-patent throughout England, strictly ordering all his sheriffs to make all the inhabitants in their several jurisdictions to swear observance to the above laws.

After this, many nobles, who had forfeited their possessions for treason, came to the King to demand their castles and lordships, as belonging to them by hereditary right. These claims the King waived for the present, and until they could be established on the oaths of legal men; and, more fully to assist the investigation, he fixed the 16th day of August as the day for them to make their claims, at Westminster; but he at once restored Rochester Castle and the Tower of London to Stephen Langton, the Archbishop.

As soon as their demands were settled at Runnemead, the barons returned to London, and there remained, under pretence of holding a tournament at Staines or Hounslow, but really to keep possession of the city.

Their first hostile movement was to send William d'Albini to take possession of Rochester Castle, which he at once did; for Langton, the holder under the King, rendered no opposition. The place was found to be completely destitute not only of arms and provisions, but even of furniture.

As soon as John heard that William d'Albini had taken possession of Rochester Castle by force of arms, he marched there to lay siege to the place, and took it in three months, receiving all the garrison prisoners; and amongst the rest William d'Albini, whom he sent, with a few others named in the Chronicle, to Corfe Castle, there to be kept in safe custody.[1]

During the three months of the siege of Rochester Castle, the army of God, in possession of the city of London, dared not, as we saw, to come to the assistance of the place.

For these outrageous proceedings in London and Rochester the Pope sent orders to Pandulph the Legate, Peter de Rupibus, Bishop of Winchester, and the Abbot of Reading, to lay the terrors of excommunication on all the disturbers of the King and kingdom of England; and to proclaim the sentence throughout all England on every Sunday and feast-day, amidst the ringing of bells, and with candles burning. Besides the above, Peter de Rupibus and Master Pandulph, the familiar of our lord the Pope, went to the Archbishop of Canterbury, ordering him to charge his suffragan bishops to publish the sentence of the Apostolic See against the barons, and also against the Archbishop himself. The Archbishop attempted delay under pretence of seeing the Pope on the business. On this, the Pope's agents at once suspended Stephen Langton from entering the church and performing divine service.

In November of this year, 1215, a great Council was held at Rome; at which the Abbot of Beaulieu, and Thomas Hardington and Geoffrey de Crawcombe, knights, appeared as proxies of the King of England against the Archbishop of Canterbury, to accuse him publicly of connivance with the English barons; and asserting that he showed favour and gave advice to the said barons, in their attempt to expel the said King from the throne of the kingdom.

The King was delighted greatly by the news from Rome: the barons were excommunicated; the Archbishop of Canterbury was suspended; and· his great and good Chancellor, Walter Gray, was made Archbishop of York.

---

[1] Roger de Wendover, vol. ii. p. 339.

On the above, with a light heart, the King proceeded from Rochester to St Albans with all his forces.

On the arrival of John at St Albans, he repaired to the chapter-house, in the presence of the monks, and ordered the letters about the suspension of the Archbishop of Canterbury to be read; and at once demanded of the conventual assembly that a confirmation of the aforesaid suspension, under their seal, should be sent to all the churches of England, conventual as well as cathedral, to be made publicly known.[1]

At this place the King divided his army into two parts: one to be left in the neighbourhood of London, under the command of William, Earl of Salisbury, the Admiral, the King's base brother, with Falkasius, a man of experience; Savaric de Mauleon with the troops of Poictou; William Briwere, the treasurer, with all his force; and Walter, surnamed Buck, who commanded the Brabantians.

The second division of the army, the King took under his own command, with the intention of going to the northern parts of England, which he intended to ravage with fire and sword.[2]

From St Albans, King John proceeded northward, in company of William de Fortibus, Earl of Albemarle, Philip d'Albini, John Marshall, and other generals, with their forces, by way of Dunstable, Northampton, &c., to Nottingham.

William, Earl of Salisbury, and Falkasius, with their forces, assisted the Castellans of Windsor, Hertford, and Berkhampstead to harass and annoy the London barons, and endeavoured to cut off their supplies.

These men roved through the counties of Essex, Hertford, Middlesex, Cambridge, and Huntingdon, collecting booty and indulging in rapine.

In 1215-16, King John kept his Christmas-day at Nottingham

---

[1] Roger de Wendover, vol. ii. p. 348.   [2] Ibid.

Castle ; and on the day following he marched to Langar and demanded the surrender of the castle, which was done after some consultation, because it belonged to William d'Albini, then John's prisoner in Corfe Castle.

The Pope, seeing that a general sentence of excommunication had little effect upon the barons, now, by the King's desire, excommunicated them by name and individually, in a letter to the Abbot of Abingdon, the Archdeacon of Poictou, and Master Robert, an official of the Church of Norwich. We give a passage from this letter:—

"It is moreover our will and command that you, by the apostolic authority, publicly, throughout all England, denounce as excommunicated, and cause to be strictly avoided by all, certain barons of England whom our venerable brother the Bishop of Winchester, and our well-beloved sons the Abbot of Reading and Master Pandulph, our subdeacon and familiar, by us delegated, have personally declared excommunicated, because they found them guilty in the aforesaid matters,—to wit, those citizens of London who have been the chief promoters of the aforesaid crime, and Robert Fitz-Walter, Saher, Earl of Winchester, R. his son, G. de Mandeville, and William his brother, Robert, Earl of Clare, and G. his son, H., Earl of Hereford, R. de Percy, Eustace de Vesci, John, Constable of Chester, William de Mowbray, William d'Albini, W. his son, R. de Roos, and William his son, P. de Brus, R. de Cressy, John his son, Ralph Fitz-Robert, R., Earl Bigod, H. his son, Robert de Vere, Fulk Fitz-Warren, W. Malet, W. de Montacute, W. Fitz-Marshall, William de Beauchamp, S. de Kime, R. de Mont Begon, and Nicholas de Stuteville, and also several others expressed in the decree by name as guilty of the aforesaid offences, together with their accomplices and abettors; and that on each Sunday and feast-day you solemnly republish this sentence, and order it to be strictly observed."

The barons being excommunicated by name, and their chief, Langton, being suspended from his office, and driven into exile by home affairs, a demand for an invasion of the realm by the son of the French king was resolved upon.

Two delegates were selected for this treasonable service—Saher, Earl of Winchester, and Robert Fitz-Walter.

Those two, fortified by letters under the seals of the barons, repaired to France; and there earnestly beseeched the father, Philip Augustus, king, to send his son to England to seize the crown, and reign there as king. Here we have feudatories of high rank under the crown of England, inviting an invasion of the realm by a foreign power. This act alone, without others innumerable, brands the whole party—Fitz-Walter and company—as traitors to the crown of England.

Not satisfied with letters under baronial seals sent by feudatories of the English crown to a foreign and hostile power, these traitors confirmed their letters and their seals by a deposit of twenty-four distinguished men from their order, as hostages, to be held by the King of France for his security, and as a guarantee for the veracity of the letters and the seals carried by Saher de Quinci and his companion in treason, Robert Fitz-Walter.

Louis wrote to the barons still in London that by Easter Sunday he would be at Calais ready to cross the sea, as they had strenuously and bravely conducted themselves in this affair; and, in the meantime, would send in arms, as his advanced guard in the invasion of the realm, the Castellan of St Omar, the Castellan of Arras, Hugh Thacun, Eustace de Neville, Baldwin Bretel, W. de Wimes, Giles de Melun, W. de Beaumont, Giles de Hersi, and Biset de Fersi, with a large retinue of knights and followers.[1]

This armed band of generals, knights, and soldiers arrived, by the river Thames, in London on the 27th of February, A.D. 1216, to the great joy of the barons, then in possession of the capital.

To verify the object and the real character, or no character, of the party pursuing it, we may state that the Pope's agents in England

---

[1] Roger de Wendover, vol. ii. p. 359.

seized upon this armed band of French invaders, and added them to their list of the excommunicated. They stated that there had arrived from the French kingdom certain nobles, with an armed band of knights and followers, all of whom they wished to fetter with the sentence of excommunication; *"for they invade the kingdom of England,* in opposition to our lord the Pope and the Roman Church, —are daily robbing it, and in part keeping possession of it, as is evident to all, in England as well as elsewhere."[1] These men were all excommunicated by name, along with those who had lent their assistance or money against the King to invade the kingdom of England.

It may not be out of place here to state that the men, barons, or traitors, or what you will, who invited an invasion from France in the year A.D. 1216, were the same men who were in France inviting an invasion of England in the year A.D. 1213; and also that these same men or barons were, under Stephen Langton, the French professor, the great actors at Runnemead of the insulting farce called MAGNA CHARTA. Put that and this together, reader. Connecting these men, Langton, De Quinci, Fitz-Walter, and De Vesci, with French intrigues and French invasions, over a period of six years at least,—and finding the getting up of the great MAGNA-CHARTA gathering at Runnemead to be entirely and altogether in their hands,—and finding, as we do, that one of their French invasions, that of 1213, drove King John, by the advice of William Marshall, Earl of Pembroke, Walter Gray, his Chancellor, and others, to take refuge for himself and kingdom in the Church of Rome, to save that kingdom from annexation to France, we make bold to pronounce that *the surrender of the crown of England to the Pope, in so far as it was blameworthy, was the act and deed of these men;* and that they were traitors to the crown of England in inviting a French invasion—a threatening of invasion that drove the King of England to the position which he had to take at Dover before Pandulph the legate.

---

[1] Roger de Wendover, vol. ii. p. 360.

Further, seeing that the getting up of 'Magna Charta' at Runnemead was theirs two years afterwards, we fearlessly affirm that 'Magna Charta' was the production of traitors, headed by the Archbishop of Canterbury, acting under French advice and French influences — in short, that 'Magna Charta' was the fruit of a French traitorous conspiracy, carried into execution by Stephen Langton, Archbishop of Canterbury, and his abettors, Robert Fitz-Walter, Eustace de Vesci, Saher de Quinci, and others. Having made these few remarks on Magna Charta and its chief perpetrators, we will now return to the invasion from France.

Soon after Easter, Louis left the port of Calais, in company with his earls, barons, knights, and numerous followers, in six hundred ships and eighty cogs, making for the isle of Thanet, where they landed at Stanshore on the 21st day of May. King John was at Dover at the time, but did not give battle to Louis on his landing, but rather strategetically retreated, leaving Dover Castle in the charge of Hugh de Burgh. He continued to Winchester by way of Guildford. Louis repaired from Sandwich to London, where he was received with great joy by all the barons. He there received homage from all of them, and homage or fealty from the citizens, as the case might require; while he himself swore on the Holy Gospels *that he* would grant good laws, and restore their inheritances to each and all of them.[1]

Louis appointed Langton, the Archbishop of Canterbury, his Chancellor, who preached to the citizens of London, as well as the excommunicated barons. Who ever heard before of an Archbishop of Canterbury to an English king being chancellor of a French king invading the realm by force of arms? Louis made an inroad into the county of Kent and subdued it, excepting Dover Castle; and, marching onward, he gained possession of the county of Sussex, with all the towns and fortresses. But here, as the monk writes, a young man named *William Collingham*, gentleman of the county of Sussex, at the head of one thousand archers, encountered

---

Roger de Wendover, vol. ii. p. 364.

Louis and his troops at every point of the great forest lying across this county, where the French troops and their allies of the "Army of God" might happen to pass to or from through the county, within the limits of this forest.[1]

The name of *William Collingham* of Sussex is an illustrious one. We class him with the two Grays, John and Walter, Peter de Rupibus, Roger de Laci, and other firm friends of the King.

From London, Louis made an incursion into Essex, Suffolk, and Norfolk, and garrisoned the castle of Norwich, which he found empty, with his own soldiers. He also sent a large force against the town of Lynn, and took it, and then returned with great booty to London. Gilbert de Gant, being girt by Louis with the sword of the county of Lincoln, was sent to check the incursions of the garrisons of Nottingham and Newark Castles.

At the same time, Robert de Roos, Peter de Brus, and Richard Percy reduced the city of York, with the whole county, to subjection to Louis; and Gilbert de Gant and Robert Roppelle took the city of Lincoln and county, without the castle.[2]

On the day of the Nativity of St John the Baptist, Louis, with a powerful force of knights and soldiers, laid siege to Dover Castle, defended by Hubert de Burgh, but could not take it. Another party of barons from London made an incursion into the country near Cambridge, and took the castle; and from this place they marched into the counties of Norfolk and Suffolk, and exacted large ransoms from Yarmouth, Dunwich, and Ipswich. Colchester also they ravaged as they returned to London.

After this the barons laid siege to Windsor Castle, but without success, as the place was so well defended by the garrison under the command of one of John's Brabanter friends, Ingelard d'Athie, a man well tried in war. We cannot follow the monk in all the marches and depredations of both parties in Cambridgeshire and neighbouring counties, and still more in the north, where Eustace de Vesci was killed by an arrow shot from Barnard Castle.

---

[1] Roger de Wendover, vol. ii. p. 366. [2] Ibid., p. 374.

CHAPTER X.

"IN THE SHADOWS:" DEATH.

WHILE John was taking vengeance on the barons of Cambridgeshire, Suffolk, and Norfolk, as the Earl of Arundel, Roger Bigod, William de Huntingfield, Roger de Cresi, and others; the barons, making no way at the siege of Windsor Castle, thinking to intercept the King in Cambridgeshire, on his way to Lincoln Castle, suddenly raised the siege and marched for Cambridge. But the King had taken refuge in Stamford for a time, whence he proceeded to Lincoln Castle, now besieged by Gilbert de Gant, Louis's newly-created Earl of Lincoln, and was pursued towards Lynn. From Lynn he marched, probably precipitately, across the river Wellstream, where he took his carts, waggons, and baggage-horses, together with his money and all his valuables. The King and his army had a narrow escape from drowning; but they did escape with their lives, and repaired to Swineshead Abbey for the night, some miles distant. This numerous party, by delay, had missed their calculation of rise of tide at the ford, and, like others similarly placed, ran every chance of drowning. No doubt but the King got a thorough ducking; and as he had to travel in his wet clothes to Swineshead Abbey, ten miles off, he got a severe cold, which ended in fever.

The King was very ill; but yet, as no time was to be lost, with the barons in pursuit, he left Swineshead Abbey at early dawn for the castle of Sleaford, distant about fourteen miles. Here he became worse; but yet on the following morning he rode on horseback to Newark Castle, a distance of twenty miles, where he became worse still. This violent exercise, in his weak state of body, increased the fever; so that at Newark he died, surrounded by some of his best friends,—one of whom, Randulph Blandeville, Earl of Chester, wrote an account of his death, the particulars of which have come down to our time, and the substance of which we are truly happy to give here, as so many fabulous and malignant statements have gone to the world from the monkish writers of the thirteenth and fourteenth centuries.

The following account of John's illness and death is from the pen of the Rev. Samuel Pegge, in a very admirable Paper prepared by him:—

"King John was at Linn, in Norfolk, on the 11th of October 1216-17, intending to cross the washes, or flooded marshes, which part the two counties of Norfolk and Lincoln.[1] In making the attempt to cross with his whole army—probably from unexpected delay or loss of time in passing so large a force in a certain prescribed time he lost his opportunity—he was overtaken by the tide flowing up the river Wellstream, which overflows these marshes at spring-tides, when all his baggage was lost, and he, with his army, had a very narrow escape of being drowned. He contrived to cross with his life, and arrived late at night, wet and worn out in body and prostrated with disappointment in mind; and was here, where he remained one or two days, laid low by fever and dysentery. On leaving Swineshead Abbey[2]—whether on the first or the second day—for Sleaford,[3] on horseback, he found that he was unable to bear the fatigues of the saddle, and so had to be transferred to a litter, on which he was carried

---

[1] These washes are between a place called *The Cross-Keys*, in Norfolk, and Fosdike, in Holland, in the county of Lincoln. Annot. on Rapin and Brady, p. 516. As for the Wellstream, see Dr Brady, p. 516.

[2] According to Caxton,—an English chronicle cited by Mr Lewis,—John Fox, and my (Rev. Mr Pegge's) MS. chronicle, he stayed two days at Swineshead. But see Brady, p. 515, and Appendix, p. 163.

[3] R. Higden makes him *dine* there. This was 14th October. Brady, p. 516.

to Sleaford,[1] and the next day to Newark Castle, where he died, as all our best authors agree,[2] a few days after; his bowels being buried at Croxton,[3] in the county of Leicester, and his body at Worcester."[4]

If there had been any truth in the story so industriously circulated centuries after the death of this King, that he was poisoned by a monk at Swineshead Abbey, surely this would have been the time for the detection of the crime. He died in his own castle, surrounded by his steadfast friends. His bowels were separated from his body, and each had a separate interment,—one in the county of Leicester, and the other in the county of Worcester; and the process of embalming that body, accompanied with all the circumstance of such an office,—superintended, too, by such friends as Peter de Rupibus, Bishop of Winchester, William Marshall, Earl of Pembroke, Walter Gray, Archbishop of York, Randulph Blandeville, Earl of Chester, and others devoted to England's King and England's interests; and yet amidst all this melancholy scene not one word of suspicion breathed against the hospitality of Swineshead Abbey; and this silence on the suspicion of poisoning remained unbroken for sixty or eighty years after this memorable death took place at Newark!

Be it remembered that at this time London, with all the south of England, was in the hands of the French king's adherents,— to wit, Langton, Archbishop of Canterbury, and his traitorous bishops, with the subservient *baronage* of England,—marshalled under the flag of France, and kept together by French promises and expectations, if not by French pay.

This state of things in the south compelled the firm adherents

---

[1] Pegge's Inquiry into the Nature and Cause of King John's Death. Archæologia, vol. iv. p. 29. Sleaford Castle and Newark Castle, mentioned afterwards, were both of them now in the King's hands.

[2] P. Langtoft says he died at *Hauche*, but read Nauche—*i.e.*, Nauerche, or Newark.

[3] The Abbot of Croxton (perhaps Ralph de Lincoln. Willis, Mitr. Abb. II., p. 109) was his physician at Newark. M. Paris, p. 288.

[4] Dr Brady, p. 515, and App., p. 164.

of the King to rally round the royal standard, as a point of security; which of necessity brought together many eye-witnesses of the first quality, in these realms, to bear evidence before the world of the last moments of the life of their friend and king.

King John died at Newark Castle on the 18th of October 1216,[1] Matt. Paris being then old enough to be professed at the monastery of St Albans the year following;[2] and Roger de Wendover, who died A.D. 1236, was also a contemporary. Thomas Rudburne was also a contemporary. Without the least impeachment or contradiction,[3] Richard de Morins, author of the Annals of Dunstable, was also living at the time, he being elected Prior of his house A.D. 1202,[4] and dying A.D. 1242.[5] Also the Annals of Margan, which terminate soon after A.D. 1232; and the Annals of Waverley, written probably about the same time, only say the King died, after three or four days' illness, at Newark.

The Annals of Mailros continued to the year 1270; and the Annals of Burton, whose author is thought to have been contemporary with Matt. Paris, agree in the same. Nicolas Trivet also, born about A.D. 1260,[6] says expressly, without transcribing from anybody, "Interim Joannes Rex, in ipso belli apparatu *morbo correptus docubuit* et post paucos dies defungitur apud Newark," &c. Matt. of Westminster too, who flourished A.D. 1307, gives the same account of the King's death at Newark.

And so we close our account of the real and actual John; and, when we have a little cleared our way, shall proceed to investigate the historic character who usurps his great name.

---

[1] So most authors. See Dr Brady, p. 517.
[2] Tanneri Biblioth., p. 572.
[3] Leland, Collectaneæ II., p. 421.
[4] Hearne's Præf., p. 21.
[5] Willis, Mitr. Abb. II., p. 2.
[6] Cave's Hist. Lit., Appendix, p. 9.

INTER-CHAPTER.

ACCESSION OF HENRY.

IT was on the 19th day of October, A.D. 1216, that King John died; and on the Eve of Simon and Jude, October 27th, an assembly was convened at Worcester,—at which Walo, the Pope's legate, Peter de Rupibus, Bishop of Winchester, Randulph Blandeville, Earl of Chester, William Marshall, Earl of Pembroke, William, Earl Ferrars, and many others, with abbots, priors, &c., were present,—to arrange for the coronation of Henry, the late King's eldest son.

On the day following, October 28th, the young King, aged ten years, proceeded in procession to the Cathedral of Worcester; and there, before the high altar, in the presence of all, swore,—as his father, grandfather, and their royal ancestors had done before,—on the Holy Gospels and other relics of the saints, that he would observe honour, peace, and reverence towards God and Holy Church; and also that he would show strict justice to the people, according to the laws and customs of the kingdom, &c.

After this, Peter de Rupibus, Bishop of Winchester, placed the crown upon his head, and anointed him King, with the usual ceremonies of prayer and chanting observed at coronations. William Marshall, Earl of Pembroke, was appointed guardian to the young King.

On the news of John's death reaching Dover, Louis at once raised the siege, and repaired to London, and from thence proceeded to Hertford, where he took the castle, nobly defended by Walter de Godardville, a knight of Falkasius.

Robert Fitz-Walter at once made a claim to the castle, which Louis, by the advice of his French knights, waved for the present, or "till the whole kingdom should be subdued."

As soon as Hertford Castle was taken, an attack was made upon the castle of Berkhampstead, under the charge of Walleran, a German, well tried in warfare, who made a brave resistance against the French, and caused great slaughter amongst them.[1]

After a protracted siege, Walleran surrendered the castle on the 20th of December.

On the day following,—St Thomas's Day,—Louis went to St Albans, and demanded homage from the abbot, which was refused.

Louis threatened to burn the convent and the whole town, but was appeased by the intervention of Saher de Quinci, Earl of Winchester, who persuaded the abbot to pay a fine for the convent and the town, when Louis returned to London.

After Easter, A.D. 1217, William, Earl Marshall, the guardian of the young King, assembled Randulph Blandeville, Earl of Chester, William de Fortibus, Earl of Albemarle, William, Earl of Ferrars, and many others, with Falkasius and his Castellans, to lay siege to the castle of Mountsorel.

Henry de Braybrooke commanded the place, along with ten knights of great valour; and these being hard pressed by the besiegers, sent to Saher, Earl of Winchester, then at the head of the barons in London, for immediate assistance.

The above invitation brought from the city of London six hundred knights and more than twenty thousand soldiers, under the command of the Count of Perche, Mareschall of France, Saher, Earl of Winchester, Robert Fitz-Walter, and others.

This army marched first to St Albans and then to Dunstable,

---

[1] *Walleran* is a name frequently met with in the "Rotuli Misæ" of the latter years of the reign of John, as one much about the King in the royal chamber. We have before classed him as a vadlet, clerk of the closet, or chamberlain of the Exchequer.

and next day proceeded northward for Mountsorel, where Randulph, Earl of Chester, and others were besieging.

As this great army approached, the Earl of Chester retreated to Nottingham Castle, there to watch the progress of their approaching enemies.

When the barons arrived at Mountsorel Castle, they determined to march to Lincoln, where Gilbert de Gant, the *French* Earl of Lincoln, had carried on a long siege without success.

This army of Robert Fitz-Walter and Saher de Quinci marched through the vale of Belvoir on their way to Lincoln, where they joined in the assault upon the castle.

While all this was passing at Lincoln, William Marshall, the guardian of the King and kingdom, by the advice of Walo the legate, Peter de Rupibus, Bishop of Winchester, and others, convoked all the Castellans belonging to the King, and knights in charge of castles in different parts of the kingdom; ordering them, on the command of the King, to assemble at Newark on the second day in Whitsun week, to proceed together to raise the siege of Lincoln Castle.

This summons was heartily responded to by the English party in the kingdom, who, when they were assembled, numbered four hundred knights, nearly two hundred and fifty cross-bow men, and a large host of followers and horsemen, who could act as soldiers, and fulfil the required duties on an emergency.

The chiefs of this army were, William, Earl Marshall, and William his son, Peter, Bishop of Winchester, William Plantagenet, Earl of Salisbury, William, Earl of Ferrars, and William de Fortibus, Earl of Albemarle.

Besides the above, there were also the barons William d'Albini, John Marshall, William de Cantelope, and William his son, the renowned Falkasius, Thomas Basset, Robert de Vipont, Brian de l'Isle, Geoffrey de Lucy, and Philip d'Albini, with many Castellans of experience in war.

These remained three days at Newark to refresh the horses, and men employed in confession, and in strengthening their bodies by partaking of the body and blood of our Lord, and asking His protection against their enemies.[1]

At length, on the sixth day of Whitsun week, after the performance of the holy sacrament, the legate rose, and set forth to all of them the injustice of the cause of Louis and the English barons who had joined him; and in order to animate the army to battle he put on his white robes, and, in company with the whole clergy there, excommunicated Louis by name and his accomplices, now carrying on the siege of Lincoln against the King of England.

To those engaged on the King of England's side, he granted a full pardon of all their sins, with a promise of eternal salvation.

After this they struck their camp and set off towards Lincoln, reaching Stowe, eight miles from Lincoln, by the evening, where they rested for the night.

In the morning, seven dense and well-appointed battalions were formed, and they marched against the enemy; the cross-bow men all the time keeping in advance of the army almost a mile.

The barons and French in the city felt such confidence of success that, when their scouts announced the approach of the enemy, they only laughed at them, and continued their attack on the walls of the castle.

Robert Fitz-Walter and Saher de Quinci went out to survey the host and estimate their numbers, and returned with a disparaging report. The army approached, and Falkasius entered the castle by the northern gate at the head of his division and all the cross-bow men, and stationed them suddenly on the roofs of the buildings and on the ramparts, whence they discharged their deadly weapons against the besieging barons—levelling at once horse and rider with the ground.

After the cross-bow men had done their work from the ram-

---

[1] Roger de Wendover, vol. ii. p. 392.

parts and roofs of the buildings, Falkasius burst forth from the castle at the head of his troops into the midst of the enemy.

He was so impetuous in his advance that he became surrounded and taken prisoner, until he was rescued by his cross-bow men and knights.

In the meantime the main body of English troops had forced the gates of the city and rushed upon the enemy.

The Count of Perche, the commander of the French troops, was slain, when the French battalions took to flight, both horse and foot, and suffered great loss at the southern gate by an impediment there, the cross-bar of the gates, left purposely to hinder the retreat.

No great effort was made in the pursuit, or not a man would have escaped.

Saher, Earl of Winchester, Henry de Bohun, Earl of Hereford, Gilbert de Gant, Louis's Earl of Lincoln, Robert Fitz-Walter, Richard de Montfitchet, William de Mowbray, William de Beauchamp, with many others, were taken prisoners.

The city of Lincoln became a scene of pillage for the conquerors, mixed up with the plunder taken from the sumpter-horses, baggage-waggons, &c., &c.; even the cathedral, churches, and religious houses taking their share in the penalties of excommunication.

This battle, named "*The Fair*," took place on the 19th day of May, A.D. 1217.[1]

It appears that Louis was not at "*The Fair*" fight of Lincoln, but in London, where he was joined by about two hundred knights, his friends in adventure, who had made their escape from Lincoln.

Walo the legate, with William Marshall and the Lincoln army, marched to London, and blockaded the place by land and water, when Louis offered to leave the kingdom and abandon the enterprise, if he could be allowed to do this on honourable terms.

Terms were agreed upon, and ratified at a place near Staines, on the Thames, when Louis returned to France, never more to lay claim to the crown of England.

---

[1] Roger de Wendover, vol. ii. p. 397.

CHAPTER XI.

THE BARONS.

By the feudal system every barony became a little kingdom, and the hereditary baron was judge in person, or by his bailiff, and carried his decrees or verdicts even to the length of capital punishment. Archbishops, bishops, abbots, and priors holding baronies of the Crown, had their baronial courts also, with similar powers; and even the barons of barons, or those holding manors by military service of the King's barons, had similar courts within their manors, but commonly without the privilege of pit and gallows, or the power of inflicting capital punishment.[1]

Before the Conquest, and for some time afterwards, the *Earl* was official in his own county, where he was governor, the general of his county in times of war, and the Chief Justiciary, or judge, in times of peace. His court, presided over by him, was the county court; and, as a reward or salary for his judgeship, he received the third penny of all the dues, amercements, and profits arising in his court.[2]

This was Anglo-Saxon justice, as well as that of William I., and was a court of great power and dignity, in which the bishop of the diocese sat with the Earl, and on which all the abbots, priors, barons, knights, and freeholders of the county were obliged to attend. In this Court all controversies arising in the county, even the most important, were determined, with appeal unto

---

[1] Spelman, Glanvil, Bracton, Fleta.   [2] Selden's Titles of Honour, p. 526, &c.

Cæsar. This judicature continued till A.D. 1085, when William I. excluded the bishops from the judicial bench, and confined them to their own ecclesiastical courts. By the removal of the bishops from the county courts, most of the legal talent and habits of business were removed from them, whereupon their reputation fell, and their usefulness too; which drove Henry II. to appoint paid judges from the bar, and plan out the circuits of assize, a measure which gave the greatest offence to the clerical pleaders, and chamber-council, attorneys and solicitors of the day; the King himself being the chief judge, who travelled the circuits with the Chief Justiciary and other judges of assize, as did also his son John, with most indefatigable industry and painful exertion,—as has been shewn.

According to William of Malmesbury, all the advocates, as well as clerks, in the law courts of the Anglo-Saxon period, were clergymen, from which the clergy got the name of clerks; and the Anglo-Saxon clergy were so generally practitioners in law, that it became a proverb—"There is no clergyman who is not a cause pleader." [1]

J. Sarisburiensis affirms that the best writers of the period represent those clerical advocates as the most covetous and venal of all men.[2]

We now come to Henry II., who was a lawyer by profession, of whom Henry, in his History of England, very justly observes:— "This great prince, in the course of his long reign, made several improvements in the law, especially in its forms, in the manner of its administration, and the practice of its courts."[3] Randulph de Glanvill was this great King's Chief Justiciary. Henry II., if we may believe one of the best of our ancient historians, was assured by his judges "that the clergy, in the first ten years of his reign, had committed no fewer than one hundred murders, besides many thefts, robberies, rapes, and other crimes, for which they could not

---

[1] William of Malmesbury, l. 4, p. 70, col. 1. [2] Vol. vi. p. 58. [3] Pp. 289-292.

punish them."[1] Henry continues: "To put a stop to those intolerable evils, and reduce the clergy to the rank of subjects, Henry, in a great council, A.D. 1164, enacted the famous Constitution of Clarendon."[2]

The 'Statute,' or 'Constitution of Clarendon,' which was passed at a great National Council, in the tenth year of the reign of Henry II., A.D. 1164, was the most grievous blow ever inflicted on the priestly order by the Crown of England. It caused that disruption between the Crown and the Church which ended with the murder of A'Becket, the Archbishop of Canterbury, and the complete subjugation of the King during the remainder of his days to priestly domination. Richard I. personally escaped sacerdotal rudeness by becoming a crusader, and by exhausting the blood and treasure of England at the gates of Jerusalem, to the great loss of strength of his kingdom. He left at home a priestly tyrant as Regent—viz., Bishop and Chancellor William Longchamp, Bishop of Ely, who was deposed and banished the realm in the "Churchyard Parliament" in the ever-memorable year, A.D. 1191, when, as we shewed, for the first time in English history, a minister of the Crown was made personally responsible for the advice which he might give to his sovereign.

In the eighth year of King John, A.D. 1206, on the death of the great Hubert Walter, Archbishop of Canterbury, and the appointment of his friend and disciple, John Gray of Norfolk, as his successor in the archbishopric, the sacerdotal flame again broke forth, as we saw, by the Pope refusing to confirm the election of Gray and insisting upon a French professor of divinity being elected Archbishop of Canterbury in his place.

This contest of A.D. 1206, on the appointment of an Archbishop of Canterbury, was only a tongue of flame from the smouldering

---

[1] Henry's History of England, vol. vi. p. 59, and William Neubrigen, l. a, c. 16, tom. 1, p. 158.

[2] Gervas's Chronicle, col. 1386, and Henry's History of England, vol. vi. p. 59.

embers of the fire of Clarendon of A.D. 1164,—that fire which was the death of Thomas à Becket.

John, supported as he was by his old coadjutor of the Churchyard Parliament, William Marshall, Earl of Pembroke; the two Grays, John and Walter; Peter de Rupibus, Bishop of Winchester; and Randulph Blandeville, Earl of Chester, and a dozen more, calmly accepted the challenge of the Church of Rome, and put both monk and priest at defiance for six years together; the King during those years being publicly denounced and cursed by book, bell, and candle at every churchyard gate and market-cross by all faithful monks and priests, because he adhered to the " CONSTITUTION OF CLARENDON."

Affairs took so high a turn that the King had to give over his crown to the Pope, in order to prevent that crown being placed upon the head of Philip, King of France, or his son, Louis, and that crown was held by the Popes of Rome for a hundred and fifty-four years, until Edward III., by the advice of his Parliament, refused to pay the £1000 annual rental for permission to wear it.

The truth is, Henry II., who had been brought up for the bar in France, where he held the situation of Seneschal of France, introduced into the cleric-haunted law courts of England great changes of administration, by having educated barristers for pleaders, and men learned in the law for judges.

This was death to all legal dignity in the sacerdotal order.

After King John had surrendered his kingdom to the Pope, the clergy were still dissatisfied with their position in England; for the great political move of the Pope and conclave of cardinals at Rome in European politics, did not embrace Henry II., 1164, and the " *Constitution of Clarendon*," that 'Constitution' which clipped the wings of the clergy of England, and confined their flights to the convocation, synod, and parish vestry, instead of the presidential chair of the county courts or hundred sessions.

At the time we are writing upon, A.D. 1164, the clergy were almost the only persons who taught and practised physic, as well as the other sciences; and we meet with very few celebrated for their medical knowledge who were not priests or monks.

This profession became so lucrative, and so many monks applied to the study and practice of it,—deserting their monasteries and neglecting their own profession,—that a canon was made in the Council of Tours, A.D. 1163, prohibiting monks to stay out of their monasteries above two months at one time, teaching or practising physic.[1]

William of Malmesbury, a Benedictine monk of the twelfth century, the most learned and truthful of that order, writes as follows on this subject:—

"Before the arrival of the Normans, learning was almost extinct in England.

"The clergy contented themselves with the slightest smattering of letters, and could hardly stammer through the offices of the Church. If any one amongst them understood a little grammar, he was admired as a prodigy."[2]

To which Dr Henry, the historian, adds:[3] "But so sudden and advantageous a change in this respect took place after the Conquest, that the same sensible writer acquaints us that learning was in a more flourishing state in England and Normandy, so early as the reign of Henry I., than it was in Italy."[4]

This happy change seems to have been owing to the following causes:—

"The accession of William, Duke of Normandy, to the throne of England contributed in several ways to the revival of learning in Britain. That prince had received a good education, was fond of reading, and the conversation of learned men, to whom he was a most munificent patron, advancing them to the highest dignities and richest benefices in the Church."[5]

---

[1] Bulæi Hist. Univers Parisien, tom. ii. p. 575. Henry's History of England, vol. vi. p. 114.
[2] Wm. of Malmesbury, l. 3, p. 57.
[3] Vol. vi. p. 117.
[4] W. Malmesbury, l. 5, p. 90.
[5] Wm. Gemitens, p. 604, edit. a Camdeno. Orderic Vitalis, p. 656.

"This had excited an extraordinary ardour for literary pursuits among the clergy in Normandy, and had afterwards the same effect in England. Besides this, many of the most learned men on the continent came over into Britain after the Conquest, and by their example and instructions diffused the love and knowledge of letters. William took great care of the education of his royal offspring, and Henry I., his youngest son, became the most learned prince and the greatest promoter of learning of the age in which he flourished. This procured him the surname of *Beauclerk*, or the fine scholar."[1]

"He married his only daughter, the heiress of all his dominions, to Geoffrey Plantagenet, Earl of Anjou, who is greatly celebrated for his learning."[2]

"The eldest son of this marriage, Henry II., received a learned education, under the direction of his excellent uncle, Robert, Earl of Gloucester, who was more illustrious for his knowledge and virtue than for his royal birth."[3]

"Henry II. never lost that taste for letters he had acquired in his youth; and through his whole life—as we are assured by one who was intimately acquainted with him—he spent his leisure hours either in reading, or in discussing some literary question in a circle of learned men.[4] His three sons—three only! (*Constitution of Clarendon* even here, in Dr Robert Henry's History of England!) Henry, Geoffrey, and Richard—had all a considerable tincture of letters, and a taste for poetry.[5] Under the patronage of these great princes learning could hardly fail to revive, and in some degree to flourish."

As Robert Henry, D.D., could only select the names of *Henry, Geoffrey,* and *Richard* as learned men, we are left to infer that another son of Henry II.—his youngest, John—had no learning,

---

[1] Martin Anec. l. 3, p. 345. J. Brompton, apud X. Scriptores, p. 978.
[2] D. Acherii Spicileg, l. 10, p. 508.
[3] Gervas's Chronicle, p. 1358, and W. Malmesbury, l. v. p. 96.
[4] P. Blesens Epi, t. 6, p. 98.
[5] Histoire Littéraire de la France, tom. 9, p. 175.

nay, had no existence at all! But it was not so. Dr Henry, the historian of the eighteenth century, has as much of the leaven of monkism and priestcraft in his pages as was ever possessed by any Benedictine monk of the twelfth or thirteenth century.

No monkish writer ever held the spirit of vengeance over the head of a devoted criminal, for the enactment of the "*Constitution of Clarendon*," with more singleness of purpose (and this after the lapse of six hundred years) than does Dr Henry, in his "History of England," as follows :—

"Though King John was certainly one of the worst princes that ever filled the throne of England, his reign will be for ever memorable for the melioration of the Constitution by the great Charter of liberties that was then obtained. His merit, however, in this melioration was very small, as he contributed to it only by rendering himself odious by his vices, contemptible by his follies, and impotent by his losses,—which both constrained and encouraged his subjects to demand, and enabled them to obtain, by means already related, this great palladium of English liberty."[1]

As the spirit of vengeance for the "*Constitution of Clarendon*" haunts the monkism and priestism of all centuries, we will pause to inquire what that great statute of Clarendon really was, and how it acted upon monk and priest.

Its sections were sixteen in number, of which the substance is as follows :—

No. 1. All pleas between clergymen and laymen shall be tried in the King's courts.

No. 2. Churches in the King's gift shall not be filled without his consent.

No. 3. All clergymen, when accused of any crime, shall be tried in the King's courts; and, when convicted, shall not be protected from punishment by the Church.

---

[1] Vol. vi. p. 64.

No. 4. Clergymen shall not go out of the kingdom without the King's leave.

Nos. 5, 6. Regulate the manner of proceedings in the ecclesiastical courts.

No. 7. None of the King's ministers or vassals shall be excommunicated without his knowledge.

No. 8. Appeals from the archbishops to be made to the King.

No. 9. Pleas between a clerk and a layman, whether an estate was in free-alms or a lay-fee.

No. 10. One of the King's tenants might be interdicted, but not excommunicated, without the consent of the civil judge of the place.

No. 11. All prelates who hold baronies of the King shall perform the same services with other barons.

No. 12. The revenues of vacant fees and abbeys belong to the King. The election of prelates shall be with the King's consent; and they shall swear fealty and do homage to the King, before their consecration.

Nos. 13, 14, 15. Direct the manner of proceeding in case any of the King's barons shall disseise any of the clergy of the lay-fees which they held under them.

No. 16. The sons of villains shall not be ordained without the leave of their masters.[1]

The above gives the substance of the celebrated "*Constitution of Clarendon*"—a statute which in its consequences has worked more important issues than any other statute which ever has been passed by a British Parliament. In the first place, it was the cause of the murder of Thomas à Becket, of the surrender of the kingdom of England to the Pope for one hundred and fifty-four years, and of the passing of *Magna Charta*, with other baleful effects, onward for centuries.

The "*Constitution of Clarendon*" was passed A.D. 1164; and in

---

[1] Gervas's Chronicle, col. 1386, &c.

A.D. 1176 Henry II., with consent of the Great Council of the nation, consisting of prelates, earls, and barons, at Northampton, divided the whole kingdom into six parts or circuits, and appointed three judges *learned in the law* to hold courts in each of these, by a commission from the King,—empowering them to hear and determine all causes not exceeding the value of one-half of a knight's fee, unless the matter were of such importance or difficulty as to require the judgment of the King's court, in his royal presence.[1]

These Justices-Itinerant took an oath to administer justice to all persons with impartiality.[2]

These itinerant judges had also authority to adjudicate in all criminal causes and pleas of the Crown, and to transact a variety of other affairs for the public good.

In 1179 a further change was made, by dividing the kingdom into four circuits, and allowing a greater number of judges to each of these circuits.[3]

We may picture to ourselves the great disturbance which these wise laws must have caused to the priestly mind in judge and pleader in the upper law-courts; where baron, squire, and knight, with bishop, abbot, prior, dean, and rector, had all the honours and all the emoluments of the legal profession to divide amongst them.

Henry II. went still further with his reforms in the administration of the law, by giving encouragement to trial by jury, instead of the superstitious modes of trial by fire-and-water ordeals, and the still more barbarous one of single combat, especially in civil causes.

No prince ever introduced such reforms into the law-courts as did Henry II.; and yet these very reforms in the law were the real cause of the clerical clamour for a return to the laws of our Saxon ancestors. Yes; the code of Edward the Confessor, with the

---

[1] Roger Hoveden's Annals, p. 313.   [2] Roger de Wendover, p. 92, col. 1.
[3] Hoveden's Annals, p. 337.

tattered scraps of Canute's code, and those of Ethelred, Edgar, Edwy, Edred, Edmund, Athelstan, Edward the Elder, Alfred Ethelred, Ethelbert, and a score of others; for in these Saxon courts and Saxon times the *personne* was the great man, and presided as judge with the baron and the squire, and with them divided the bribes, fees, and fines of the court.

We might have supposed that the total surrender of the kingdom to the Pope by King John, after his terrific struggle with the Church of Rome for six years, would have afforded unmixed satisfaction to the clergy.

But no! The clergy were overruled and outwitted altogether by that surrender; for they had intended it to have been made to the King of France, from whom they could have extorted a better bargain in restoration of those times,—the Saxon times of fees and fines, legal honours and social positions, as judges and pleaders at the bar,—those times when "darkness covered the earth, and gross darkness the people." The flood-tide of French civilisation and learning, so fatally cherished by Henry II. as to make clerical or monkish judges and clerical special pleaders and king's counsel altogether out of fashion, was the real grievance of the monks and priests in the reigns of Henry II. and King John. The gift of the kingdom to the Pope did not flush back the flood of French advancement introduced by Henry II. No! That gift did not repeal the "*Constitution of Clarendon*," and the providing judges learned in the law for his new assize courts.

The gift of the kingdom to the Pope threw the clergy; and was an act which they wished to ignore altogether by clamouring in the face of that gift for the "Great Charter"—the professed copy of the charter of Henry I. As for poor Henry II., his name was never once mentioned in all the contest for "Magna Charta." Henry I. was the god of monkish idolatry; and why? Henry I. was a great builder and endower of churches and monasteries; while Henry II. was the reformer of the law-courts—the firm-handed clearer-out of the clerics.

CHAPTER XII.

TITLE OF "MAGNA CHARTA" INVALID—NOBLE "BROKERS"—
DETAILS OF CHARTER EXAMINED.

IT may be impatiently asked, How came King John to submit so tamely to the Runnemead dictation? Was it cowardice? John and his ministers knew well that the whole document of MAGNA CHARTA was invalid in title, and therefore utterly worthless as a national legislative enactment. Here we find the explanation of his 'smile' when it was first proposed to him at the house of the Knights-Templars in London. Stephen Langton was the ostensible mover of the whole sedition. Who and what was he? Who and what his tools?

Stephen Langton was a baron of the realm, who had been five years in France exciting the king and people of France to invade and take possession of these realms by force of arms. Consequently he was a traitor to the crown and realm of England. William, Bishop of London, was in France for five years, similarly inciting the French king and his people to an invasion of these realms, he being at the time a baron of England. Self-convicted, he too is branded as a traitor.

Eustace, Bishop of Ely, also a baron of these realms, was in like manner in France for five years, urging upon the king and nation the advantage of an invasion of England. Again a traitor!

Giles, Bishop of Hereford, was in France with Stephen Langton, William, Bishop of London, and Eustace, Bishop of Ely, and was a participator in their acts and deeds when in France for five years. Once more—a traitor!

Jocelyn, Bishop of Bath, was in France with Stephen Langton

and the above-named bishops, partaking of their traitorous actions at the court of France for five years together, while still a baron of the realm of England. Yet again—a traitor!

Hubert, Bishop of Lincoln, was of the same conspiracy in France, and also, like them, a baron of the realm of England; and thus also a traitor!

Robert Fitz-Walter was a traitor who had fled the realm to avoid worse personal consequences. He had been outlawed.

Eustace de Vesci, another baron, a traitor who had fled the realm, and been outlawed to save worse personal consequences.

Saher de Quinci, Earl of Winchester, a baron of the Exchequer, —a needy money-borrower of the Jews, as the Tower records fully shew,—was a leader in this conspiracy. We imagine that he alone possessed any legal knowledge, and had a good deal to do with drawing up the document,—especially those parts on borrowing money of the Jews, and only paying it back again under certain favourable circumstances.

Saher de Quinci may represent a large body of the barons of Runnemead—hungry scoundrels ready for the scramble on an invasion from France, and a redistribution of baronial and knights' fees from the hands of the King of France; made King of England either at Paris or Westminster.

As Walter Savage Landor once wrote to a friend of ours, of Charles I., "These men I would not have beheaded. No, sir! I would have *hanged* every one of them." But it may be retorted, that although these men had been traitors to King John, runaway traitors, they yet had been pardoned by the King. "Pardoned by the King"—yes! and this pardon alone gave them standing-room in England. And this is urged as a defence. "O Shame, where is thy blush?" How did they return the King's gracious favour, solicited by the Pope? By dragging the King to Runnemead, to insult him there. Noble patriots! Poltroonly ingrates rather! But, technically, we are non-suited on the traitor-charge brought against the conspirators of Runnemead because of a condoning pardon. We must, therefore, fall back upon other evidence to shew the utter worthlessness of the title-deed of MAGNA CHARTA.

In the year A.D. 1213, as we have seen, King John surrendered his crown and kingdom, his Lord-Paramountship of England and Ireland, to Pope Innocent III., and received them back again in vassalage at a "*ferm*" of one thousand marks of sterling money, to be paid half-yearly for the two. This money was paid to Pandulph, the delegate of the Pope, in advance; and the King's charters of supremacy and surrender were handed over to the delegate and taken to Rome, where they now are.

This act of surrender broke the bond of feudalism in England. John became a vassal of the Pope; and as his baronage only held of him, as all feudatories and sub-infeudatories held, on the pleasure of the lord-in-capite, the pleasure or will of holding departed on the death of the lord-in-chief. John was feudally dead. He had ceased to exist as Lord-Paramount, and all his baronage and other sub-infeudatories were dead too. The Pope was the risen man. Had these barons done homage to the new lord, and received a renewal by letters-patent of their baronies? Had they done homage to the Pope for their fees? No. They were excommunicated by the Pope, the head of the fee; they were a broken baronage, and as such *were no barons at all*, but yeomen or copyholders only—only copyholders—of King John, the freeholder of the Pope. The barons who assembled at Runnemead were out of the pale of the law. They were outlaws in a state of insurrection against the lord-paramount the Pope, and his freeholder, King John.

THE TITLE TO MAGNA CHARTA IS INVALID. Copyholders could not legislate as barons of the realm.

Copyholders could not attest legislative enactments with baronial seals.

In A.D. 1213 the baronage was broken, and remained so for one hundred and fifty-four years at least; for during those years the rent was paid to the Pope.

But we must look a little more closely at this famous or infamous and ignorantly lauded 'Charter,' and, in detail, expose its worthlessness as a thing of LAW.

Matthew of Westminster,[1] when writing on King John's surrender of his crown and kingdom to the Pope as a free gift, gives the following as the confirming Charter of surrender :—

"Therefore we, holy grace itself inspiring us, in accordance with the excellent counsel of our barons, do offer and freely grant to God, and to his holy apostles Peter and Paul, and to the holy Roman Church our mother, and to our lord the Pope, Innocent III., and his successors, all the right of patronage which we have in the Anglican churches, and the whole kingdom of England and the kingdom of Ireland, with all their rights and belongings, for the remission of our sins, and those of our whole race, both living and dead. And receiving them back again, as it were, from God and the Roman Catholic Church, as their feudatory,[2] and holding them so, with the presence of the wise Pandulph, the sub-deacon and friend of our lord the Pope, we, from this time forward, doing liege homage to our lord,[3] Pope Innocent, and his Catholic suc-

---

[1] Vol. ii. p. 116 of Chronicle.

[2] "*Their feudatory*" does not mean vicegerent. A vicegerent finds no place or name in the feudal system, while the highest place in that system for feudatory is a "libere tenens"—freeholder.

[3] What is "*doing liege homage to our lord?*" Is it the mere formality of a vicegerent, or is it the reality of feudalism? Does it imply vassalage? "*Liege homage to our lord*," what is it? In the fairest sunshine in which you can behold it, you see the "FREEHOLDER."

Allowing King John to be *freeholder*, what were his sub-infeudatories? Were they equals, feudatories —"hail, fellow, well met?" Certainly not; they formed a lower grade as his tenants. They were *his inferiors* in the system of feudalism. They were copyholders, and copyholders only, *every man of them*. They were farm-tenants, farmers, yeomen, every man of them. THEY WERE YEOMEN ONLY!

This was feudalism—an institution which no Popery could tamper with without vitiating. To tamper with it, was to destroy it. The Pope could not alter the system; for feudalism stood above and beyond Popery. The Pope could destroy, and did destroy King John's position as lord-paramount; and by that destruction he rendered the proud legislators of Runnemead COPYHOLDERS, and as such their laws, not worth the skins upon which they were written.

cessors, and to the Roman Church, according to the form set down below, would do the same in the presence of our lord the Pope, if it were possible for us to be in his presence : Obliging our successors and our heirs by our wife for ever, that they in the same manner shew loyalty and fidelity, without any contradiction, to the supreme pontiff, who shall for the time be the president of the Church, and to do him homage; and, moreover, we and our successors do resign for ever the guardianship of the vacant churches. And, in proof of this, our perpetual offering and concession, we do will and establish that, from our own proper and especial revenues, which proceed from our kingdoms before-mentioned, the Roman Church shall, in lieu of all customs which we are bound to pay for those things, (besides, in all cases, the penny of Saint Peter,) receive a thousand marks sterling every year,—that is to say, five hundred marks at the Feast of Saint Michael, and five hundred marks at Easter—of which thousand marks seven hundred shall be for the kingdom of England, and three hundred for the kingdom of Ireland; and this shall be done without injury to ourselves, our heirs, our laws, liberties, and royal privileges. And we, willing that all these things shall be ratified and perpetual and lasting, as they have been above set down, do bind ourselves and our successors not to contravene them. And if we or any of our successors shall presume to attempt any such thing, whoever he may be, he shall be declared an outlaw, unless, on being admonished, he come to his senses. And that this Charter of our obligation and concession may remain unalterable, I swear that for the future, from this hour forth, I will be faithful to God and to the blessed Peter, and the Roman Church, and our lord the Pope Innocent, and to all his successors who become so in accordance with the Catholic faith.

"Moreover, I will be a helper in upholding and defending the patrimony of the blessed Peter, and especially of the kingdom of England and kingdom of Ireland, against all men, as far as my power extends.

"So help me God and these holy gospels; I myself being the witness, in the house of the military order of the Temple."

Philip Augustus, King of France, when remonstrating with his son Louis and the barons of the realm, observed, "The kingdom of England never was the patrimony of Peter or of the Roman Church; nor is it now, nor will it ever be," &c. [1]

"The nobles of France began to cry out, as it were with one voice, that *they* would stand to the death in defence of that article —namely, that no king or prince could, by the impulse of his own private will, give away his kingdom, or make it tributary; by which conduct the nobles of his kingdom would be rendered slaves."

What does this mean? Does it mean that the barons of France affirmed to their king that for a king, being lord-paramount, to give away his fee, and receive it back again in vassalage from the grantee, was to become a lower member in the feudal system, and his baronage still lower, or so low as to become slaves?

They meant this; and they said this with reference to the position of the baronage of England, after John had ceased to be Lord-Paramount and become a FREEHOLDER. Thus, once more it has to be repeated, that John's becoming a freeholder broke the letters-patent of nobility of all his baronage, and rendered the body or class of nobility copyholders.

In short, the proud baronage of England ceased to be peers of the realm.

The gift of the nation to the Pope was a formal legislative enactment, as well as the confirmation of the vassalage-tenure by the King. The following attesting witnesses, given in the language of Matthew Paris, will verify the transaction; and also shew that it was not a capricious, drunken, or thoughtless act on the part of the King:—

"Et hæ charta obligationis et concessionis nostræ semper firma

---

[1] Matt. Westminster, vol. ii. p. 126.

King John of England. 147

permaneat. Teste meipso apud domum militum templi juxta Doveram coram—

H. Dublinensi archiepiscopo.
Johanne Norwicensi episcopo.
Galfrido filio Petri.
W. comite Sarisburiæ.
Willielmo comite Pembroc.
R. comite Bononiæ.
W. comite Warennæ.
S. comite Winton.
W. comite Arundel.
W. comite de Ferarriis.
W. Briwere.
Petro filio Hereberti.
Warino filio Geroldi.

15th die Maii anno regni nostri decimo quarto."

"Randulph Higden, in his book entitled 'Polychronicon,' saith indeed that King John did not only bind himself, but his heirs and successors, being kings of England, to be feudatories unto Pope Innocent and his successors, popes of Rome; that is to say, that they should hold their dominions of them in fee, yielding and paying yearly to the See of Rome the sum of seven hundred marks for England, and three hundred marks for Ireland."[1]

From the above, as well as a dozen other testimonies, it is plain to demonstration, King John gave his dominions absolutely to the Pope, and received them back again as a vassal, or as *libere tenens*, a *freeholder;* which transaction made at once all his sub-infeudatories copyholders, yeomen, or farmers, and broke their nobility as holding by first-class baronage tenures.

Surely somewhat of the 'sacredness,' somewhat of the 'glory,' of this vaunted 'Charter' vanishes in the light of these facts and elucidations; and we might well stay here our commentary as

---

[1] Holinshead's Chronicle, vol. iii. p. 177.

being on an invalid title-deed—a worthless parchment. But although the whole getting-up of the Magna Charta insult has been shewn to have been a French conspiracy to serve Louis, the husband of Blanche, the daughter of King John's sister Eleanor, who had married the King of Castile, yet, as this document has always been held up to the public gaze as a miracle of patriotic legislative wisdom, we feel ourselves compelled to touch upon its merits somewhat. Let us glance rapidly at some of the details:—

1st, "That the Church of England shall be free, and enjoy her whole rights and liberties inviolable."

This might appear to be the design of Langton and his traitorous bishops,—those preachers of treason in France,—and their tools, Robert Fitz-Walter and Saher de Quinci; but it is not so. This placing the Church above the secular power is the very corner-stone of the fabric of feudalism.

When Joseph, the prime minister of Pharaoh King of Egypt, enslaved the people of Egypt, he left the Church property above and beyond the legislative reach of the secular power.[1]

All the provisions of Magna Charta respecting the Church of the nation are as old as the feudal system itself; and had been carried out by King John during the whole of his reign.

2d, "We have also granted to all the freemen of our kingdom, for us and for our heirs, for ever, all the underwritten liberties: to have and to hold, them and their heirs, of us and our heirs."

What is a freeman? Is he not a man holding in chief, or *libere tenens*, of the lord-paramount of the fee? Was not King John the *libere tenens* for the whole kingdoms of England and Ireland? Was he not tenant-in-chief of the Pope? He was. He took the fee at a rental—an annual rental. He was the tenant, the *libere tenens*, the *freeholder*, the *freeman*, and the *only freeman* in the realm; and his sub-infeudatories were copyholders, and copyholders only.

---

[1] Genesis xlvii. 22-26.

This clause provides for them "*to have and to hold, them and their heirs, of us.*"

What is this? Is it a sub-infeudation under a freeholder. It is. The people of England were all copyholders; and the clause is as worthless as informal.

3d, "If any of our earls or barons, or others who *hold in chief* by military service, shall die," &c., &c., &c.

This is absurd. King John was tenant-in-chief by military or baronial service, and he alone in his fee-ferm. He paid the rent, he was tenant-in-chief; and the so-called earls were the copyholders of the realm, and had no standing as peers of the realm—especially when the lord of the fee, the Pope, protested against their insurrectionary and tumultuous gathering.

11th, "If the principal debtor fail in the payment of the debt, not having wherewithal to discharge it, then the sureties shall answer the debt; and if they will, they shall have the lands and rents of the debtor until they be satisfied for the debts which they have paid for him, unless the principal debtor can shew himself acquitted thereof against the said sureties."

This was the law of England for generations before the passing of this document. Every boy of fourteen years had to find twelve sureties for his production when wanted by the lord-paramount, and to pay his debts, and answer as bondsmen for his general good conduct as a citizen, and pay any fines required by the State for any deficiency of honest membership.

12th, "If any one have borrowed anything of the Jews, more or less, and dies before the debt be satisfied, there shall be no interest paid for that debt so long as the heir be under age, of whomsoever he may hold; and if the debt falls into our hands, we shall take only the chattel mentioned in the charter or instruments."

13th, "And if any one die indebted to the Jews, his wife shall have her dower, and pay nothing of that debt; and if the deceased left children under age, they shall have necessaries provided for them according to the tenement (or real estate) of the deceased;

and from the residue the debt shall be paid, saving, however, the service of the lords. In like manner let it be to other persons than Jews."

The above provisions are not new, for prejudices against usury were of very old standing, even as far back as our Saxon kings; but whether Magna Charta be honoured by the above way of checking usury, is very doubtful to us. The heir under age is protected from interest; the dower of the widow is secured from payment; the lord's rent is secured from payment; the provision for the children must be secured; and then, if there should be any residue, from that residue the Jews' debt may be paid, but not otherwise.

17th, "And for the assessing of scutages we shall cause to be summoned the archbishops, bishops, abbots, earls, and great barons of the realm, singly, by our letters."

Previous to the 15th of May, A.D. 1213, when King John was lord-paramount, he always summoned "*the great barons of the realm*" by letter, personally addressed to each, and signed by the royal sign-manual. John did this when he was lord-paramount; but when he became a freeholder under the Pope, and "*the great barons of the realm*" became his copyholders, the charter of incorporation or letters-patent of nobility was broken, and no sophistry of the Roman Catholic Church could heal the fracture. The institutions of feudalism were superior to the conjuring tricks of popes and cardinals. Feudality in England was broken; and what followed afterwards was sham and nonsense.

18th, "And furthermore, we will cause to be summoned in general, by our sheriffs and bailiffs, all others who hold of us in chief (as citizens and burgesses) at a certain day,—that is to say, forty days before their meeting, at least,—to a certain place; and in all letters of such summons we will declare the cause of the summons."

All minor barons or burgesses "*who hold of us in chief*" are to be summoned by the sheriffs of the counties, and high bailiffs or constables of the cities or boroughs.

All this was done by the sheriffs, bailiffs, and constables so long as John was lord-paramount, and *they* were freeholders under the crown; but when the King himself became freeholder, the bond or charter of incorporation was broken, and the summons of the county sheriff or city bailiff became a sham,—and such a sham as the Church of Rome could not gloss over or conceal.

38th, "We will retain the lands of those convicted of felony but one year and a day, and then they shall be delivered to the '*lords of the fee.*'"

What could the "*lords of the fee*" mean in 1215, when the King himself had become the sole freeholder of the realm in 1213? Copyholders or yeomen could not be "*lords of fees.*" No! nor summon a jury to a court-leet or court-baron; nor fine a constable, bailiff, or tenant of the manor for non-attendance. King John's becoming a vassal of the Church of Rome in the year 1213 broke every court-leet and court-baron of the realm. We do not believe that there is a single court-leet or court-baron in England or Ireland which could stand a sifting investigation in a court of equity. The court-leet and court-baron of the lordship and manor are feudal institutions all over; and on the legalities—*the technicalities in law*—they must stand or fall. If the charter of incorporation of the manor court be informal, where is the authority of the steward of the court for summoning and impannelling of the jury? Where stands the authority for fining a delinquent tenant, or a contemptuous constable or juryman? A mere freeholder certainly could not grant a court-leet or court-baron to a copyholder.

41st, "There shall be one measure of wine and one of ale through our whole realm; and one measure of corn,—that is to say, the *London quarter;* and one breadth of dyed cloth and *russet* and *haberjects*,—that is to say, two ells within the list; and the weights shall be as measures."

This measure was really good, though unnecessary; for the King had striven more than ever king strove before or since, through his great minister, *Hubert Walter,* to make the wine-merchant and the innkeeper place the legal measure within *the decanter.*

Considering the position in which King John had placed the peerage of England, by himself becoming a vassal of the Pope, it is quite impossible to wade through the several provisions of Magna Charta without a feeling of impatience occasioned by their absurdity. As the necessity for the Great Charter was never named till after King John had become a vassal of the Pope, we must regard this "great" declaration of rights at Runnemead by the baronage of England as a *whitewashing* of their order. The peerage of England was broken by King John in 1213; and the barons assembled in 1215 to whitewash their order and ignore the breakage.

We believe the gathering at Runnemead to have been an attempt to filch from Pope Innocent III. his TITLE-DEEDS TO ENGLAND.

There was nothing new in Magna Charta, nothing but what had been acted upon for fifty years at least; the last innovation being introduced by that enlightened king, Henry II., under the advice of Randulph de Glanville, the English lawyer.

Most of the provisions went back for generations, and formed the great staple of all coronation oaths from the time of Edward the Confessor. But suppose new laws had been required, was Stephen Langton or was Robert Fitz-Walter the man to introduce those laws to the King and realm of England? Certainly not the latter.

We have been curious to find how the tampered page of monkish history gets over the anomalous position of the King and baronage of England by John becoming the "*libere tenens*" of the Pope.

Roger de Wendover gets over the difficulty by placing King John outside the pale of feudalism, when he had been lord-paramount of the fee of England;[1] and for this honour of annihilation in feudality, John is allowed to pay a rent of £20,000 a year; for a thousand merks, A.D. 1213, is equal to £20,000 a year of our time and money.

This piece of trickery is made out to save the position of the "*baronagii Angliæ*" at the King's expense.

Did King John surrender absolutely his crown and kingdom to the Pope of Rome?

He did, and became "*vicegerent*" in return for £20,000 a year of our money and time.

What is "*vicegerent*" in feudalism? It is nothing; and for that nothing King John has to pay £20,000 a year of our money and time.

Is this likely? No. Again the monkish story has been garbled to save the position of the "*baronagii Angliæ.*"

The truth is, John became a vassal of the Church of Rome—a "*libere tenens*" or "*freeholder*"—and at a rental. England became his "fee-ferm," and he was the tenant-in-chief of the Pope.

Well! but what were the barons of England? Were not they tenants-in-chief also? No, certainly not. John was the tenant, for he paid the annual rental for the tenement. John could not pay his rental for his tenement, and have besides half of England partners in the ferm, without the express consent of the lord of the fee, and declaration made in the charter of feudation.

The King of England became the only "*freeholder*" in England; and all his barons, knights, and esquires, of high and low degree, became his sub-infeudatories as "*copyholders.*"

The Papistry may be full of trick and sophistry, but feudalism stood above Popery; and no Pope of Rome or Constantinople could throw down the ancient landmarks of feudalism as it stood in its integrity.

---

[1] Flowers of History, vol. ii. p. 269.

"*Vicegerent*" indeed! Feudalism recognised no such order; and Pope Innocent III. could not create it.

John was freeholder, and his barons were copyholders; and no Pope could upset the order of precedency.

Copyholders assuming to be legislators at Runnemead !—yes, at Runnemead! The thing was a sham, *for copyholders could not legislate there.*

Their signatures, their escutcheons, their seals attesting, what were they?

All sham!—all! The MAGNA CHARTA was a farce, a delusion, and a fraud; invalid in title, and *utterly worthless as a legal document.*

On the 15th day of May, A.D. 1213, the English King and Pandulph the legate, with the nobles of the kingdom, met at the house of the Knights-templars, near Dover, and there the said King, according to a decree pronounced at Rome, resigned the crown, with the kingdoms of England and Ireland, into the hands of our lord the Pope, whose functions the said Pandulph was then performing.

After having resigned them there, he gave the aforesaid kingdoms to the Pope and his successors, and confirmed them to the latter by the underwritten:—

"*John, by the grace of God King of England, &c., to all the faithful servants of Christ who shall behold this charter, health in the Lord.*[1]—We wish it by this our charter, signed with our seal, to be known to you, that we, having in many things offended God and our mother the Holy Church, and being in great need of the Divine mercy for our sins, and not having wherewithal to make a worthy offering as an atonement to God, and to pay the just demands of the Church, unless we humiliate ourselves before Him who humiliated Himself for us even to death; we, impelled by the inspiration of the Holy Spirit, and not by force or from

---

[1] Roger de Wendover, Flowers of History, vol. ii. p. 268.

fear of the interdict, but of our own free will and consent, and by the general advice of our barons, assign and grant to God and His holy apostles Peter and Paul, and to the Holy Church of Rome, our mother, and to our lord, Pope Innocent, and his Catholic successors, the whole kingdom of England and the whole kingdom of Ireland, with all their rights and appurtenances, in remission of the sins of us and our whole race, as well for those living as for the dead: and henceforth we retain and hold those countries from him and the Church of Rome as vicegerent, [*vicegerent, indeed*]; and this we declare, in the presence of the learned man, Pandulph, subdeacon and familiar of our lord the Pope. And we have made our homage and sworn allegiance to our lord the Pope [*homage from a vicegerent—homage !*], and his Catholic successors, and the Church of Rome, in manner hereunder written; and we will make our homage [*homage* again!] and allegiance for the same, in presence of our lord the Pope himself, if we are able to go before him; and we bind our successors and heirs by our wife for ever, in like manner to do homage [HOMAGE for what?] and render allegiance, without opposition, to the supreme Pontiff for the time being, and the Church of Rome.

"And in token of this lasting bond and grant [*bond and grant ?*], we will and determine that, from our own income, and from our special revenues arising from the aforesaid kingdoms, the Church of Rome shall, for all service and custom which we owe to them, saving always the St Peter's pence, receive annually a thousand marks sterling money—that is to say, five hundred marks at Michaelmas, and five hundred at Easter—that is, seven hundred for the kingdom of England, and three hundred for Ireland; saving to us and our heirs all our rights, privileges, and royal customs [*saving to us rights, privileges, and customs in feudality ?*]. And as we wish to ratify and confirm all that has been above written, we bind ourselves and our successors not to contravene it; and if we, or any one of our successors, shall dare to oppose this, let him, whoever he be, be deprived of his right in the kingdom. And let this charter of our bond and grant [*what bond and grant?*] remain confirmed for ever.

"Witness myself, at the house of the Knights of the Temple, near Dover, in the presence of Henry, Archbishop of Dublin; John, Bishop of Norwich; Geoffrey Fitz-Peter; William, Earl of Salisbury; William, Earl of Pembroke; Reginald, Count of Boulogne; William, Earl Warenne; Saer, Earl of Winton; William, Earl of Arundel; William, Earl Ferrars; William Briuere; Peter Fitz-Herbert; and Warin Fitz-Gerald, this fifteenth day of May, in the fourteenth year of our reign."

By the above charter it is quite evident that King John did homage to the Pope of Rome as a vassal, and that for the kingdom of England and Ireland, held in *free-tenancy* of the Pope. *Homage* is only paid by a tenant in *capite* to his superior lord. John paid this *homage* to his lord the Pope, and by the payment realised his position as a *tenant-in-chief* of the Church of Rome. By this *homage* paid he sealed his own position, and that of all his baronage; he was the tenant-in-chief, the *freeholder*, and all his barons were *copyholders*. The barons of Runnemead, the sealers of MAGNA CHARTA, were no barons at all, but copyholders; and as copyholders, farmers, or yeomen, but NO LEGISLATORS.

Each Chronicler has his own version of this charter of surrender to the Church of Rome; for Matthew of Westminster speaks of John receiving his kingdoms back again from Pandulph " as *their feudatory*, and as doing liege *homage* to our lord Pope Innocent and his catholic successors." [1] John did homage to the Pope as a *freeholder;* and his sub-infeudatories, his baronage of all degrees, rendered *fealty* to him as copyholders.

Of this there can be no doubt. John was a freeholder to the Church, and the barons were copyholders to John. Copyholders have no seals for legislative purposes, consequently all the show of

---

[1] Chronicle, vol. ii. p. 116.

heraldry attached to MAGNA CHARTA goes for nothing. MAGNA CHARTA can shew no valid title.

This being the case, we have not thought it worth our while to go into and examine the details, section by section, of Magna Charta, save only as a thing of curiosity and imposture, and to the extent of our notes and comments in the present chapter.

The chief movers were traitors, and the whole scene was a traitorous French conspiracy. So much for Magna Charta.

CHAPTER XIV.

FEUDALISM—VASSALAGE—COWARD-CHARGE.

MAY we ask how old the institution of feudalism is? In looking back for its original, we find ourselves led to the Book of Genesis.[1] In that book we read that Joseph, great-grandson of Abraham, was prime minister to Pharaoh, King of Egypt, and that he introduced the feudal system there. We do not wish to indulge in vague speculation; but may ask, Was the institution transmitted to the Greek Empire? Did the Romans borrow it from the Greeks? Did they leave it, with other of the wreck of their institutions, to the empire of the Franks, under Charlemagne? If this descent could be made out, we should have that feudalism which was flourishing in France in all its glory about the time of Hugh Capet. It originated in Egypt by the advice of Joseph, the son of Jacob, when he was prime minister there, under Pharaoh the king. Let us read verse 20th of the above chapter:—"And Joseph bought all the land of Egypt for Pharaoh; for the Egyptians sold every man his field, because the famine prevailed over them: so the land became Pharaoh's." Here we obtain the lord-paramount of feudalism. Again: in verse 21st we have, "And as for the people, he removed them to cities, from one end of the borders of Egypt even to the other end thereof." Here we have serfdom all over—the people bought, and the people removed at will from their homes, at the caprice of the purchaser.

---

[1] Chap. xlvii. 20-25.

Further, verse 23d: "Then Joseph said unto the people, Behold, I have bought you this day, and your land, for Pharaoh: lo, here is seed for you, and ye shall sow the land" (as tenants). Verse 24th: "And it shall come to pass, in the increase, that ye shall give the fifth part unto Pharaoh; and four parts shall be your own, for seed of the field, and for your food, and for them of your households, and for food for your little ones." Again, verse 25th: "And they said, Thou hast saved our lives; let us find grace in the sight of my lord, and we will be Pharaoh's servants."

In the above three verses we have the free tenants of the crown of a later day, and the homage or fealty pledged on entrance to the grant of land. This is feudalism completed.

That Joseph, then, the son of Jacob, introduced feudalism into Egypt is certain; but whether the institution was transmitted to the Greeks and Romans by them, awaits proof. But to end speculation on origin, let us proceed to the facts of the case.

In France and Italy, about the time of Hugh Capet, there were large monastic institutions, independent of each other, with fortified cities and small principalities, all similarly independent of each other; and many of them hostile in spirit, and some even practically antagonistic.

All these little republics did what they could to strengthen their positions by alliances with stronger powers; in short, they all more or less entered into a frank-pledge of nationalities with stronger powers, for protection. One looked to France and its king; another to Germany and its earls, or some powerful sovereign prince, king, or bishop there; one to Italy; and some even to the Dansker men, just pitching their tents upon the banks of the Seine—their seized locality of the future North-man-dy.

No fortified city, castle, or monastery existed without its patron prince or bishop, and he too a fighting prince or bishop. The patron prince was chosen for his prowess in the battlefield; he became the resident chief or lord; and he in his turn made all the members of the little community fighters too. No tenant entered upon his farm without doing homage and swearing fealty to the lord of the fee, whether he might be prince or priest; and every neighbouring outlying independent vine-growing Naboth hastened to the lord of the fee to surrender his title to that lord, and become a vassal or tenant-in-chief of this sovereign prince,—and this he did to save himself and his from the covetous grasp of an Ahab and the urging vengeance of a Jezebel. There was no cowardice imputed to the thousands who surrendered their rights of freedom to the vassalage of feudalism under these circumstances. The alliance became fashionable and truly honourable; and the man who held by his own right of purchase had a dangerous possession, besides no position in society. The proprietor of fifty thousand acres, allied by baronial tenure to the powerful principality or monastery, was a greater man than the mere lordly squatter, whom nobody knew, or even cared to know.

The man of less possessions, in becoming a knight by knight-tenancy, became a greater man than the small country gentleman with great desires and contracted means could possibly be; and so the smaller man, or soc-man, raised himself by raising the position of his landlord. Who now would not sooner be a Brocklesby tenant in England than a small holder of a little water-mill, toft, and homestead by fee-simple, in some obscure village or hamlet?

Four generations before the birth of William the Conqueror, this state of national frank-pledge existed in all its glory in France and Italy, and took possession of Normandy too, when the "*Dansker*" boatman or barge-hauler had become respectable, and changed his name to '*Norman.*'

The chivalry of feudalism was very infectious, and soon reached England—England's king and England's nobles and gentry. All must be barons or knights, and wear the state-livery of vassalage and position, at the expense of (so-called) independency and of obscurity. The connexion between the courts of England and Normandy, in the Saxon period, was constant and intimate for at least three generations before the birth of William the Conqueror; so that on his landing in England, in A.D. 1066, he found the spirit of feudality pervading the land as much as he had left it in France and Normandy. It is quite a mistake to suppose that William the Conqueror forced the spirit of feudality, or any other institution on the State, by a legislative enactment.

Do we not know that the first step taken by the Conqueror was to call a national council of the tenants holding by baronage-tenure, and also summoning by the vice-count of each county four knights, *ancient in years* and *learned in the law*, to shew him in council what were the laws and customs of the government of Edward the Confessor?

When William the Conqueror landed at Hastings, what was he? A duke of Normandy, holding his dukedom by baronial tenure of the king of France. All his earls, barons, knights, esquires, and gentlemen,—what were they? Vassals holding by baronial or knight's service, every man of them; for they were all vassals either of the crown of France or the dukedom of Normandy. The opposing forces, the earls of England, the knights and esquires too,—what were they? Vassals every man, to earl or king; and the man who was not vassal to the great was 'soc-man' or small-tenant to the obscure and little. All the holders of Normandy—from the first recognised '*Dansker*' plunder-dukes, down to King John—were dukes holding Normandy of the crown of France by vassalage. The holding would not have been a respectable tenure if not so held. Vassalage was fashionable, overwhelmingly so, for ten generations; and where is the man or woman who even now against 'fashion' dare to walk down the town-street in hat, glove, bonnet, or crinoline? John was a vassal to the crown of France by inheritance, without the imputation of cowardice; and we ask whether John might not, in self-defence, place his kingdom of England in vassalage to the Church of Rome in the face of the sixty thousand men encamped on the heights of Boulogne, invited there for the invasion of his kingdom by his own Archbishop of Canterbury and five English bishops and other traitors? In this national crisis, could not the kingdom of England be placed in vassalage to the Church of Rome without the scurrilous charge of COWARDICE being made against the King? John, as can't be too often repeated, saved his kingdom by treaty-annexation to Rome. He did so to keep it from annexation to France by strife and plunder; and for this kingly act he has been branded coward by all disappointed, outwitted Langtons, Fitz-Walters, De Vescis, and 'historians' (save the mark!) for six hundred and fifty years.

John, to save his kingdom, surrendered his crown in vassalage to Rome at the house of the Knights-Templars at Dover. He did this openly, and with the concurrence of his ministers and friends —William Marshall, Earl Marshall of England; John Gray, Bishop of Norwich; Walter Gray, Bishop of Worcester; Peter de Rupibus, Bishop of Winchester; Geoffrey Fitz-Peter, Earl of Essex, the Chief-Justiciary; William Briwere, the Treasurer; and others, judges and chamberlains: with his friends William de Fortibus, Earl of Albemarle, and Randulph Blandeville, Earl of Chester, and others; with the Master of the Temple, and 'Cornhill,' the Government banker. All these were friends to the King before he placed England on the same level as Normandy had stood for generations—*in vassalage;* and all these were friends to him afterwards, even until death parted them. These were not men to be and remain the ministers and friends of a coward in life and in death. No. These men, these great men, were not as Langton, Fitz-Walter, or Eustace de Vesci—French-paid traitors; but they were men of whom England has ample reason to boast to this day. They were an honour to their own times; and they would be an honour to all times in which they might happen to be cast, either as citizens or as statesmen. These were men worthy of more propitious times than those in which they lived. To King John they were true, and for King John they died; for those who survived John fought at '*Lincoln fair*' for the boy-king, his successor, Henry III.

CHAPTER XV.

FEUDAL SYSTEM—WRITS—JOHN'S VIGILANCE.

HAVING seen what Feudalism was, we wish now to give a glimpse into its working; and this we think may best be done by translating from the Tower Records specimens, from among many hundreds, of the 'Writs,' every one bearing John's signature, and, what is better, the stamp of his own vigorous intellect and well-nigh ubiquitous vigilance. Little commentary is demanded; for the old words interpret themselves, and carry vindication of the actual John in their every line. Let us read :—

Confirmation of the same [the Knights-Templars] of the Flette.

"*John, by the grace of God, et cetera.*—Know ye that we have granted, and by this present charter have confirmed, for the safety of our soul, and of King Henry our father, and E. the Queen, our mother, and of all our ancestors and successors, to the Knights of the Temple of Jerusalem the place upon Flette, near to the Castle of Baynard, and all the course of the water of the Flette, to make there a mill and a messuage upon the Flette, near the bridge of the Flette. Wherefore we wish and firmly enjoin that there they may have and hold the aforesaid place, with the whole course of the stream and the aforesaid messuage, free and acquitted of all customs, as our father King Henry gave and confirmed by his charter. And we forbid, under a penalty of ten pounds, any one occupying anything, or doing anything to annoy or injure them, from this time forward. Attested, et cetera. Given by the hand of Hubert, Archbishop of Canterbury, our Chancellor, at Sagium, in the first year of our reign."[1]

"*The King, et cetera, to Geoffrey Fitz-Peter, et cetera.*—Know ye that for C pounds and j palfrey we have granted to our dearly-beloved and faithful Peter de Stokes the marriage with her who was the wife of Jordan de Anneville."[2]

In the Roll of Fines.

"*The King, et cetera, to Geoffrey Fitz-Peter, et cetera.*—Know ye that William Ruffus has paid to us xx marks for having the marriage of Isabell, the daughter of Gilbert de Arches, which [he has] by our gift; and therefore we command you that, security being received from him for paying those xx marks at periods which you require, and you carefully introduce as a suitor the man who may have her. I myself attesting at Montfort on the xxviij day of July."[3]

William Ruffus is to have the marrying of the daughter of Gilbert for 20 marks; and Geoffrey Fitz-Peter, the Chief-Justiciary, is to see that he selects a suitable husband.

Custodiam Commisimus.

"*The King, et cetera, to Geoffrey Fitz-Peter, et cetera.*—Know ye that we have granted to our dearly-beloved and faithful S. Ridell the guardianship of the land and heir of Ganfridus Ridell, his brother, who is dead, to keep the same as long as it shall please us; and therefore we command you that you may make him to have them without delay. I myself attesting at Alençon, on the xj day of August (A.D. 1203)."[4]

The "tenendam quamdiu nobis placuerit" of the above writ is the very foundation of all freehold tenures, guardianships, and royal grants of any kind.

---

[1] Rotuli Chartarum, by Thomas Duffus Hardy, p. 2, vol. i.
[2] Rotuli de Liberate, p. 42.
[3] Ibid., p. 55. [4] Ibid., p. 57.

There is not an acre of land of real ancient freehold tenure but what stands upon the continued favour of the royal pleasure.

"*The King, et cetera, to Geoffrey Fitz-Peter, et cetera.*—We command you that you should make Ascelin de Guatervill to receive our dearly-beloved Peter de Ripia for a husband, because we wish that she should do this; but if she refuse this, and levy her fine with us for marrying herself according to her wish, you may make the same Peter to have Matilda de Diva, the sister of the same Ascelin, without delay, with her land. Attested by Peter de Pateshull at V'nol on the xxj day of August (A.D. 1203)."[1]

The above fee, held by knight's or baronial service, was not properly filled up by a woman, as a fighter was required at the head. The elder sister was to marry a fighter, we suppose; but if she objected, she might pay the fine for refusal, and let her younger sister take the man. One must have him, because the free tenement must have a man at the head of it.

"*The King, et cetera, to Geoffrey Fitz-Peter, et cetera.*—We command you to take into our hands the lands, edifices, and chattels of Thomas de Kirkby, from his lay-fee in Norfolk and Suffolk, and hold the same until we may have the debt which Roger, his brother, has owed to us. I myself attesting at Trianon on the xxiij day of August. By G of the Exchequer."[2]

By the above writ we find Roger in debt to the exchequer, and Thomas, the brother, having his lay-fee, with all its appurtenances, seized for the debt.

Either the above was a family property held *in capite* of the crown, or else the one brother was bound for the other in the bond of 'frank-pledge.' In the feudal times, every freeman had to find ten neighbours for his bondsmen, as a 'frank-pledge;' and if anything went wrong with the party assured, the crown could come down at once upon all the ten sureties.

---

[1] Rotuli de Liberate, p. 59.   [2] Ibid., p. 59.

The Castle of Bowes is committed to Robert de Veteriponte by the letters-patent of our lord the King; and is freed to Eudon, his nephew, to keep.

"*The King, et cetera, to Geoffrey Fitz-Peter, et cetera.*—Know ye that we have committed C Bowes, with their appurtenances, to our faithful Robert de Veteriponte; and therefore we command you that you make him to have that castle, with all its appurtenances, without delay, when he will be responsible on that account to us at our exchequer. I myself attesting at Hébertot on the xij day of September (A.D. 1203)."

Land given for Fee-farm.

"*The King, et cetera, to the men of the Manor of Wirkesworth and of Essburn, and of the Wapontake of Wirkespurth, et cetera.*—We have enjoined you that ye be inclined to William, Earl of Derby, according to the tenor of our charter which we have given him for the manors of Wirkespurth and Essburn, and the wapontake of Workespurth, our fidelity being safe. Attested by William de Braosa at Montfort on the xvi day of September (A.D. 1203)."

These two manors and the wapontake were granted to the Earl of Derby according to the old charter; for in all these grants, forfeitures, and re-grants the "*salva fidelitate nostra*" was always preserved and enforced, let the original grant be made by baronial or by knight's-service tenure.

Land Given.

"*The King, et cetera, to Geoffrey Fitz-Peter, et cetera.*—We command you to give, without delay, to Theobold Frusser, our crossbowman, ten pounds of land from the land which was Guidon de Toarc's in Angoleime, for his land which he lost through our service; but if there should have been there the sum of C shillings or L or less which may remain to us, nevertheless you must free the whole to him, so that he may answer at our exchequer annually for that which remains beyond the aforesaid x pounds of land which we ordered to be assigned to him. I myself attesting at Moreton, on the xxiij day of September (A.D. 1203)."[1]

The above writ is very characteristic of King John. The crossbowman was to have land worth x pounds a year, but no more. If the grant of land should be worth C or even L shillings more, the surplus should be paid by the said Theobold annually at the exchequer. The above writ was signed '*Teste meipso*,' as thousands of writs were signed; and the document carries the author of it in its every word.

"*The King, et cetera, to Geoffrey Fitz-Peter, et cetera.*—We have pardoned Robert de Veteriponte C marks of silver and C marks he has returned by our precept to our exchequer by his fine which he has levied with us for having the sons and heirs of Hugo Gernagan in wardship, with all their land, and for marrying them, and for marrying the widow of the said Hugo, and for all the chattels of the said Hugo which the heirs possess; and therefore we command you that the aforesaid Robert, for the aforesaid CC marks, be acquitted; and you may make the aforesaid guardianship in its integrity, and the aforesaid marriages, and the aforesaid chattels, to be freed to the same Robert, or to his appointed messenger."[2]

The Charter of the Canons of Langele Deo dono of Robert Fitz-Roger.

"*John, by the grace of God, et cetera.*—Know ye that we have conceded to the petition of our faithful subject Robert Fitz-Roger, and by this our present charter have confirmed the donation

---

[1] Rotuli de Liberate, p. 64. [2] Ibid., p. 66.

which the same Robert has made to God and the Church in honour of the Blessed Mary at Langele built, and of the canonical order of Premonstrancensis, at the same place, serving God at the abbey there appointed, to minister there for ever, for possessing all the manor of Langele in free, pure, and perpetual charity or frankalmoigne, with the church of the same village, and with the marsh of Ravenesness, and with all the appurtenances of the same manor. Besides, we have granted, and by the present charter have confirmed to God and the Church of Saint Mary of Langele, and the canons there serving God, all donations of lands and men and gifts of charity [frankalmoigne] which may reasonably be made to them in churches, and all other things and possessions.

"Wherefore we wish and firmly enjoin that the aforesaid canons and their men may have and hold all their lands and possessions and frankalmoignes with soc and sac[1] and tol and them and infengenthef,[2] and with all their liberties and free customs and acquittances, in wood and open country, in meadows and pastures, in waters and mills, in ways and footpaths, in stagnant pools and duck-ponds, and marshes and fisheries, and granges and willow-holts, within the borough and out of it; and in all things and in all places unfettered and free, and acquitted from the usage of shires and hundreds, and pleadings and defendings, and from giving money for injury, and for murder, and for wapontake and scutage, and for gelds and danegelds and hidages and

---

[1] *Soc and sac* were of the laws of Edward the Confessor, so much coveted by the great agitators Langton and his bishops at Runnemead. Soc and sac were the old manor-court, where pleas of trespass were held, and fines and amercements levied, on the suitors at the court, by the knight and squire and 'personne' who presided; and divided their own perquisites of their own court between themselves in some defined proportions. This institution was superseded by the great innovator in law-matters, Henry II., by his court of assize,—innovations carried out by his never to be forgiven "*Statutes of Clarendon.*"

[2] This 'infengenthef' was a Saxon court, where thieves taken in the manor with the stolen property upon them could be at once tried, and, if found guilty at this manor-court, be executed. The Halifax Gibbet Court was the latest example known.

assizes, and for the works of castles and parks and bridges and the public roads, and for fledwite and for hangwite and flemenesfreuithe [receiving a fugitive,] and for hamsoken [burglary] and ward-penny and for aver-penny, and for bloodwit and frodwit and for leirwit, and for hundred-pence and for tithing-pence, unless on entry; and they and their men may be acquitted through all our land of all toll, and of all things which the canons themselves and their men could secure for themselves,—those things for the proper use of the canons themselves or their men, which they might buy or sell without making a sale further, [We suppose a fictitious sale, for the evasion of duty,] and for passage and pontage, and for market or fair-toll and stallage, and for all secular service and servile work and exaction, and all other occasions and secular customs, the justice for death and member being alone excepted."[1]

"*The King, et cetera, to William the Treasurer, and William and Robert, Chamberlains, et cetera.*—Know ye that we have lent to Roger de Lacy, Constable of Chester, a thousand pounds from our treasury, on the pledge of Robert Fitz-Roger, who has taken [security] upon all his land in England, which, within the first month in which the same Roger should have come into England, he should make us to have the bond of the said Roger for the repaying the aforesaid thousand pounds to us, at the times which we have provided for ourselves; and, therefore, we command you that, when the aforesaid Robert shall have brought his pre-placed bond to us, you may give him the aforesaid thousand pounds, which we have lent to the same Roger for his redemption. Besides, know ye that we have lent to Randulph [Blandeville],

---

[1] We see by this reservation alone the Saxon or Danish resolve to punish murder and maiming on the highways or in the fields. This was carried so far, that all deaths sudden, and not to be accounted for, were returned as *mur*ders, and the hundred or wapontake was fined for that murder. May not the office of coroner have been instituted to collect the tax, and so look after the interests and revenues of the crown?

Earl of Chester, for the redemption of the said Constable, CC marks upon the manors of Tiwe and Carpedene, as the bond of the said earl affirms; and, therefore, we command you that, when you receive on this account the bond of the said earl, you may give him the CC marks. *Teste meipso*, at the Tower of London, on the xxix day of May (A.D. 1204.) By the Justiciary."

The above writ is important, as shewing on what terms the valiant Roger de Laci, Constable of Chester, regained his liberty when he was taken prisoner in the French war, and so honourably set at liberty on his parole, in consideration of his great bravery.

Land Given.

"*The King, et cetera, to Geoffrey Fitz-Peter, et cetera.*—Rannulph le Fol has shewn to us that one virgate of land [forty acres, the fourth part of a hide of land] in Craneburgh, which Goofrey Fitz-Johette held, is in our hand, and is our escheat; and, therefore, we command you that, if that virgate of land is our escheat, and you see it to be best for us, you may make the aforesaid Rannulph, for his service, to have without delay that virgate, if there were there not more than one virgate of land. Attested by Master Robert de Stoke, at Rouen, on the fifth day of October (A.D. 1203.) From the lord the King."

Here we have another glimpse of John's real character—astute vigilance. The "*si* ibi amplius non fuit, quam j virgata terræ" runs through all John's proceedings. We have met with so many examples of this in the Tower writs, that we consider love of truth and keen insight to be the great leading characteristics of the man. But these characteristics are never to be found in your profuse prodigal, your reckless spendthrift; and, moreover, this watchfulness and truthfulness of character are not usually accompaniments of your coarse and brutal man. Oh, how unlike the actual John was to the 'historical' John, as credulously accepted from monkish and priestly slanderers!

"*The King, et cetera, to Geoffrey Fitz-Peter, et cetera.*—Know ye that Robert the Falconer has levied a fine with us for x marks, for having the sergeantry of the land, which was his father's, at Hurst and Wudeton; and, therefore, we command you that, on good security being received from him for discharging those x marks, at periods which you may appoint, you may make him to have the aforesaid land of his father; but if he should have alienated anything of his aforesaid father's from the aforesaid land, that justly, and according to the custom of Angoleime, you may cause to be revoked, and the same Robert you may arrest for his liberties, according to the tenor of his charters. Attested by W. de Breosa [William Briwerr the Treasurer], at Montfort, on the xxviij day of July. By the same."

Land Given.

"*The King, et cetera, to Geoffrey Fitz-Peter, et cetera.*—Know ye that we have given to our dearly beloved clerk, Thomas of the Exchequer, all the lands and buildings, with all the appurtenances, which were William Aurifaber's in London, who was taken [as frank-pledge] for William with the beard [a seditious barrister and demagogue, who was executed for treason in the reign of Richard I.]; and, therefore, we command you that you may make him to have those plenarities, or his messenger, without delay or difficulty. I myself attesting at Montfort, on the xxix day of July (A.D. 1203.)" [1]

Land Given.

"*The King, et cetera, to Geoffrey Fitz-Peter, et cetera.*—We command you to make our dearly beloved John Marescall to have all the land of Hugo de Aure, with its appurtenances, in Angoleime, which we gave to him, unless another was seised of it by our precept. I myself attesting, at Cambray, on the xviij day of August. Per ipsum Norwich." [2]

---

[1] Rotuli de Liberate, p. 55.   [2] Ibid., p. 58.

Custody of an Heiress.

"*The King, et cetera, to Geoffrey Fitz-Peter, et cetera.*—We command you that, without delay, you make Walter de Saint John, the dearly beloved and faithful knight of our Jno. de Pateshull [a baron of the Exchequer], to have the heiress of Dun Bard, such as she is. I myself attesting, at Montfort, on the xxix day of July (A.D. 1203.)"

No money is named as fine in the above writ. That, we suppose, is a present to the knight; but such as she was he was to have her, rich or poor.

"*The King, et cetera, to Geoffrey Fitz-Peter, et cetera.*—We command you that you should inquire into the value of the castle of Hellesmere, with its appurtenances, and that you should make Audoen Fitz-David to have the value of it elsewhere; for we wish to have that castle, which is situated in the Marches [of Wales], in our possession. Attested by the Bishop of Norwich, at Auriwall, on the ij day of August. By the same."

The loss of Normandy, and consequent war with Philip Augustus, formed John's resolution to uphold the integrity of the nationality. The cowardly conduct of the feudatories of the crown—the "BARONAGII ANGLIÆ"—drove the King to granting 'knight's fees' upon the Exchequer, with countless payments of debts to Jew and Gentile at the same Exchequer, producing a 'monetary pressure' in Fleet Street and Cornhill, and so drove the King to apply the feudal screw with redoubled energy to all marriages, forfeitures, and wardships, so as to meet the augmented expenditure.

Pope Innocent III.'s release of all vassals shook the system, as we have seen, to its foundation. As for the system of ·'government' that succeeded it, and the real as opposed to the alleged motives of the priestly muster of Fitz-Walter's army in the ings of Runnemead, all looked to the treasonous helping of the King of France, not to advantaging the nation of England. Commentary on the facts is really needless.

CHAPTER XVI.

SPORTS—HUNTING—DOGS.

WE find that in the times immediately succeeding the Norman Conquest, the tenants of the crown, who held by tenure of soccage and petit-sergeantry, paid their rents in a variety of small matters, —as provisions, services, and even horses, dogs, hawks, &c.; as palfreys, destriers, chaseurs, leveriers, with hawks and falcons— English, Scotch, Norway, and Spanish. In the reign of Stephen, Barnard the Scribe paid as fine for a grant of land by the Bishop of Exeter one palfrey.[1]

Outi of Lincoln was fined in one hundred *Norway* hawks and one hundred girsals: four of the hawks and six of the girsals were to be white.[2]

In King John's journeyings on the circuit of assize from his residence at Marlborough Castle to Bristol, then to Gloucester, Hereford, Shrewsbury, and Burton-on-Trent, in Staffordshire, Melbourne, in Derbyshire, Nottingham, Lincoln, Sleaford, Stamford, Northampton, with a dozen other places or more, within five weeks, it could not be supposed that the huntsman could keep up this constant run of twenty-five or thirty miles a day, and follow the chase besides, without some assistance of carriages and horses to convey him from one point to another,—perhaps across the country, over two or three counties.

These carriages and horses and men to drive, supplied by the sheriff of the county for the conveyance of the King's huntsman,

---

[1] Madox's History of the Exchequer, vol. i. p. 273. Mag. Rot. 5 Steph.
[2] Ibid.

would imply a considerable load. The roads at that period over the clay or the old red marl formation of Herefordshire and Worcestershire must have often been well-nigh impassable from the deep ruts in kneaded clay. Would not these carriages have also to convey bows, arrows, ropes, nets, and other implements of the chase?

The carriages, horses, post-boys, and attendants employed in conveying the court of the King on circuit of assize, were the same in every respect as were employed in the hunting season for the huntsmen, game-beaters, pages, grooms, dogs, crossbows, arrows, nets, ties, traps, and other engines of destruction; for all these formed part of the royal retinue in the winter months.

The writs extracted from the Tower documents are on all subjects connected with sport and game. We give a few examples out of the enormous mass:—

Mem. 3 in Dorso.

"Richard de Muntfichet has letters from the lord the King, directed to Hugo de Neville, on having C as well bucks as does, from the forest of Windsor, for renewing his park of Langley. At Barnevitt, xxviij day of October (A.D. 1202)."[1]

Again:—

"*The King, et cetera, to Hugo de Neville, et cetera.*—We command you that you should give Guarin Fitz-Gerard ten bucks from our forest of Essex. Peter de Stoke attesting, xj day of June."[2]

Once more:—

"*The King, et cetera, to Hugo de Neville, health in the Lord.*—We command you that you may take xl does and x bucks in the park of Woodstock, far off from our hall; and you may make Gerard de Camvill to have them for re-stocking his park of Midelinton. *Teste meipso* at Rouen on the xvj day of June (A.D. 1203.)"[3]

---

[1] Rotuli de Liberate, p. 33. [2] Ibid., p. 41. [3] Ibid., p. 43.

Further :—

"*The King, et cetera, to Hugo de Neville, health in the Lord.*— We command you that you would permit Gerard de Caville to take and to have xx does in Syrwude ; yet, nevertheless, that he should not have there greyhounds nor any bow, unless the ranger have his bow. *Teste meipso* at Rouen xvj day of June."[1]

Again :—

"*The King, et cetera, to Hugo de Neville, health in the Lord.*— We command you that you shall make Thomas Fitz-Bernard to have L bucks in Essex, for re-stocking his park. *Teste meipso* at Aurivatt the xviij day of June (A.D. 1203)."[2]

Once more :—

"*The King, et cetera, to Hugo de Neville, et cetera.*—We command you that you shall make Walter de Muscegros to have iij stags and v bucks from the forest of Mauverne, to make our dogs which he has in his keeping to run. *Teste meipso* at Alençon on the xiiij day of August."[3]

Yet again :—

"*The King, et cetera, to William de Falais, et cetera.*—We have sent Henry Fitz-Gerard lx and x dogs, and Guido and Wall Oiselur the huntsmen, and three berners and one valtrar, as well as with his horse and boy for each ; and therefore we command you that, when he cannot find the necessaries of life any more for them, you may cause to be found those subsistences for them, and it shall be computed to you at the Exchequer. Attested by Hugo de Neville at Ongar (in Essex) on the xvij day of December (A.D. 1203)."[4]

Further :—

"*The King, et cetera, to the Bailiffs of Southampton, et cetera.* —Find a good and secure ship, and one well crated, for William de Neville, for transporting our wild beasts, which he may take in the New Forest, without paying for them, and it shall be reckoned

---

[1] Rotuli de Liberate, p. 43.
[2] Ibid., p. 43.
[3] Ibid., p. 58.
[4] Ibid., p. 76.

to you at the Exchequer, et cetera. Attested by Geoffrey Fitz-Peter, et cetera." [1]

The sending wild animals—as fallow deer, or red deer, or hares, and perhaps other animals—with dogs and huntsmen to hunt them, from England to Normandy, appeared to be a common practice at this time. From whatever cause, the nationality in game-pursuing with horse and hound, is English altogether, not French.

Again:—

"*The King, et cetera, to the Vicecount of Southampton, et cetera.*—We enjoin upon thee, when William Neville shall inform thee, that thou mayest make to be summoned the men of thy bailiwick, to come to our chase in the New Forest, to take wild beasts for our use; and, on the view of legal men, you may find for him ropes and ties and staves to take them, and hay and oat-straw to sustain them, until they may come to Normandy; and what for you both may be put to for having this done, it shall be reckoned to you at the Exchequer. Attested by Geoffrey Fitz-Peter, et cetera." [2]

Once more:—

"*The King, et cetera, to the Vicecount of Dorsetshire, et cetera.*—We send to you Randulph Portar, with his falcon, commanding that you should make to be found what shall be necessary for him and the falcon and the horse and his boy from your farm, and it shall be reckoned to you at the Exchequer, et cetera. Attested by Geoffrey Fitz-Peter, et cetera, on the vj day of March (A.D. 1204)." [3]

Yet again:—

---

[1] Rotuli de Liberate, p. 82.

[2] It is difficult to speculate upon the precise time when the spaniel, in all its varieties of setters, pointers, &c., was imported from the south of Europe, and the destructive spirit of game-pursuing therewith; but certainly it must have been long before the reign of John, or even before the Norman Conquest. We have met with nothing yet of importing hounds from Spain; but have found hounds, huntsmen, and deer sent to Normandy, to hunt or be hunted there by English huntsmen, A.D. 1204.

[3] Rotuli de Liberate, p. 82.

"*The King, et cetera, to Richard de Riveriis, et cetera.*—We command you that you may find the necessaries of life for Richard Leporus, with one horse and one man and vij dogs, until we shall have come into Normandy, and it shall be reckoned to you at the Exchequer. Attested by Geoffrey Fitz-Peter, et cetera."

Further :—

"*The King, et cetera, to William de Neville, et cetera.*—Find from your farm of the New Forest the necessaries of life for Richard Leporus, with one horse and one man and vij dogs, which we send to the sea to be transported with our beasts, so long as he shall have been beyond the sea, and it shall be reckoned to you at the Exchequer. Attested by Geoffrey Fitz-Peter, et cetera."[1]

Once more :—

"*The King, et cetera, to William de Falaise, et cetera.*—Free from our pence to Ganfred de Hauville C shillings, to train our birds at Fairford, and it shall be reckoned to you at the Exchequer. Attested by Geoffrey Fitz-Peter, et cetera, at Southwick, on the viij day of May (A.D. 1204.) By the same."[2]

Again :—

"The lord the King has acquitted Warin the huntsman and his men, for the last tallage placed upon them by Hugo de Neville."[3]

Further :—

"*The King, et cetera, to the Vicecount of Gloucestershire, et cetera.*—We enjoin upon you to give Richard Fitz-Edwin and the other huntsmen who are at Tewkesbury, lxviij shillings, to make their discharges for xij days : to wit—Richard Fitz-Edwin xviij shillings and vj pence, Burnell xxiij shillings, Herbert de Colloel xix shillings, and two boys with vij greyhounds, vij and vj pence,

---

[1] Richard Leporus means Richard the Hare-hunter, and the dogs—vij only—are greyhounds, and the wild beasts to be pursued, hares. We have seen seventy dogs and damos being sent, which were staghounds and bucks. Here Leporus has only hares.

[2] Rotuli de Liberate, p. 99.

[3] Ibid., p. 100.

and it shall be reckoned to you at the Exchequer, et cetera. Attested by Peter de Stoke at Westminster on the xxiiij day of March (A.D. 1204.)"[1]

To proceed:—

"To William de Go . . . . . who came from the parts of the King of Scotland, with one girfalcon, xx shillings."

"To Simon de Sircis, who brought another girfalcon, xx shillings."

"To Thomas the Welshman, who brought one girfalcon from the parts of the same King of Scotland, one mark. By the King."[2]

"On the day of Venus, in the feast of Saint Edmund, [November 20, 1209, at King's Cliffe,] to Henry de M'c going to Uphaven with one falcon gentill, ij shillings."[3]

"To Watekin Fitz-Wi . . . . . and William de Siwell going with falcons to Lewelin the Welshman, in Anglesea, xx shillings. By the King."[4]

"On the day of the moon next, [February 1, 1210,] at Windelsour, to Siwell the huntsman with xiiij dogs, and to Richard Pincon with xv dogs, going to hunt in the bishopric of Chichester, iiij shillings and ij pence. To John Stultus with xliij dogs going to hunt with Brian de Insula at Cawood, half a mark. By the King."[5]

"At the same place, [Odiham,] to Thomas Porcherez with xxiij greyhounds and iiij valtrars and his galoway for six days going to Gerard de Canvill at Stowe, xiij shillings and vj pence. To Helic and Oliver valtrars with vj greyhounds going to Henry Fitz-Warenn, vij pence. To Bello Campo one valtrar with v greyhounds going to Jacob de P . . . . . for three days, ix pence. To Richard the valtrar with two whelps going to William de Nevill, iij pence, for j day. To Patricius with v greyhounds going to Peter de Scudemore for two days, x pence . . . . . To Walter

---

[1] Rotuli de Liberate, p. 107.
[2] Rotulus Misæ, p. 136.
[3] Ibid., p. 139.
[4] Ibid., p. 145.
[5] Ibid., p. 148.

de Pikering with vj greyhounds going to Godfrey de Saint Martin for ij days, x pence."[1]

"On the Lord's-day next after the feast of Cineres, at Winchester, to Randulph Stultus and Hugo Norreis going with xij greyhounds to Henry Fitz-Garin for one day, x pence. To Clench and Norman and Doket with x greyhounds for five days going to Roger Rastel, iiij shillings and vij pence. To Scot and Roger with viij greyhounds going to the wife of Garner the huntsman during one day, viij pence. To Robin and Michael and another Robin with x greyhounds going to William de Nevill in one day, xj pence. To Adam and Alan with viij greyhounds going to Peter de Maulay in one day, viij pence. To Garin and Nicholas Grass, Thomas Chanterel, Simon Long, Robert de Heleneia, with xix greyhounds to Philip de Ulecot in ten days, xvj shillings and iij pence. To Walkelin, Cointerel, and Alan the brother of Watt, Buchard, Walkelin Grass, and Watt Permentar, with xxiij greyhounds going to Brian de Insula in six days, x shillings and ix pence. By the King."[2]

"On the day of Mars, [March 9, 1210,] to buy fowls for the falcons of the lord the King, ij shillings, freed to Henry de Merc."[3]

"On the Sabbath-day next, [March 13, 1210,] at the same place, Saint Bride's, to Wilekin de Subir, valtrar, with xx valtrarian dogs, and four scores and four greyhounds, remaining for one night by the precept of the lord the King at Guildford, vij shillings, freed to the same Wilekin; and Adam, the man of Henry Fitz-Harvey,[4] for fowls bought for the falcons of the lord the King, iij shillings."[5]

"To William de Merc, for buying fowls for the falcons of the lord the King, ij shillings."[6]

---

[1] Rotulus Misæ, p. 150.
[2] Ibid., p. 153, A.D. 1210.
[3] Ibid., p. 154, A.D. 1210.
[4] Ibid., p. 153, A.D. 1210.
[5] Ibid., p. 157.
[6] Ibid., p. 160, A.D. 1210.

"To Randulph Lutrar and his companion going to hunt at Nottingham with the Vicecount, x shillings. By the King."[1]

"At the same place, [Northampton,] on the day of Mars, April 27, 1210, for thirty and three valtrars and six score and seven greyhounds, which had for the day x shillings and ix pence halfpenny for going to London in three days, as above, xxxij shillings and iiij pence halfpenny, freed to Michael and Philipp, the men of Henry Fitz, Earl [of Saxony]."

"On the Sabbath-day next after the Finding of the Sacred Cross, [Saturday, the 8th of May, A.D. 1210,] at Westminster, for the expenses of six scores and eleven greyhounds and xxxvj valtrars for three days going to and remaining at Cold Mantell, xxxiij shillings and iiij pence."[2]

"At the same time and place, to Walen and William Doget, with Flit and Bidon, going to and being at Cold Mantell, xij pence."

"On the day of Mars, [the 9th of May, A.D. 1212,] at Freitmantell, for the expenses of xli valtrars, each of whom had ij pence a-day;[3] and four greyhounds, each of which had a halfpenny a-day; and xv large hounds, and xxi dogs of mota, each of which had a halfpenny a-day; and for the expenses of Ferling the huntsman, and Thomas the wild-boar huntsman, each of whom had for the day vij pence halfpenny; although tarrying for one night by the way—namely, on the Sabbath-day next after Ascension day, [Saturday, May 5th, A.D. 1212,] when the lord

---

[1] Rotulus Misæ, p. 160, A.D. 1210.
[2] Ibid., p. 166, A.D. 1210.
[3] The valtrars received twopence a day each, or three shillings and fourpence a day of our time and money, as forest-drivers or covert-beaters, and took their name from vallum, a fence or enclosure. Now, as these valtrars received ij pence a day each, or three shillings and fourpence of our time and money, the sum paid to the four coachmen of the garderobe each, and the sumpters of the garderobe, they must have held a respectable position in the hunting establishment of the King, though below Ferling the huntsman, and Thomas the porkerer, and the three berners, who had sevenpence halfpenny a day each, or twelve shillings and sixpence a day of our time and money.

the King went from Lambeth even to Odiham, the sum of xiij shillings, freed to William Fitz-Richard. By the King."[1]

[On Friday, 11th May, A.D. 1212, at Odiham,] "for the expenses of xlii valtrars, each of whom had ij pence a-day; and eight scores and vij greyhounds, each of which had a halfpenny a-day; and xxxviij dogs of mota and xv valtrar-dogs, each of which had a halfpenny a-day; and xxxij spaniels or park-hunting dogs, each of which had a halfpenny a-day; and ix boys who have charge of these park-hunting dogs, and Ferling the huntsman, and Thomas the wild-boar huntsman, each of whom has vij pence halfpenny a-day, tarrying at Basingstoke for one day; the sum of xx shillings and iij pence; freed to William Fitz-Richard. By the King."[2]

"On the same day, [Monday, May 14th, A.D. 1212,] at Ditton, for the expenses of xliij valtrars, and eight scores and ix greyhounds, and xv dogs of the valtrars, and xxxviij dogs of mota, (mutes,) and j berner, and xxxij [dogs to hunt within the enclosure of a park, probably small hounds, beagles, or spaniels]; Thomas the porkerer and Ferling the huntsman, each of whom had vij pence halfpenny a-day, delaying by the command of the lord the King at Chertsey, for two days; the sum of xlj shillings and iiij pence, freed to William Fitz-Richard. By the King."[3]

"On the day of Mercury next, [May 23d, A.D. 1212,] at Lambeth, for the expenses of xliij valtrars, and lvj greyhounds, and xv dogs of mota, and j berner, and ij boys who had the care of the bracketts, [southern hounds, perhaps staghounds,] and xij valtrar dogs, delaying at Chertsey for one night, the sum of xj shillings and three halfpennies, freed to William Fitz-Richard. By the King."

"At the same place, [Odiham,] Thursday, May 31st, 1212, to Burnell the huntsman, with one horse, and j berner, and xvij dogs going to hunt at Durham with Philipp Ulecot and the Archdeacon

---

[1] Rotulus Misæ, Anni Regni Regis Johannis Quarti Decimi, p. 231.
[2] Rotulus Misæ, p. 231.
[3] Ibid., p. 232.

of Durham, for x days; xij shillings and vj pence. By the King. Freed to the same."

"On the day of the Sabbath, [Saturday, June the 9th, A.D. 1212,] next before the feast of Saint Barnabas the Apostle, at Kingshaugh, [in Nottinghamshire,] for the expenses of xliij valtrars, and ij boys having the custody of the southern hounds, [brackettos,] and j berner; and Thomas the wild-boar huntsman, and Ferling the huntsman, who had xv pence; and eight scores and iij greyhounds, and xxxviij dogs of mota, and ix bracketts or southern hounds, and xv valtrar dogs, delaying for one day at going, by the command of the lord the King, from Kingshaugh [near Tuxford] towards Knaresborough, for two days; the sum of xxxix shillings and vij pence, freed to William Fitz-Richard. By the King." [1]

"At the same place, [Kingshaugh, in Nottinghamshire,] to Henry Doget, the berner of Adam de Stawell, going with the dogs of the same Adam to Randulph de Ralegh, to buy a tunic, iij shillings." [2]

"Also, at the same place, [Kingsley, in Buckinghamshire,] for the expenses of xxxvj game-drivers, and two boys who had the custody of the southern hounds, and j bear-huntsman, and seven scores and nine greyhounds, and xxxviij dogs of mota, and ix southern hounds; and Ferling the huntsman, who had vij pence halfpenny a day, going from Chertsey even to Huntingdon in three days, and delaying there for one day. By the command of the lord the King, the sum of lxj shillings and vj pence." [3]

"On the day of Jove next, [Thursday, June 14, A.D. 1212,] at the same place, [Knaresborough,] for the expenses of xij bracketts

---

[1] Rotulus Misæ, p. 233.

[2] As bears were unknown as wild beasts in England in the year A.D. 1212, the berner could not be considered a bear-hunter, but a bear-ward; and his dogs, so often mentioned in these writs, could not be considered as hunting dogs, but baiting dogs; therefore we must consider bear-baiting to have been one of the sports of the day during the reign of King John. Bull-baiting is not once met with in these writs; so we conclude the practice did not exist.

[3] Rotulus Misæ, p. 233.

and iij boys of Robin de Samford delaying at Knaresborough for one night, xij pence."[1]

"Also, at the same place, [Kirk-Oswald, in Cumberland,] for the expenses of twelve scores and two greyhounds, and twenty-three dogs of mota; and fifty-three valtrars, [who had ij pence a-day each;] and Ferling the huntsman, who had sevenpence halfpenny a-day, for two days' journeying towards North Allerton, the sum of xli shillings, freed to William Fitz-Richard. By the King and the Earl of Salisbury."[2]

"On the same day, [Sunday, July 1, A.D. 1212,] at York, for the expenses of fifty-eight valtrars, and two hundred and sixty-one greyhounds, and twenty-three dogs of mota, and Ferling the huntsman, who has sevenpence halfpenny a-day, for one day at York, the sum of twenty-two shillings and three halfpence. Also for the expenses of forty valtrars, and one hundred and seventy-eight greyhounds, and twenty-three dogs of mota, and the aforesaid Ferling the huntsman, who has sevenpence halfpenny a-day, for two days at Danecaster and Blythe, [Nottinghamshire,] the sum of thirty-one shillings and fourpence, freed to William Fitz-Richard."[3]

"On the day of Mercury, in the feast of Saint James the Apostle, [July 25, at Trowbridge, in Wiltshire,] to Adam the huntsman, and his bear-ward, and twenty-four roebuck hounds, going with Fitz-Richard towards Devizes, during two days, twenty-one pence, at the same place for the expenses."[4]

"The lord the King has pardoned Randulph de Hanvill a gir-falcon which is owing from him at the Exchequer; and it is commanded the Treasurer, et cetera."[5]

"On the day of Mercury, [Sept. 2, 1209,] at Geydinton, in Northamptonshire, for a carriage and pair of horses for the conveyance of stags' horns, for three days, even to Gloucester,

---

[1] Rotulus Misæ, p. 233.
[2] Ibid., p. 234.   [3] Ibid., p. 234.
[4] This is the first time I have met with "*canibus capreolariis*"—chamois or roebuck dogs.
[5] Rotuli de Liberate, p. 77.

ij shillings and vj pence. Freed by the Seneschal to Geoffrey de Ardenn."

" On the day of Venus, [Friday, Sept. 4, 1209,] at Pateshull, to William Colomose for venison of the larder, iij shillings. By the Seneschal."

" On the Lord's-day, [November 15, 1209,] at Rockingham, in posting a carriage which brought the crossbows from Nottingham even to Mountsorell, vj pence." [1]

" On the day of Mars, [December 15, 1209,] at Gillingeham, to Geoffrey Gascon, the servant of Robert de Torneham, who brought goshawks of Asturia from Pictavia, for a gift, iij marks. By the King."

" On the day of Mars next, before the feast of the Nativity, [December 22, 1209,] at Odiham, to Richard Luverez and Odo, valtrars, for two wolves taken at Clarendon, xv shillings. By the King." [2]

" On the day of Mercury next, [January 13, 1210,] at Beer Regis, to Robin de Samford, to buy fowls for the falcons, xij pence."

" To Walerand, going with hooded falcons to Wilton to hawk, j mark. By the King."

" On the day of Jove, in the vigil of Saint Lawrence, [Thursday, August 9, 1212,] at Woodstoke, for the expenses of one esquire of the household, and six boys, and six horses of the lord the King, and four coachmen of the hunting-carriages, and eight horses of the hunting-carriages, delaying at Winchester on the Sabbath next after the feast of Saint James, [Saturday, July 28, 1212,] during one night, by command of the King."

These glimpses into long-vanished sports open up a new chapter in the history of England, and we lay them up here in detail

---

[1] From the Itinerary, the King appears to have spent at this time one whole month in the forests of Northamptonshire and Nottinghamshire.

[2] Rotulus Misœ, p. 144.

as materials to be fallen back upon in the sequel of our Vindication. For even herein the detractors of John have not been slow to accuse him, while accusation has been deemed proof by your 'historians' (so called.)

NOTE.—It is much to be desired that some persevering student would go into the Dog-question fully. The early Tower Records afford ample testimony to the fact, that all our sporting dogs were as well defined in breeds and uses, at the time of the Saxons and Normans in England, as they are at present. The question to be solved is this, Did the Romans import our sporting dogs from Spain or Italy, or were they imported by the Phœnicians in the ships of Tarshish and of the Isles, long before the Roman period in Britain? Who will decide whether Carthage or Rome introduced the taste for field-sports into Great Britain? for the Normans did not, neither did the Saxons.

CHAPTER XVII.

ALLEGED PROFLIGACY OF KING JOHN.

As we have seen, on becoming King of England, John considered it necessary to make some change in his family arrangements, on account of the barrenness of his wife Hawis, or Avis, daughter of William, Earl of Gloucester, his own cousin.

A.D. 1200, King John obtained a divorce from his above-named cousin in the third remove, and married Isabella, daughter of Aymer, Earl of Angouleme, who had been affianced to Hugo le Brun, Earl of March,—but with whom the marriage had never been fulfilled,—in infancy.[1] She was crowned Queen of England by Hubert, Archbishop of Canterbury, at Westminster in October;[2] and at the Whitsuntide following the King, with his Queen, embarked for Normandy from Portsmouth, and, after a rough and dangerous passage, landed in Normandy.

At Easter, A.D. 1201, the King and Queen were again crowned at Canterbury, when guests of Hubert Walter, the Archbishop, at Canterbury.[3] This, probably, was owing to the absence of John on the former occasion.

But looking away from his marriages to his ordinary life, we are confronted with monkish charges of immorality, profligacy, licentiousness. Let us see what can be said about them. Thus Matthew Paris affirms that he defiled many noblemen's wives and daughters, and by these means made to himself as many enemies as there were great men.

---

[1] Roger de Hoveden, f. 457. n. 10.
[2] Roger de Wendover, vol. ii. p. 193.
[3] Ibid., vol. ii. p. 201.

King John of England.

King John had two sons, Henry III., and Richard, afterwards King of the Romans.[1]

He had three daughters, Joane, the eldest, married to Alexander, King of Scots.[2]

Alienor, the second daughter, was married to William Marshall the younger, who died without issue, A.D. 1231. She remarried Simon de Montfort, Earl of Leicester, A.D. 1236.[3]

Isabell, the third and youngest daughter, was married to Frederic II., Emperor of Germany, A.D. 1235.[4]

John had five bastard children:—
Richard, the eldest.[5]
Geofrey Fitzroy.[6]
Osbert.[7]
Oliver.[8]
Joan, married to Llewellen the Great, Prince of North Wales.

John's matrimonial alliance with Isabella was not a happy one, which may account for some of these children at least, if not all. It were satisfactory if we could get nearer to the royal "hearthstone" and family circle. But mists hang over his domestic life, which his mortal enemies, monks and priests, have peopled with all phantasmagorian shapes.[9] The Tower Records and gossipage of monkish chronicle fail us here, in so far as true insight is concerned; and sorry is the substitute offered by Miss Strickland and Dr Lingard. We shall allow priest and spinster equally to speak for themselves, and shall have something to say as we proceed, and still more when we have concluded our gatherings from the "History of the Queens of England,"—a work that passes for "history," and is, nevertheless, mere tattle. First of all we have this from Lingard:—

---

[1] Matt. Paris, f. 225, n. 10; and f. 226, line 1.
[2] Patent Roll, 5 Hen. III., M. 6., Dors., dated York, June 28, 1221.
[3] Matt. Paris, f. 465, n. 40.
[4] Ibid., f. 414, n. 30, 40.
[5] Ibid., f. 298, n. 40.
[6] Sandford's Genealogical History, f. 86.
[7] Rotuli, Pat. 17, John, Part ii. M. 16.
[8] Rotuli, Clan. 1, Hen. III., Part ii., M. 23.
[9] Sandford's Genealogic History, f. 87.

"The passion of John for his queen, though it was sufficiently strong to embroil him in war, was not exclusive enough to secure conjugal fidelity; the King tormented her with jealousy, while on his part he was far from setting her a good example, for he often invaded the honour of the female nobility. The name of the lover of Isabella has never been ascertained, nor is it clear that she was ever guilty of any dereliction from rectitude. But John revenged the wrong that, perhaps, only existed in his malignant imagination in a manner peculiar to himself. He made his mercenaries assassinate the person whom he suspected of supplanting him in his queen's affections, with two others supposed to be accomplices, and secretly hung their bodies over the bed of Isabella."[1]

Now Miss Strickland:—

"After this awful tragedy the queen was consigned to captivity, being conveyed to Gloucester Abbey under the ward of one of her husband's German mercenaries. In a record-roll of King John he directs Theodoric de Tyes[2] 'to go to Gloucester with our Lady Queen, and there keep her in the chamber where the Princess Joanna had been nursed, till he heard further from him.'"

As Miss Strickland appears to know more than can be gathered from the Tower Records, we are compelled to follow her through the "History of the Queens of England." So we continue:—

"Although the most extravagant prince in the world in regard to his own personal expenses, John was parsimonious enough toward his beautiful queen. In one of his wardrobe-rolls there is an order for a gray cloth *pelisson* for Isabella, guarded with nine bars of gray fur.

"'In King John's wardrobe-roll is a warrant for giving out cloth to make two robes for the Queen, each to consist of five ells; one of green cloth, the other of brunet. The green robe, lined with cendal or sarcenet, is considered worth sixty shillings. The

---

[1] Dr Lingard, vol. ii. p. 72.
[2] The above is taken from Miss Strickland's "History of the Queens of England," and may be correct in quotation and references.

King likewise orders for his Queen cloth for a pair of purple sandals, and four pairs of women's boots, one pair to be embroidered in circles round the ankles. There is likewise an item for the repair for Isabella's mirror.'

"The dress of John was costly and glittering in the extreme, for he was, in addition to other follies and frailties, the greatest fop in Europe. At one of his Christmas festivals he appeared in a red satin mantle embroidered with sapphires and pearls, a tunic of white damask, a girdle set with garnets and sapphires, while the balbrick that crossed from his left shoulder to sustain his sword was set with diamonds and emeralds, and his white gloves were adorned, one with a ruby and the other with a sapphire."

As Miss Strickland is so full on these obscure points of King John's history, we continue to avail ourselves of her researches:—

"The Queen, soon after her return to England in A.D. 1214, [October 15th, or precisely seven months before the great gathering at Runnemead,] was superseded in the fickle heart of her husband by the unfortunate beauty of Matilda Fitz-Walter, surnamed the Fair. The abduction of this lady, who, to do her justice, thoroughly abhorred the royal felon, was the exploit which completed the exasperation of the English barons, who flew to arms for the purpose of avenging the honour of the most distinguished among their class—Lord Fitz-Walter, father of the fair victim of John."

Because King John ran away with Robert Fitz-Walter's daughter, the father became the field-marshal of the army of God and the Church of England! Good reader, what think you of this original of the be-lauded 'Charter'?

All hail to Miss Agnes Strickland and her good conceit of herself, so well expressed in

> "*The treasures of antiquity, laid up
> In old historic rolls, I opened.*"

For further evidence on this abduction we fall back again on Miss Strickland's collections :—

"The unfortunate Matilda, who had roused the jealousy of the Queen and excited the lawless passion of John, was supposed to be murdered by him in the spring of the year 1215."[1]

Having given Miss Strickland large space for her old-maid gossip on King John's (so-called) flagitious conduct toward Robert Fitz-Walter's daughter, we have now to turn to actual history, as found in the Tower Records, as these bear on John's marriage, and on his queen, Isabella. When we have exhausted both charters and letters-patent on these subjects, we may again take a flight into the regions of romance and quote fully Henry Knighton on Eustace de Vesci's wife and the Prioress of Saint Botulph, the sister of the Prior of Swineshead Abbey; and so again confront the "Pleasures of Imagination" with FACTS. We shall do little more than quote the 'Records,' and ask the reader to "look on *that* picture and on *this*," — that he may decide whether John, under notorious provocation, was the careless and penurious husband of his libellers.

Mem. 5. Charter of the Lady the Queen I. on her Dower.

"*John, by the grace of God, et cetera.*—Know ye that we have given, have conceded, and by this present charter have confirmed, to our dearly-beloved wife Isabella, by the same grace Queen

---

[1] "About the year 1215," saith the book of Dunmow, "there arose a *great discord between King John and his barons because* of Matilda, surnamed the Fair, daughter of Robert, Lord Fitz-Walter, whom the King unlawfully loved, but could not obtain her nor her father's consent thereto.

"Whereupon the King banished the said Fitz-Walter, the most valiant knight in England; and caused the castle in London, called Baynard, and his other dwellings, to be spoiled.

"Which being done, he sent to Matilda the Fair about his old suit in love; and because she would not agree to his wickedness the messenger poisoned an egg, and bade her keepers, when she was hungry, boil it and give her to eat. She did so, and died.

"Tradition points out one of the lofty turrets perched on the top, at the corner of the White Tower of London, as the scene of this murder. She was conveyed there after the storming of Baynard's castle in 1213.

"Like Count Julian, her enraged father brought the French into England, to avenge his daughter."

of England, et cetera, who by the common assent and unanimous wish of the archbishops, bishops, earls, barons, clergy, and of the population of the whole kingdom, was crowned for Queen of England, all things below written, for dower: to wit,—in Devonshire—the City of Exeter, with the fair of the same city, with lestage and stallage and lifftom, which William de Gattesden and Agatha, his wife, held through all her life by responding for the service of that land to the lady the Queen, after whose death that land returned to the dominion of the same Queen; and besides, Kenton and Ailricheston and Wike: in Somersetshire—Ivecester: in Wiltshire—Wilton, Maumesborough, Betesdem, which Henry de Bernavall holds, who will respond to the same Queen for service of the same land, and Wiltereslawe: in Sussex—the city of Cycester, the tenement of Simon [de Wells,] the elect of Cycester being saved for all that city, with its appurtenances, through ancient firm as by our charter, which on that account he has, he may be continued: in London—the heath of the Queen: in Essex —the manor of Waltham, which the abbot and canons of Waltham hold in tenancy: in Hertfordshire—the honour of Birkhampstead, with all its appurtenances, as well in lordships as in fees, and besides, the county of Roteland and the manor of Rokingham: and in Normandy—Falais and Daufront, with their appurtenances, Bonavilla upon Toke; and besides, all others which were assigned in dower, as well on this side as on the other of the sea, to our dearly-beloved mother A., Queen of England: and if anything from that should be subtracted or taken away, through wer or otherwise, we wish that a competent and sufficient exchange should be made for her in England, against dictation or any diminution.

"Wherefore we wish and firmly enforce that the aforesaid I., Queen, our wife, in the kingdom of England, as solemnly as was stated before, was crowned to the Queenship of England, may have and hold for her whole life all the aforesaid, with all their appurtenances, liberties, and free customs, as well and in peace, free and acquitted, honestly and fully, as any our predecessors,

Kings of England; even we will have those in our hand better, and more fully. We forbid, also, that any Justiciary, Sheriff, or forester, or any other bailiff—the bailiffs of the Queen herself being excepted—may send a force into the aforesaid lordships, or from another introduce himself from thence, unless with the wish and assent of the Queen herself. But if we may have assigned more in augmentation of the dower of the dearly-beloved Queen, our wife, by the advice of our faithful [barons], we wish and firmly enjoin that she may have that in its integrity, and may hold fully, through her whole life, by the same liberties and immunities by which we have granted other privileges, above written, to her.

"Attesting, the Lords P. of Durham and H. of Salisbury, bishops; Brother Aymeric, master of the Militia of the Temple in England; G. Fitz-Peter, Earl of Essex, et cetera, Justiciar of England; Earl Roger le Bigot; W. Earl of Arundel; A. de Veer, Earl of Oxford; Henry de Bohum, Earl of Hereford; W. de Braosa, Robert Fitz-Roger, William Briwerr, Hugo de Nevill, Robert de Trasgoz, Robert de Veteriponte, Stephen de Tornham. Given by the hand of S., the Elect of Cycester, at Porchester, v day of May, in the v year of our reign, (A.D. 1204.)"

These granted testimony to be made to the Mayor and Secretary, and his master; to be subscribed as well by the ordained in the word of truth as the laity, standing erect on the oath being taken, that all the aforesaid ordinances were faithfully and firmly to be observed with all their power; and they strengthened the same by placing their seals, to wit, Lord ———, and Lord Durham and Salisbury, bishops before named; G. Fitz-Peter, Earl of Essex; Earl Roger le Bigot; W. Earl of Arundel; A. de Veer, Earl of Oxford; H. de Bohum, Earl of Hereford; William de Braosa, Robert Fitz-Roger, W. Briwerr, Hugo de Nevill; G. Winton, bishop; S. Bath, bishop; Robert de Tresgoz, Robert de Veteriponte, Stephen de Turnham.

Theodore de Tyes, constable of Birkhampstead, the Queen's

manor and residence, takes a prominent position in the Queen's affairs; therefore we take early notice of him.

"*The King to Theodore de Tyes, et cetera.*—We command you to procure for the lady the Queen a competent and domestic robe; such as is becoming for her to wear, the like make her to have. I myself attesting, at Winchester, on the xiiij day of December, (in the 17th year of the reign, and A.D. 1215.)"[1]

On Finding the Necessaries of Life.

"It is commanded Robert Cordwainer, and other honest men of Bristol, that they may find for the lady the Queen her necessaries of life, as Theodore Teuton orders them; and the lord the King will cause to be reckoned in the farm of their city the outlay which they may be put to for this, or he may return to them from his pence, [the privy purse.] The King attesting at Salisbury, xiij day of June, (anno regni 18, and A.D. 1216.)"

"It is commanded the Mayor of Bristol that he shall cause Theodore Teuton to have xv marks for the use of the lady the Queen from the fine which the burgesses have laid with the lord the King." Attested as the writ above. [Rege.]

Henry III. was crowned on the 28th of October, A.D. 1216; and on November 1st, the following charter was signed at Gloucester; and because the great seal was not then present, the seal of William Marshall, Earl of Pembroke, the guardian of the boy-King, and Regent of the realm, was used on the occasion:—

Mem. 25.

"*The King to the Sheriff of Devonshire, health in the Lord.*—We enjoin upon thee immediately, and without delay, to make Isabella the Queen, our mother, to have full seisin of the city of Exeter, with the fair, lestage, and stallage of the city. And of

---

[1] Rotuli Litterarum Clausarum, p. 242.

Lifton, which William de Gatesden and his wife hold; and, besides, of Kenton, and of Aldricheston, and of Wike, which were assigned to her for dower. And, since we have not the seal, these letters we have made to be sealed with the seal of our faithful Earl, William Marescall. Attested by me myself, at Gloucester, on the 1st day of November."

In the same manner it is written to Theodore Teuton for the same purpose, with respect to Berkhampstead, with all its appurtenances;—to the Sheriff of Southampton, on the manor of Wilfrinton;—to the Sheriff of Essex, on the farm of the manor of Waltham, which the abbot and canons hold at an annual rental;—to the Sheriff of Wiltshire, on Wilton, and the farm of Malmesborough, and on Betesdon;—to the Sheriff of Somersetshire, on Ivecester;—to the Sheriff of Sussex, on the city of Cicester;—to the Sheriff of Northamptonshire, on the county of Roteland, with the manor of Rokingeham, which have been assigned to the same lady the Queen in dower, with all their appurtenances. Given at the same time, under the same seal.[1]

Again:—

"It is commanded Peter de Maulay and Robert de Curtenay that they should hold faith towards Theodore Teuton in those things which he shall have spoken to them on the part of the lady the Queen, for the fidelity, profit, and honour of the lady the Queen. Attested by the same Earl [W. Marshall] as above."[2]

Again:—

"It is commanded the Archbishop of Burdegal to make Theodoric Teuton to have a hundred pounds to sustain himself in our service while he shall be in your parts. Because truly not yet, et cetera. Attested by the same Earl, [William Marshall, the Regent,] at Oxford, on the xxv day of July, (A.R. 1.) By J. Marshall."[3]

This Theodore Teuton being the Queen's Constable at Berk-

---

[1] Rotuli Litterarum Clausarum, p. 293. [2] Ibid., p. 302 b. [3] Ibid., p. 310 b.

hampstead, and being in connexion with the Government of
Henry III., we think it right to insert every trifle of charter, letters-
patent, or writ referring to him, to see in what company, and by
whose commands, this Queen's 'Constable' of Berkhampstead
was acting.

For Theodore Teuton.

"It is commanded Peter de Malo Lacu that he shall make
Theodore Teuton to have full seisin of his land of Peretun, with
its appurtenances, from whence he has made him to be disseised;
and that, without delay, he may make to be restored to him all
the chattels which were taken from thence, or removed afterwards,
on account of his being disseised. Attested by Earl, [William
Marshall, the Regent,] at Worcester, on the xiiij day of March,
(A.R. 2.) By the Lord Bishop of Winchester, [Peter de Rupibus.]"[1]

Of the Seisin of the Land of Andrew de Vitery.

"The lord the King commands Henry, the son of the Earl [of
Saxony,] as he has commanded others, that without delay he
shall make Theodore Teuton to have full seisin of the land which
was Andrew de Vitery's, which he had in the baileywick of the
Lord John, the father of the lord the King, and which you have
taken from him by force. Attesting, Henry, et cetera, at Westminster, on the ij day of November, (A.D. 1219.)"[2]

That no one may buy from the Woods appertaining to the Manor of Berkhampstead.

"*The King to the Sheriff of Hertfordshire, health in the Lord.*
—It is given us to understand that the Constable of Berkhampstead makes sale, felling, and destruction in the woods appertaining to the manor of Berkhampstead, in many ways, to our loss
and inheritance. And therefore we enjoin upon thee that thou
make it to be proclaimed in thy full county court, and likewise

---

[1] Rotuli Litterarum Clausarum, p. 355.   [2] Ibid., p. 407.

through the hundred and the market of thy baileywick, that no one, as he values his body, may buy anything from those woods; and if by chance you may be able to discover any one buying or selling from thence contrary to this our prohibition, immediately you make his body to be arrested and safely guarded, until you have, on this business, from us another injunction. Attested by Henry, [the King,] et cetera, at Warwick, as above."

In the same manner it is written to the bailiff of the Queen at Berkhampstead for Geoffrey de Lucy, *ut supra*, (as attested above by the Earl himself, William Marshall.)[1] The above writ was written for Geoffrey Lucy, a sub-infeudatory of the manor of Berkhampstead, to have full seisin of his farm as he had previous to the late war between King John and his barons.

The following writ is one of the most important in connexion with the reign of John, inasmuch as it is the writ, or one of the writs, upon which King John's alleged cruelty to his wife, Isabella, is founded. This writ was signed at Corfe Castle on the 4th day of December, A.D. 1214, when John had been in England only seven weeks, after a sojourn in Normandy of nearly nine months.

At this very time the barons were in a state of insurrection in London and its neighbourhood; and this writ points to the King's measures taken at this critical juncture for the Queen's safety, in removing her from her manorhouse of Berkhampstead, in Hertfordshire, to the more secure retreat of Gloucester Castle, which was far removed from Saint Albans, and the New Temple, near the Fleet Bridge, in London, and Windsor, and Runnemead.

The Queen was removed for security to Gloucester Castle, under the charge of her husband's old faithful vadlet, promoted, for his tried fidelity over a course of years, to the important position of Constable of Berkhampstead, the Queen's manor.[2]

---

[1] Rotuli Litterarum Clausarum, p. 326.

[2] We had been at considerable pains to extract several writs from the "Rotuli Litterarum Clausarum," to shew the position and connexion with the King, as *vadlet*, of Theodore Teuton, before his elevation to the Constableship of the Queen's manor of Berkhampstead; but finding these foreign and appar-

King John of England.

"*The King to the Sheriff of Gloucestershire, et cetera.*—We send to you the lady the Queen, our wife, with Theodore Teuton, and one horse,[1] commanding you to find what is necessary for them until we have commanded you otherwise; and you will make her to have the bedroom where our daughter was nursed. And you shall receive Master Peter, the crossbowman, with our crossbows, which he will take care of; and you shall find for him the necessaries of life until we order otherwise for you. I myself attesting at Corfe, on the iiij day of December, (A.D. 1214.)"[2]

The purport of the above writ appears in another form:—

"*The King to Theodore Teuton, et cetera.*—We command you that without delay you go even to Gloucester with the lady the Queen, and there you shall guard her in the chamber in which Johanna her daughter was nursed, until we order otherwise on this business. For we have commanded the Sheriff of Gloucester by our letters directed to him which we send to you, that he shall receive her, and find for her and for you the necessaries of life. I myself attesting at Corf, on the iij day of December, (A.D. 1214, and the 16th of the reign.)"[3]

The Delivery of a Hostage.

"*The King to the Queen of England, health in the Lord.*—We command you that without delay you make to be liberated to the bearer of these presents, Roger,[4] the hostage, the brother of the Constable of Chester. And in testimony of this, et cetera, we send

---

ently trifling notices only clogging this important subject, we have (not without reluctance) omitted them.

[1] The Queen travelling with her Constable *on one horse* would imply a flight; in the night perhaps, and a double horse-ride, the Queen sitting on the pillion behind the Constable. Perhaps "*Peter,*" the well-known *brother, son, captain,* and *friend* of the King, might accompany the Queen, and take the Constable's seat occasionally on the saddle, the two working upon the *ride-and-tie principle*.

[2] Rotuli Litterarum Clausarum, p. 180 *b*. (A.R. 16, A.D. 1214.)

[3] Rotuli Litterarum Patentium, p. 124 *b*.

[4] Rotuli Litterarum Patentium. After Roger de Laci died, in 1209, he was succeeded by a very different man, a friend to the traitorous barons, and from him security had to be taken.

to you. Attested as above. Runnemead, xix day of June, in the xvij year of our reign."

"*The King to Theodore Teuton, health in the Lord.*—We command you that you free from the pence which are in your possession, to the bearer of these presents, xxx marks, to be sent to Walerand Teuton to pay the wages of the servants who are with him in our castle of Berkhampstead; and in testimony of this we send to you. I myself attesting at Canterbury on the xiiij day of September, in the xvij year of our reign, (A.D. 1215.)"[1]

From the above writ it is evident that although the Queen had been despatched on a pillion behind the Constable of Berkhampstead, and accompanied by the old '*Peter*' of the crossbowmen at Marlborough Castle; the home of the Queen at Berkhampstead Manor was not broken up, but left, with the servants in it, under the care of "*Walerand*," a name of frequent occurrence in the Tower writs as that of a vadlet in the closest confidence of the King.

Guardianship Appointed.

"*The King to all Archbishops, Bishops, Earls, Barons, Knights, and all others of the county of Hertford, et cetera.*—Know ye that we have committed to our dearly-beloved and faithful Walerand Teuton the county of Hertford, with all its appurtenances, to keep, as long as it shall please us; and therefore we command you to be anticipating and answering to the same Walerand in all things as to your sheriff, and in testimony of which we send to you. I myself attesting at Saint Albans on the xviij day of December, A.D. 1215, and the 17th year of the reign."

As all King John's appointments were good, we are led to believe the appointment of Walerand Teuton to the sheriffship of Hertfordshire, as a reward for his services in the Queen's house-

---

[1] Rotuli Litterarum Patentium, p. 155.

hold at Berkhampstead Manor, to have been alike gratifying and honourable to both parties—the king and the subject.

Having disposed of the Tower Records, up to Isabella being removed to Gloucester for security, on the first outbreak of the insurrection in 1214,—only five months before the great insurrectionary meeting at Runnemead,—we leave these historic FACTS to make their own impression, and would now turn to the lighter pursuit of gossip, falsehood, and slander in the pages of Henry Knyghton's Chronicle—a chronicle written one hundred and seventy years after the time of King John, and therefore rich in monkish accumulations; for historic marvel always increases in force and interest in proportion to the remoteness of the event concerned.

Henry de Knyghton, Canon of Leicester,[1] observes :—

"This King John, by always continuing his tyranny, provoked many of his nobles to anger. It was not the fair in person and modest in conduct which excited his lust, for he went after the married portion; and, relying upon female extravagance, in a more odious form lusted after the wives and dames of all his nobles, and derided their husbands after the perpetrated enormities. That which indeed stood prominently as the chief cause and origin of the universal war and great sedition was this. There was at that time among the boon companions of the King the most noble baron and strenuous knight, Eustace de Vesci, having a most fair and chaste wife, whom the King had desired beyond measure, but could not possess on account of her husband, and could not endure a longer separation from his sight and favours. It happened on a certain day when they sat at meat together, the King and Eustace, the King saw a ring on Eustace's finger, and accosted him, saying that he had a stone which he wished to be set in gold by the same artist. He, suspecting no

---

[1] Liber ii. folio 2422.

ill, lent the King the ring, who immediately despatched the same
by a boy to the wife of Eustace,—the boy saying, on the part
of the husband, that she should come in all haste to London if
she wished to see him alive, for he was at the point of death.
She, seeing the ring and hearing the boy's story, immediately
did as she was ordered. But it happened that on a certain day,
while she journeyed, her husband by chance met her, and won-
dering to see her, asked, 'Where go you, O my lady?' She told
what had occurred. Who, knowing the fraud of the King, said in
grief, 'Thou hast been called that the King might deceive thee.
Make therefore a lotrix, [*i.e.*, strumpet,] set off in thy vest, to be
brought to the King in thy place, and thou, without delay, return
to the place from whence thou hast come;' which being done, on
a certain day, whilst the King and Eustace were conversing with
one another, the King, glorying in his worst deeds, said to Eustace,
'O Eustace! you have a most fair lady, and one very pleasing in
nocturnal silence.' To whom Eustace replied, 'By what means
knowest thou that, O King? for thou hast not had my wife, but in
her place a shameless strumpet.' The King, enraged, with an oath
threatened him with death; and when he attempted to rise up
against him, Eustace leaped away from and escaped him. In
retreating from the King even to the northern parts, he demolished
the houses of the King, together with the manors of the King, on
the way; and there were joined to him many of the nobility, and
they chiefly of those whose wives the King had violated. And
they arose in rebellion unanimously against the King, and increased to a great multitude. They occupied royal castles and
fortifications, and destroyed the 'allegiances' of the King."

Now for still more incredible Romance.

After King John's final disaster on crossing The Wash above
Lynn, Henry Knyghton, the chronicler, observes, "that King
John himself went aside to the monastery of Swineshead, which
is distant from Saint Botulph five miles, for the sake of hospitality.

He had heard that the Abbot of the same place had a fair sister, who was the Prioress of the neighbouring place, [Saint Botolph;] and inflamed after this manner by desire, he sent his satellites that they should bring her to him. Which when the Abbot her brother had heard, he was sad and very much affected; nor would he receive consolation from his brethren. To whom one of his confidential friends said,—he who took the charge of the hospitality and friendship to strangers, and known to the lord the King, —'What is the matter with you, brother? Why does your countenance fall, and more sad with care you go about your business?' To whom the Abbot replied, 'I have a sister, one who is the spouse of Christ, one in whom I delight, and the King proposes to degrade her.' But he replied, 'Pardon me, father, and pray for me, and I will take away his life from this wicked world, and the fear of him from the conversation of men.' To whom he replied, 'I might wish these things, truly, my son; yet it is not lawful to raise a hand against the person of the King.' Wherefore he, being turned away, proceeded and took new perry, of which he knew that the King would partake freely, and put poison in each cup except three, which, placed amongst the rest, he especially marked. At last, when the King had seated himself at the table, and had conversed with his knights, who were seated with him, one piece of bread being received, not, indeed, that he should make a lordly supper, but that he might converse to his hurt and death, the King inquired of the servants what was the value of the bread which he had eaten, and they replied one halfpenny. He then said, that great prosperity followed the insurrection of the barons and people against him; 'but moreover, if life and health be my companions for a whole year, I will make bread of that weight to be worth twelve halfpennies.' His servants were offended with that speech, and certain of them retired. They all conspired against his life. Wherefore he [the monk] turned, came, and applauded the King, as he had been accustomed to do at other times, and said to him, 'Does it please thee, O King, to eat of new fruit?' He replied, that it pleased him; 'go and bring it.' And he took the prepared perry, and placed them before the King. Presently the precious stones which were before the King were misted with perspiration, [*in sudorem.*] And the King said, 'What hast thou brought, brother? hast thou spread out poison?' When he replied, 'Not poison, O King, but the best fruit.' And the King said, 'Eat thou of thy fruit.' And immediately, one being taken from the marked fruits, he eat. And the King said to another, 'Eat.' And he did eat. He repeated, 'Give,' also a third time, and he did so. Nor could the King contain himself any longer; for he eat from one taken from the poisoned ones; and the same night he died. Nor, indeed, was he changed in appearance; but was amongst them as one who had fallen down [in a fit.] And God freed, by the death of the wicked King, the aforesaid sacred character, [the Prioress of Saint Botolph,] His espoused, from a new, as is believed, diabolical suitor. Wherefore John, being dead; as extinct, at length after death, he was buried at Worcester, on the day of Saint Luke the Evangelist, A.D. 1216, and the 17th year of his reign."

This whole hobgoblin story of the poisoning with perry or fruit is proved to be untrue by the King's death, at Newark Castle, three or four days afterwards, in the presence of William Marshall, Earl of Pembroke, the Earl Marshall of England, William de Fortibus, Earl of Albemarle, William d'Albini, Earl of Arundel, and Randulph Blandeville, Earl of Chester, and others of the King's court equally respectable. As for the above party, half-drowned, seeking shelter at Swineshead Abbey, late at night; and the King wishing to seduce the Prioress of Saint Botolph, five miles off, and she the sister of the Prior of Swineshead,—absurdity lies on the face of every item. We shew quite enough in the sequel concerning Robert Fitz-Walter and Eustace de Vesci, to account for the

King's estrangement from them, without requiring the aid of either daughter or wife to embellish the story.¹

We do not mean to say or think that King John was strictly a virtuous or moral man, for he left five bastards; but this is one thing, and to be the abandoned reprobate which he is constantly represented to have been by the Benedictine monks of the thirteenth and many following centuries, is another, and atrociously different thing. The clerical corporation of the Church of Rome was above *and dangerous to the civil power of the realm of England;* and King John attempted to curtail its power; but, owing to the wide-spread influences of superstition and priestcraft amongst his barons and people, he failed. Yes! he made a stand against the assumptions of the Church of Rome—*a brave, single-handed stand*, and failed. He did! and monks and priests, for six centuries and a half, have told, without check or contradiction, their priestly and malignant slanders *on this Church Reformer,*—writing their slanders in monkeries and confession-cells, that were as sties of pollution, and themselves the swine.

---

¹ The monkish fable of King John's death, like other monkish fables, gathers bulk and weight by the process of rolling. At the time of the King's death, only a faint surmise or report was heard of "*some say;*" but this faint suggestion of poisoning, after a while, ripens into the fact that *the King was poisoned* by a monk of Swineshead Abbey. After another two centuries, the fact is confirmed by money being left to Swineshead Abbey for two monks to say or sing continued mass and prayers for the soul of the monk of Swineshead Abbey who poisoned King John. This bit of *mythus* is found in one of our later chronicles, copied, no doubt, from F, who had it from E, who took it from D, and he, in turn, received it from C, who got it from B, who had it from A, some obscure chronicle of some obscure monk, whom nobody ever heard of, saw, or knew but A himself.

CHAPTER XVIII.

JOHN'S ALLEGED CRUELTY TO THE JEWS.

As Roger de Wendover in his Chronicle[1] has brought a very serious charge against King John of cruelty to the Jews, which charge is the foundation of the wider charge of John's inherent cruelty, transmitted through six hundred and fifty years, we shall adduce the Benedictine monk at length, and then offer our Vindication from the Tower Records.

Wendover records that in the year 1210,—when the kingdom was under the Papal INTERDICT, and the King himself was personally excommunicated from week to week by all true and faithful Roman Catholics throughout England,—King John ordered all the Jews throughout England, of both sexes, to be seized, imprisoned, and tortured severely, in order that he might do what he liked with the Jews' money.

Some of the Jews, the monk averreth, after being tortured, gave up all the money they had to avoid future torture.

A Jew at Bristol, even after being dreadfully tortured, still refused to ransom himself and so put an end to his sufferings. In order to enforce submission, and so obtain the hidden treasure, the King,—KING JOHN,—saith Wendover, ordered his agents to knock out one of his cheek-teeth daily, until he had paid ten

---

[1] Chronicle, vol. ii. p. 252.

thousand marks of silver to him. This knocking out of teeth continued for seven days; each day having its tooth, till the poor Jew gave in through fear of further pain, on the eighth day, and paid the required sum.

Such is the stuff Benedictine monks and superstitious priests wrote against John, because he wished to depress the priestly power. It was all false, but what of that? They were true, obedient sons of the Catholic Church; they did as they were ordered; they tried to destroy him. Let us confront the babblement with the Tower Records. They will shew the truth. We have need of patience to trace document after document; but there is reward in so doing.

Mem. 28. *A Confirmation to the Presbyter [High Priest] of the Jews of London.*

" John, by the grace of God, et cetera, to all his faithful subjects, and also to all the Jews of England, health in the Lord.— Know ye that we have granted and confirmed, by this our present charter, to Jacob the Jew, the Presbyter of the Jews of London, the Presbytership of all the Jews throughout England, to have and to hold as long as he lives, freely and quietly, and honourably and in its entirety, so that no one may presume to inflict upon him, after this caution, any annoyance or injury. Wherefore we wish and firmly enjoin that you shall guarantee, maintain by force, and peaceably defend the same Jacob as long as he lives, the Chief Priest of the Jews, through the whole of England. And if any one after this shall presume to hurt him, you may make that to be amended, our interest in the revision being saved to us, from our injury, as well as to our Chief Jew, whom we have specially retained in our service; also, we prohibit any cause relating to him being taken into any court of justice, unless before us or our Chief Justiciary, as the charter of our brother Richard affirms. Attested by S., [Sanaricus,] Bishop of Bath, et cetera. Given by the authority of H., [Hubert,] Archbishop, our Chancellor, at Rouen, on the **xxxj** day of July, in the first year of our reign, (A.D. 1199.)"[1]

"Benedict the Jew has letters from our lord the King for simple protection."[2]

Carta Deusaie Jude.

"*John, by the grace of God, et cetera.*—Ye have known that we have taken Deusaie, the Jew of B'nai, under our guardianship and protection, as our especial Jew, who will give each year to us iij marks of silver for annual return, and those returns at our Exchequer at Caen, [in Normandy,] in the feast of Saint Michael. Wherefore we wish and enjoin that you shall guard and defend the said Deusaie and his things, neither bearing nor suffering to be borne towards him and his things any molestation or injury. And we have granted to the same Deusaie, that he shall be acquitted from all taxation of the Jews. And we wish that he shall be governed by those liberties and free institutions by which he and other Jews were accustomed to be held in the time of Henry our father [Henry II.] and King Richard our brother. Attested by myself at Vernolium, on the xij day of October, (A.D. 1199, and the first year of the reign.)"

The above writ is most important for the characters of Henry II., Richard I., and King John, and shews that the spirit excited against the Jews was in the teeth of the constitution of the realm. This is a fact which cannot be too well known, for the sake of the reputation of Richard I. as King of England, seeing it was in his reign that the most diabolical acts ever heard of were perpetrated against the Jews.

This is not the first charter of John's reign referring to the rights and free customs of the Jews. So far as it goes, it is only

---

[1] Rotuli Chartarum, p. 6 *b*.   [2] Ibid., p. 98.

a charter of confirmation; but, like others confirmatory, it is most important.[1]

From this charter we must hold that the laws of this realm have been just and impartial towards the Jews; and that the cruelties exercised towards this devoted people did not arise from any injustice in the laws, but from an ignorant, excited mob, urged on to violence by the monks and priests of the Roman Catholic Church. The great crusading preachings of the twelfth century by Popish monks and Popish priests are alone responsible for the villainies perpetrated upon the Jewish race in the twelfth century.

Mem. 13. In Dorso.

"*John, by the grace of God, et cetera, to all the acknowledged* ('*constitutio*') *Jews throughout England, health in the Lord.*— Know ye that we have appointed William d'Albini, [Earl,] and William de Warenne, [Earl,] and Thomas de Neville, [a clergyman learned in the law,] and Gaufridus Norwich, [Neville, son of Alan de Neville, Chief-Justice of the Forests throughout England,] our bailiffs of the Jews of England, through the counsel of Geoffrey Fitz-Peter, our Justiciary; and therefore we command and enjoin upon you, as our bailiffs, by every obligation which belongs to us, to be sufficiently attentive to them."[2]

Every one must feel that the above charter of King John, appointing the guardianship of the Jews in the first year of his reign, presents a singular contrast to the gabble and slanders of Wendover and the like.

William d'Albini losing Belvoir Castle into the hands of the King, the Lord-Paramount, the year following, he became one of the discontented barons, and was put forward prominently for the seizure and defence of Rochester Castle by his confederates, the barons then holding the city of London.

Probably William d'Albini very soon ceased to hold his appoint-

---

[1] Rotuli Chartarum, p. 27. A.R. 1, A.D. 1199.   [2] Ibid., p. 61. A.R. 1, A.D. 1200.

ment as Jew-bailiff or guardian; for in a thousand transactions of all kinds with the Jews, over a period of eighteen years, we invariably find William de Warenne, Earl of Surrey, mentioned as chairman of the commission, he being Chief Justiciary of the Jews and a baron of the Exchequer. Still further, we find that all these transactions were, without exception, carried on by the ministers of the crown; the commission for protection of the Jews of these 'Records' acting as barons of the Jews' Exchequer, in concert with the barons of the King's Exchequer.

Rogamus.

"*The King, to all his Jews in England, et cetera.*—We beg of you, if it please you, to be serviceable to Leo the goldsmith, the Jew of Norwich, bearer of these presents. Witness ourself at Tewkesbury."[1]

Protection to Leo the Jew.

"*John, by the grace of God, et cetera.*—Know ye that we have received into our hand, custody, and protection Leo the Jew, our goldsmith, and all his goods; and therefore we command you that you preserve by force, keep and defend Leo himself and all his goods, bearing no annoyance or injustice to him or to his goods, nor permitting it to be borne from any one; but if any one from without do unjustly to him or his in anything, you may make that to be amended to him without delay; and you may forbid his being put to the payment of tallage; nor shall any tallage be exacted from him unless before us ourselves. Attested by myself at Niort on the fifteenth day of November, (A.D. 1199, A.R. 1.)"[2]

Here we have Saer de Quency obtaining the assistance of the King for the payment of his debts to the Jews in Normandy, A.D. 1202, as the following acquittance will shew:—

---

[1] Rotuli de Liberate, p. 47.   [2] Rotuli Chartarum, p. 62 *b*.

"*The King, et cetera, to Richard de Wilek, et cetera.*—Know ye, that we have acquitted our dearly beloved Saher de Quency of £260, Andeleys, for the stock and interest which he owes to Brun and Josce, the sons of Bonevie de Rouen, and Affaite de Mosterviler, and Abraham de Insula Bona, Jews. And, therefore, we command you, as far as the making him acquitted, and his sureties likewise. And that you cause the charters of Saher himself, and his securities, which they hold for the same debt, to be restored by them without delay. Attested by myself, at Genour, on the 16th day of August, A.D. 1202. By Earl William Marshall."

"*The King, et cetera, to Geoffrey Fitz-Peter, et cetera.*—Know ye that Thomas d'Arcy may keep himself, with iij horse-soldiers for his first guard, that is to say, for one year, that is from the day of Mercury next before the feast of Saint John the Baptist, in the fifth year of our reign, for as that we may forgive the same Thomas CC and xxv marks which he owes to the Jews and Jewesses upon his note and signature, and which note and signature may be returned to him; and besides, Thomas himself may perform his suit or service to us for his barony, as other barons do for us; and therefore we command you so far as to make Thomas himself to be acquitted on the aforesaid CC and xxv marks, and you may return his note and signature without delay; and you may compel the horse-soldiers of the same Thomas that they shall perform their service to him as they ought; and you may give to the same Thomas nine marks of silver from the same debt, which we have committed to William Fitz-Walter for liquidation. I myself attesting, at Aurivall, xix day of June, (A.D. 1203.)"[1]

In the above writ for paying a debt due to the Jews and Jewesses by Thomas d'Arcy, we must bear in mind the law-

---

[1] Rotuli de Liberate, p. 45.

abiding words, "*which we have committed to William Fitz-Walter for liquidation.*"

Land Given.

"*The King, et cetera, to Geoffrey Fitz-Peter, health in the Lord.*—Know ye that we have given to our dearly beloved R., Earl of Leicester, fifty shillings of land in Bellegrave, which should have been Aaron the Jew's, and on which account the same earl shall return fifty shillings per annum to our Exchequer; and therefore we command you that you make the said earl to be acquitted for the payment of the aforesaid L shillings. I myself attesting, at Montfort, on the xxviij day of July, (A.D. 1203.)"[1]

"*The King, et cetera, to Geoffrey Fitz-Peter, et cetera.*—Know ye that we have pardoned our dearly beloved William de Maro xxv pounds and ten shillings of sterling money, from the debt of the Jews, with usury which he owes to the Jews of London, provided that the same William will hold in our service, from this time forward to the feast of the Paschal Lamb, three horse-soldiers and five attendants on foot; and therefore we command you make him to be acquitted, and his bonds or securities, which the Jews have had quiet possession of for the same debt, you may make to be returned to him. Attested by Peter de Stokes, at Aurivall, on the xv day of June, in the fifth year of the reign."

In the same form it is written to William de Warenne [Earl of Surrey] and his companions, [the guardians of the Jews.]

As all feudal obligations seemed to be unrecognised by the vassals of the crown in these Norman wars, in consequence of the head of the fiefs, the King of France, absolving from their oaths of allegiance to the Duke of Normandy—*i.e.*, King John—the subinfeudatories of these Norman fiefs, or holders of properties by

---

[1] Rotuli de Liberate, p. 54.

knight's service in Normandy, because Arthur, the son of Geoffrey Plantagenet, the direct heir of the Dukedom of Normandy, had disappeared when in John's custody; and John had refused to surrender himself for trial to his superior lord, the King of the French, the head of the fee.—John was forced to recruit his army in Normandy from the reckless, the prodigal, and the spendthrift, by paying their debts to the Jews, by way of enlistment bounty. In the Tower Records we come upon hundreds of cases of the Crown helping all classes of society by discharge of debts of all amounts to the Jews; and these releases or acquittances were the bounties paid upon enlistment for Normandy in King John's army. But we resume our documentary Vindication:—

" *The King, et cetera, to William de Warenne, [Earl of Surrey,] G. de Norwich, and T. de Neville, et cetera, Guardians of the Jews, Justiciaries of the Jews' Exchequer, and Barons of the King's Exchequer.*—Know ye that we have satisfied our dearly beloved and faithful Geoffrey de Say for CC and L marks; a fine which he made with the Jews of London for two complete years before the feast of the Paschal Lamb, of the fourth year of our reign; and therefore we command you that he be acquitted on that account, and that you make his bonds to be returned to him on that business. Of the usury and debts of the Jews, if he owed anything beyond the aforesaid CC. and L. marks, you may make him to be satisfied, from the time when he came into our service, with horses and arms, through our request. *Teste meipso*, at Rouen, on the xij day of July, (A.D. 1203.)"[1]

This paying of debts at the Treasury to the Jews for spendthrifts, or soldiers of fortune, was most common, and was perhaps the only way in which King John could officer his Continental armies at this time. The King, or one of his ministers, notified

---

[1] Rotuli de Liberate, p. 48.

the business to the Justiciaries and Guardians of the Jews, when they settled the matter for the Jew creditor at the Treasury at the quarterly or half-yearly clearing on exchange day. No money passed through the King's hands in these transactions, but William, Earl Warenne and Surrey, received the account from the King, and settled it with William Briwerr, the treasurer. There is not a particle of evidence to shew that aught of this Jewish money ever reached the King himself during the entire eighteen years of his reign; though a hundred upon a hundred spendthrifts were sent to the Norman wars on the King himself writing to William, Earl Warenne and Surrey, to receive the Jews' debt at the King's Treasury, and to leave the bonds or securities there at the same time. This was a daily business with the King and his ministers during the years 1203-4, as innumerable Tower Records remain irrefragably to prove. Be it kept in mind, therefore, over against Wendover and other monkish mendacities, that as few or none of the old feudal barons or knights of Normandy, Acquitaine, Anjou, &c., would engage in such a contest as John was involved in,—spendthrifts, gamblers, and soldiers of fortune had to be secured by a payment of their debts in England; and that, as these debts were for the most part contracted with Jews, the King himself became a party to these payments, but only through the Jews' own Justiciaries, Barons, and Guardians on the one part, and the King's ministers, Geoffrey Fitz-Peter, Chief Justiciary of England, William Briwerr, the Treasurer, and his Chamberlains at the Exchequer, on the other. With such Lombard Street machinery as this, it is quite evident that any personal attempt at Jewish tooth-drawing by the King, or by his ministers, is a monstrous figment. There is not a tittle of truth in the charges of King John inflicting acts of cruelty upon the Jews, or on any others. These writs go an hundred times over to prove the fact, and disprove the monkish falsities.

We continue our evidence :—

"*The King, et cetera, to Geoffrey Fitz-Peter, et cetera.*—Know ye that we have acquitted Matthew de Seltford, and William his brother, for xl. pounds sterling, which they owed to the Jews of Canterbury, as well for chattels as for usury; on which account we command that you should make them to be satisfied. *Teste meipso*, at Molinett, xvj day of May, (A.D. 1203.)"[1]

Two brothers, Matthew de Seltford and his brother William, owed £40 of sterling money, in principal and interest, to the Jews of Canterbury, which sum is to be satisfied at the Exchequer, through the instrumentality of Geoffrey Fitz-Peter, Earl of Essex, the head of the Treasury. The payment of such debts, by writs on the Exchequer, was of very common occurrence at this period, and might be one way of the King's shewing his gracious favour. It was no cancelling or denying of the debt, but a paying of the money to the Jews, under the royal sign manual, at the Exchequer, by a writ directed to Geoffrey Fitz-Peter, Earl of Essex, at the head of the Treasury, Chief Justiciary of England,—a man not very likely to lend his name and office to robbing some Jews of £40 at Canterbury. It is true, the great, boasted, and glorified Magna Charta had a clause for cheating Jews deftly inserted into it; but that Charter was not originated by John's ministers, but by a band of needy barons,—borrowers of money of the Jews, —monks, priests, French and English traitors, and soldiers of fortune; and, moreover, Geoffrey Fitz-Peter was dead before that gross insult was perpetrated by the priestly rabble on the ings of Runnemead. At the time on which we are now writing, the Jews had four or six Justiciaries or Barons of their own Exchequer, appointed by the Crown to look after their interests; and, in the face of these specially appointed judges, the Judges of the King's Bench at Westminster, the Barons also of the Exchequer there, the Justices Itinerant, at the head of whom stood this said Geoffrey Fitz-Peter, Earl of Essex, and his assistants, as chamberlains and clerks of the Treasury, always travelling along with the King in

---

[1] Rotuli de Liberate, p. 38.   [2] Ibid., p. 34.

his constant circuit of assize of *eighteen years*, we are asked to believe the not less silly than impossible cruelties and robberies by tooth-drawing, &c., &c. No, no. These debts were paid to the Jews, at the Exchequer, by the King's command, without hindrance and without fraud, and reveal a benevolent vigilance on the part of John for a deeply-injured class of his subjects; and at the same time an astute obligation laid upon unwilling rascaldom-soldicry to 'serve.'

Still further :—

"*The King, et cetera, to Geoffrey Fitz-Peter, et cetera.*—Know ye that we have satisfied our dearly-beloved Hugo de Chaucumbe for usury xxxiiij pounds, which he ought to return to Moses of Paris and Leo of Warwick, Jews, for Nigell de Mandeville, from the beginning of the feast of Quadragesima even till the feast of Pentecost; and therefore we command you that you should satisfy him on that account. *Teste meipso* at Molinell xix day of May, in the fifth year of our reign."

In the same form it is written to the Guardians of the Jews.

Here we have Hugo de Chaucumbe borrowing money of the Jews of Paris, [a very gay place at this time,] and Warwick, [perhaps equally gay,] and allowing the interest to accumulate to £34, which he could not pay. He went to the King as a friend, and borrowed this money of him till the feast of Pentecost; but the King, who was styled *Lackland* when a boy, was *Lackland* when a king, and had no money to spare.

But he had kindly feelings toward his friend Hugo, and would lend him the money for these Jews till Pentecost; and he accordingly wrote to Geoffrey Fitz-Peter, Earl of Essex, then head of the Exchequer, to advance the money for the liquidating this debt, but not to Nigel de Mandeville the spendthrift, but to his friend Hugo, from the feast of Quadragesima till the feast of Pentecost. The King himself wrote to Geoffrey Fitz-Peter on this business, and also, in addition, to the justiciaries, guardians, barons, or trustees of the Jews.

The style and caution and precision in the above writ, stamp the character of the King, but not for thoughtless, reckless prodigality; in short, for the very reverse of these, for John was very methodical and very careful in all his pecuniary and general business matters.

"*The King, et cetera, to Geoffrey Fitz-Peter, health [in the Lord]*.—We command you that from this time, that, for as much as that Henna, the Jewess of Oxenford, requires payment of the debt of Walter de Bolebec from Helias de Bello Campo and Constancia his wife, you may make them, Helias and Constancia, to be satisfied [by receipt of the money] so far as the restoration to them of that which belongs to them. Attested, et cetera, at Pont Arch, xxxj day of May, (A.D. 1203.)"

From these numerous writs of the King to the head of his Exchequer—Geoffrey Fitz-Peter, Earl of Essex—on satisfying these claims of money to the Jews, we are led to believe that King John was truly a kind-hearted man, who would do a good turn to anybody, even at the cost of personal inconvenience. There was not any attempt made to evade these payments to the Jews by repudiating the debts or promises to pay; for they were paid by the King's order at the Treasury for the distressed or needy party,—sometimes by way of a gift, and at others as a loan for a fixed period of time. We see in John a great desire to assist the necessitous; and we find him subjected to innumerable applications for relief, all of which appear to be attended to, and that with the promptness of a banker's clerk.

We proceed :—

"*The King, et cetera, to Geoffrey Fitz-Peter, et cetera.*—Know ye that we have pardoned our dearly-beloved William de Maro xxv pounds and ten shillings of sterling money from the debt of the Jews with usury, which he owes to the Jews of London, provided that the same William will hold in our service, from this time forward to the feast of the Paschal Lamb, iii horse-soldiers and v [servientes] accompanying foot-soldiers [as crossbowmen or archers who accompanied the horse or cavalry, in certain proportions, perhaps five to three]; and therefore we command you make him to be quiet [give him a '*quietus,*' or receipt for the money]; and [*cartas suas*] his bonds or securities, which the Jews have had quiet possession of for the same debt, you may make to be returned to him. Attested by Peter de Stokes [one of the chamberlains of the Exchequer and Seneschall to the King] at Aurivall on the xv day of June, in the year, et cetera, fifth."

In the same form it is written to William de Warenne [Chief Justiciary of the Jews] and his companions.

"*The King, et cetera, to W. de Warren, G. de Norwich, and T. de Nevill, et cetera.*—Know ye that we have satisfied our dearly-beloved and faithful Geoffrey de Say for CC and L marks—a fine [which] he made with the Jews of London for two complete years before the feast of the Paschal Lamb of the fourth year of our reign; and therefore we command you that he be acquitted on that account, and that you make his bonds to be returned to him on that business. Of the usury and debts of the Jews, if he owed anything beyond the aforesaid CC and L marks, you may make him to be satisfied from the time when he came into our service with horses and arms through our request, so long as he should be in our service with horses and arms through our request. *Teste meipso* at Rouen xij day of July, (A.D. 1203.)"

Terra Data.

"*The King, et cetera, to William de Warren, [Earl of Surrey,] and his Companions the Guardians of the Jews, et cetera.*—Know ye that we have given to Geoffrey Salsarius, our servant, the land which was Benedict's, the son of Jacob the Jew, at Lincoln, with the appurtenances which [is now] in our hand, and returns ij marks per annum, as is said. We have given to the same Geoffrey the land, with the appurtenances, which Godard de Antioch holds at London, by returning, on its account, annually xx shillings, as is said; therefore we command you that you make him to have those lands, with their appurtenances, in their integrity, without delay, unless more shall be returned from us. *Teste meipso*, at Rouen, on the xv day of July, (A.D. 1203.)"[1]

By the above writ, we find the King himself writing to William de Warren, (Earl of Surrey,) and his companions, the Guardians of the Jews, on certain grants, regrants, escheats, or forfeitures of land—businesses always occurring, in these feudal times, between the head of the Government and the officials of the Government. Of these writs, written to the Guardians or Justiciaries of the Jews, we have met with several signed as this is, "*Teste meipso*," by the King himself, or by one of his ministers of the Exchequer, some of whom he always appears to have had about him.

We look still in vain for those cruelties which occurred in the previous disgraceful and tyrannical reigns; and also for those fabulous tooth-drawing operations for the extraction of Israelitish wealth, imputed to the phantasm-King-John of monkish history.

But yet further:—

"*The King, et cetera, to Geoffrey Fitz-Peter, et cetera.*—We command you that you give a receipt of payment of a debt and usury of vii pounds of sterling money to William de Parco, which he owes to Helie the Jew of Gloucester. *Teste meipso*, at Bona Villa, on the xiij day of November. Per William Briwerr, (the Treasurer.)"[2]

"*The King, et cetera, to his dearly-beloved and faithful William de Warenne, and his companions, Guardians of the Jews, health in the Lord.*—Know ye that we have pardoned William de Hasting a hundred pounds of sterling money from the debt which he owes to the Jews, on which account we command you that you should give him a receipt for the hundred pounds. And know ye to give your counsel to us, when we may come into Angoleime,

---

[1] Rotuli de Liberate, p. 49.   [2] Ibid., p. 73.

for taking the fine from him; and you shall consult upon what terms, [or times half-yearly,] for payment to give. And you may take into your hand and keep possession of the charters of the said William which the Jews had, until we have enjoined something else for you; and inform us how much remains of the same debt. *Teste meipso,* at Bona Villa, on the xiij day of November, (A.D. 1203.)"[1]

There is no indication here of any reckless neglect of business, nor yet of justice; for this chairman or president of the Board of Guardians for the Jews was none other than William de Warren, Earl of Surrey, of the family of Earl de Warren of Normandy, nephew of William the Conqueror, and companion, too, in arms, at the Battle of Hastings, A.D. 1066, of the Conqueror his uncle. In the face of these writs, attested by the King himself, especially in the face of this of the 13th day of November, A.D. 1203, commencing, "*Rex, et cetera,*" we ask every impartial reader if it be not monstrous to accredit that King John drew the teeth of the Jews, and otherwise wronged them, to compel them to disclose their treasures?

We proceed:—

"*The King, et cetera, to Geoffrey Fitz-Peter, et cetera.*—Know ye that we have pardoned William de Hasting one hundred pounds of sterling money of the debt which he owes to the Jews, on which account we command you that you may make him to be quiet, [give him an acquittance,] and his land, which is in the hand of the Jews, you may make him to have, with reference to the debt aforesaid. Attested, et cetera."[2]

The above two writs, authorising debts to be paid to the Jews at the Treasury by means of the Chief Justiciary, William Briwerr, the Treasurer, and two or more Chamberlains always in attendance, shew a publicity in King John's dealings with the Jews, as well as fairness in his transactions, which annihilate monkish slanders and fables.

---

[1] Rotuli de Liberate, p. 73.   [2] Ibid.

"*The King, et cetera, to William de Warren, G. de Norwich, T. de Neville, [Justiciaries of the Jews,] et cetera.*—Know ye that Robert de Pinkeny has found securities to us for returning to us six hundred and twenty marks, which his father Henry owed to Muriell the Jew, and Abraham his son, to wit, Gavin Fitz-Gerald for one mediety, and Robert de Veteriponte for a fourth part, and Thomas Basset for a fourth part; so that one mediety ought to be returned to us on the Lord's day next before the middle of the feast of Quadragesima, and the other mediety at the close of the feast of the Paschal Lamb, in the fifth year of our reign; and therefore we command you that you should make them to be reckoned to the aforesaid Jews, below the fine which they have levied with us; and you may return to the aforesaid Robert the charters of his father, which they held on that account with his bond. Attested by Geoffrey Earl of Essex, at Windsor, on the 28th day of March, A.D. 1204."[1]

The above writ, attested by Geoffrey Fitz-Peter, Earl of Essex, and Chief Justiciary of England, and addressed to Earl Warren, Chief Justiciary and Baron of the Exchequer of the Jews, contains nothing within it tending to supersede the law of the land, and substituting in its place the King's capricious will and pleasure. All these writs, or orders, for paying money to or for the Jews, are similarly written or attested by earls, justiciaries, minsters of state, and, as we have seen, very frequently by the King himself.

Finally:—

"*The King, et cetera, to William de Warenn, et cetera, guardians of the Jews, et cetera.*—Know ye we have granted to Robert Agulun the land of Geoffrey de Mard, in Dudecote, which was in the hand of Bonechose the Jew, for the debt of the same Geoffrey, by returning on that account to us yearly xvij pounds, and to Geoffrey de la Mara lx. shillings, at the times [rent-days] at which the Jew had that land; and therefore we command you that you

---

[1] Rotuli de Liberate, p. 87.

should give that land, with all appurtenances, to the aforesaid Robert, the chattels of the same land being reserved to us. Attested by Geoffrey Fitz-Peter, et cetera, at Portsmouth, on the v day of May, (A.D. 1204.)"[1]

And so the alleged 'cruelties' to the Jews vanish into 'thin air.' A more impudent falsehood could not be imagined. These old Tower Records, lifted out of that long-gathered dust, hundred-tongued proclaim that never has England had a monarch who watched with such vigilance, such thoughtfulness, such kindliness over the interests of this too often trampled on race. The men, also, who were on the commission for "the Jews" need only to be recounted, to satisfy that John gave in them surety that nothing but justice, nothing but what was within the Law, would be permitted to come upon the Jews. The same might be said of John's attitude toward all classes of his subjects. He possessed a strange ubiquity of oversight, a self-denying application to official duty, and a large-hearted interest in everything that interested his people, beyond our estimate, and beyond every sovereign of his age. The 'John' of history, so-called, is a myth, a phantasm. The 'John' who reigned right royally in "this England" was "every inch a king," and a man by nature gentle as a girl, and softened with all tender charities. He fell on an "evil day;" and his memory has had no defender.

---

[1] Rotuli de Liberate, p. 98.

CHAPTER XIX.

JOHN'S ALLEGED SKULKING IN ISLE OF WIGHT.

IT has been stated by Roger de Wendover, the Chronicler,[1] and the statement has been retold by all writers for the last six hundred years, that as soon as the barons repaired from Runnemead to London, where they never disbanded, the King proceeded secretly in the night to the Isle of Wight, with a few followers whom he had begged from the retinue of the Bishop of Norwich.[2] In this retreat, we are asked to believe, the King turned pirate, and employed himself in gaining the goodwill of the sailors of the Cinque Ports; that he lived the life of a wanderer, seeking shelter in the open air in the island near to the sea-coast, and without any regal show. For three months together the King is represented as leading a solitary life on the water, and in the company of sailors, inasmuch as he preferred to die rather than to live unrevenged of the insults of the barons. All this time, during these three months, different reports were circulated by different people concerning him. By some, John was said to have turned fisherman; by others, that he had turned trader and pirate. By some, he was represented to have become apostate, and turned Mohammedan. And what wonder if he had, when the world swarmed with such Christians as Stephen Langton, and Eustace the Monk—Bishop of Ely? After he had been searched for in vain by several parties, it was believed that he had been drowned, or had perished some other way. This

---

[1] Vol. ii. p. 325.
[2] John Gray, Bishop of Norwich, died six months before this occurred, or on the 1st of November 1214.

story of the King's secret flight to the Isle of Wight, and there turning fisherman and pirate, has been told an hundred times by as many different writers during the last six centuries. Some of these writers, voluminous as poor in materials, have embellished the story considerably. We think we have seen one version wherein the *two Grays, John and Walter*, went with him for company. This Isle of Wight story is, like a great many other monkish stories, untrue, and is easily proved to be so by the published Itinerary of King John, from the Records of the Tower. KING JOHN NEVER WENT TO THE ISLE OF WIGHT AT ALL.

Mr. Thomas Duffus Hardy, in his description of the Patent Rolls in the Tower of London, furnishes the unquestionable data. Let us read:—

"Previously to the sealing of Magna Charta, namely, from the 1st to the 3d of June 1215, the King was at Windsor, from which place he can be traced, by his attestations, to Odiham, and thence to Winchester, where he remained until the 8th.

"From Winchester he went to Merton; he was again at Odiham on the 9th, whence he returned to Windsor, and continued there until the 15th.

"On that day he met the barons at Runnemead by appointment, and there sealed the great Charter of English liberty.

"The King then returned to Windsor, and remained there until the 18th of June, from which time until the 23d he was every day both at Windsor and at Runnemead, and did not finally leave Windsor and its vicinity before the 26th of the same month.

"John then proceeded through Odiham to Winchester, and continued in that city until the end of June.

"The first four days of July he passed at Marlborough, from which place he went to Devizes, Bradenstoke, and Calne, reached Cirencester on the 7th, and returned to Marlborough on the following day.

"He afterwards went to Ludgershall, and through Clarendon into Dorsetshire as far as Corfe Castle, but returned to Clarendon on the 15th of July; from which place he proceeded through Newbury and Abingdon to Woodstock, and thence to Oxford, where he arrived on the 17th of that month; and in a letter dated on the 15th of July between Newbury and Abingdon, the King mentions the impossibility of his reaching Oxford by the 16th, according to his appointment with the barons.

"The statement of historians that John went to the Isle of Wight immediately after signing Magna Charta is thus clearly shewn to be erroneous, as it is unquestionable that the King did not then visit the Isle of Wight, nor is there any evidence of his having ever been in that island, except when he was at Yarmouth in the year 1206, in the months of May and June, and in February 1214."

So disappears another of the mendacities and libellous fables.

CHAPTER XX.

JOHN'S CARE FOR THE POOR.

As against the monkish maligning of John as 'cruel,' 'suspicious,' 'callous,' we wish briefly to shew how he discharged one Christian duty, viz.,—feeding the poor.

Perhaps no king of England exerted himself more in this than did King John, through the whole course of his eventful reign of eighteen years.

In the fifth year of his reign, the King appointed the Archbishop of Canterbury—Hubert Walter, his trusty and well-beloved Chancellor—his almoner, for the distribution of one ounce of gold to God every Lord's-day and holy day,—a sum which the said Archbishop disbursed and was repaid at the Exchequer, as the following record shews:—

"*The King to the Barons of the Exchequer, et cetera.*—Compute what is due to us by the Lord Archbishop of Canterbury in debt, and what subscribed debts we owe to him from our oblations, which are in a dry state: to wit,—for the day of Saint John the Baptist, in our fifth year, one ounce of gold; for the day of Saint Peter ad Vincula next following, one ounce of gold; for the day of the Nativity next following, one ounce of gold; for the day of All Saints next following, one ounce of gold. Attested by myself at Westminster on the first day of November, A.D. 1204.

"Moreover, you may make to be reckoned to him, for debt, that which is owing from us in subscriptions due, which we owe to them for our oblations, which are in a dry state,—to wit, for the Lord's-day in the Branches of the Palms, in the fifth year of our reign, one ounce of gold; for the day of the Paschal Lamb next following, one ounce of gold; for the day of the Lord's Ascension, one ounce of gold. Attested by myself at Rouen, June 14, A.D. 1203."

From Roger de Wendover, the chief authority for the period, it appears that in the year A.D. 1204-5 there was such a frost in January, February, and March, as to put a stop to all agricultural operations,—from the 14th of January until the 22d of March; and in the following summer a load of corn was sold for fourteen shillings.

No doubt but that a famine prevailed throughout the land; and writs that are extant shew how King John exerted himself to alleviate the distress, in the height of its pressure, previous to the coming harvest.

Mark, fourteen shillings the load, in July 1205, would be equivalent to £19 a load in July 1864, at the very least. A halfpenny a day was the ordinary wages for a freeman, postboy, hostler, &c. The great mass of the population—the agricultural labourers—were only serfs, and were paid no money-wages. Handicraft men of cities, towns, or villages were free, and entitled to receive wages. The following writ gives us a glimpse of the King,—the actual, not the historical John,—in his efforts to meet the calamity in London :—

"*The King, et cetera, to the Mayor and Vicecounts [Sheriffs] of London, et cetera.*—We enjoin upon you that, on the inspection of the Prior of Saint Trinity and iiij legal men of the city of London, you make the crop of your farm to be bought, and you cause bread to be made, so that four loaves of bread may be of the value of one penny, and you cause flour to be ground for making pottage; and from the day of the receipt of these letters you may feed at London CCC paupers, even to the day of the Assumption of the Blessed Mary, [the 15th day of August following,] so that each of them may have daily one loaf of bread; and you shall have made as much pottage from the flour as they [the mayor and sheriffs] may be able to receive; wheat-flour may be found; and when this cannot be found, as much pottage is to be made from beans and pease, from which they may be sustained, that they perish not; and it shall be reckoned to you at the Exchequer. I myself attesting at Clarendon, on the 2d day of May, (A.D. 1205.)"

This feeding of three hundred paupers in the city of London by King John was not the only exertion of the royal benevolence on this very trying occasion; but even when taken alone, it rebukes the monkish story of the King's cruelty, profanity, and recklessness of character generally. There are hundreds of examples in the writs extant, and published by the Record Commissioners, of the unwearied kindness and religious feeling of the King in feeding and assisting the poor and indigent on this and other occasions.

Under the same form it was written to the Vicecount of Wiltshire, that, "through the supervision of the Abbot of Stanley, and iiij legal men of Marlborough, he might feed C paupers for the term written above, (from the 2d of May to August 15th following, A.D. 1205.)"[1]

Under the same form it is written to the Vicecount of Southamptonshire, that, "on the inspection of the Prioress of Hilda, and iiij legal men of Winchester, he may feed CCC paupers for the term written above, (from May 2d to August the 15th following, A.D. 1205.)"[2]

Under the same form it is written to the Vicecount of Devonshire, that, "under the inspection of the Prior of Saint Nicholas of Exeter, and iiij legal men of the same city, he may feed CCC paupers for the term written above, (from May 2d to August the 15th, A.D. 1205.)"

---

[1] Rotuli de Liberate, p. 95. [2] Ibid.

Under the same form it is written to Hugo de Neville, "on the inspection of iiij legal men of Marlborough, for feeding C paupers."

Mem. 2.

Under the same form it is written to the Sheriff of Somersetshire and Dorsetshire, et cetera, that, "on the inspection of the Abbot of Binedon, and four legal men of Ivelchester, at Ivelchester, and four legal men of Saint Edwards, at the same place, and four legal men of Wareham, at the same place, he may feed CC paupers at Ivelchester, and at Saint Edwards CC paupers, and at Wareham C paupers, at the times above written."

Under the same form it is written to the Sheriff of Gloucester, that, "under the inspection of the Prior of Lantonary, at Gloucester, and four legal men of the same city, he may feed CC paupers at the same place; and, under the inspection of the Abbot of Saint Augustine, at Bristol, CC paupers, at the times above written."

Under the same form it is written to the Sheriff of Oxfordshire, that, "under the inspection of the Abbot of Osen, and four legal men of the same city, he may feed C paupers at the times above written."[1]

On the same day, at the same place, "in charity to five hundred paupers, three shillings a day for fifty days—namely, from the xxix day of March even to the xvij day of May, reckoned to vij pounds x shillings, freed to the Abbot of Binedon. To the same abbot, for charity to D paupers, because . . . . eat fishes and drank wine on the day of the Adorable Cross at Northampton, xlvj shillings and x pence halfpenny."[2]

To the same, "for charity to four score paupers, because the King was in trouble of mind, that the Chief-Justiciary [Geoffrey Fitz-Peter] and William Briwerr [the treasurer] should have eaten flesh with him on Wednesday [April 8, 1209] next after

---

[1] Rotuli de Liberate, p. 96.   [2] Rotulus Misæ, p. 110.

the closed Feast of the Paschal Lamb, at Laxington, x shillings and v pence halfpenny."[1]

To the same, "for charity to C paupers, because the lord the King twice eat on Friday, in the house of Saint Mark the Evangelist, at Alnewic, ix shillings and iiij pence halfpenny."

Also "for charity to C paupers, because the same King eat twice on Friday in the Feast of the Apostles Philip and James, at Laxington, ix shillings and iiij pence halfpenny."[2]

Also "for charity to C paupers, because at the same place he twice eat on Friday, on the morrow of the Ascension of our Lord, at Fromton, ix shillings and iiij pence halfpenny."

Also, at the same place, "in charity to C paupers, because William Briwerr [the treasurer] eat flesh at Bath on Wednesday next after the Ascension of our Lord, xiij shillings and vj pence halfpenny."

Also "in charity to C paupers, because the King repented that he twice eat on the Friday next after the feast of Saint Trinity, at Cnapp, ix shillings and iiij pence halfpenny."

Also "in charity to C paupers, because he twice eat on the Friday next before the feast of Saint John the Baptist, at London, ix shillings and iiij pence halfpenny."

Also "in charity to C paupers, because he twice eat on the Friday next after the feast of Saint John the Baptist, ix shillings and iiij pence halfpenny."

We forego the pleasure of producing more of these acts of benevolence to the poor on the part of the King; but if we chose to write them out further, we might produce hundreds of these poor-relieving accounts, from the prebendal stall of the value of twopence a year to the highest church benefice—to be given to the applicant, on the next vacancy occurring of the required value—"*in our gift.*" Surely here, in the real and actual 'King John,' we have something very different from the 'John' of History, (so-called!)

---

[1] Rotulus Misæ, p. 110.   [2] Ibid., p. 111.

CHAPTER XXI.

KINGLY KINDNESS REWARDED WITH TREASONOUS INGRATITUDE.

As Robert Fitz-Walter, Saher de Quinci, and Eustace de Vesci were the principal actors in the troublous reign of King John, we devote this chapter to Charters, Letters-Patent, and Writs referring to them exclusively, whereby insight will be given to their belauded 'patriotism,' &c., &c.

We begin with payment of a debt by the King to the Jews, for Saher de Quinci, Earl of Winchester :—

"*The King, et cetera, to Richard de Wilek, et cetera.*—Know ye that we have acquitted Saher de Quinci of two hundred and sixty pounds Andegavian for chattel and usury, which he owes to Brunus and Josce Fitz-Bonevie de Rouen, and Affaite de Mostervilers, and Abraham de Insula Bona, Jews; and therefore we command you as far as that you acquit him, and his pledges likewise; and the charters of the said Saher, and his securities, which they hold for the same debt, you may cause those to be restored to him without delay. I myself attesting at Cenomann, on the 16th day of August. By Earl William Marshall." [1]

Below we have an order from the King to Robert Fitz-Walter, the Castellan of Ruyl, to allow ten pipes of wine to pass his fortress on the Seine without the exaction of blackmail, for Saher de Quinci :—

---

[1] Rotuli Normanniæ, vol. i. p. 61. A.R. 4, A.D. 1202.

"*The King, et cetera, to Robert Fitz-Walter, et cetera, and to Robert Fitz-Heremer, et cetera.*—We command you to allow Saher de Quinci to have ten pipes of wine at Valle Rodol acquitted from blackmail. I myself attesting at Rouen, on the 7th day of March, (A.D. 1203.)"

Under the same form it is written to the Constable of Chester (Roger de Laci) and Henry de Rolleston, for ten pipes of wine (to be allowed to pass their fortress of Rock Andely.)[1]

"*The King, et cetera, to William de Warenne [Earl of Surrey] and Thomas de Neville and G. de Norwich, Justiciaries of the Jews, et cetera.*—Know ye that we have acquitted our faithful Saher de Quinci three hundred marks, which he owes to the Jews, and therefore we command you to acquit him of the same; and for the other three hundred marks which he owes to the Jews, make him to be acquitted from usury, even from the feast of Saint Michael, in the fifth year of our reign, for one year. I myself attesting at Rouen, on the 28th day of May, (A.R. 5, A.D. 1203.)"[2]

These payments of debts were no doubt bounties paid to spendthrifts on their enlistment into the Norman army. They amount to all sums; and paid *ad infinitum* to all sorts of characters, high and low.

"*The King, et cetera, to the Sheriff of Gloucester, et cetera.*— You may know that we have committed to our dearly-beloved and faithful Saher de Quinci[3] all the land which was the Earl of Leicester's, which is in our hand, in demesne as well as in fee; and therefore we enjoin upon thee to give him full seisin on that account in thy bailiwick. And chiefly to all knights and freeholders

---

[1] Rotuli Normanniæ, vol. i. p. 82.
[2] Rotuli de Liberate, p. 38.
[3] Saher de Quinci married the co-heiress and younger daughter of Robert,

Earl of Leicester; and this accounts for his connexion with lands of the Earl of Leicester.

of that fee, who are in our hand in the bailiwick, that they be dependent on the same Saher in all things, our fidelity being secured. Attested by the Lord of Canterbury at Abbedon, on the 30th day of March, (in the 6th year of the reign, and A.D. 1205.)"[1]

"*The King to the Sheriff of Leicestershire, et cetera.*—We command you that without delay you make our dearly-beloved and faithful Saher de Quinci to have Baggeworth, Weston, and Seneby, which were the Earl of Leicester's; on which account thou hast received our command to liberate them to the Countess of Leicester, to be retained in guardianship as long as it should please us, provided they be not of the honour of Grentemenuill nor of the dower of the aforesaid countess,—since we have committed them to the aforesaid Saher in guardianship, until we shall have given another to him in the place of them. I myself attesting at the Tower of London, on the 28th day of April, (A.D. 1205.)"

Under the same form it is written to the Sheriff of Berkshire, on the manor of Hungerford.

"*The King to the Sheriff of Leicestershire, et cetera.*—We enjoin upon you without delay to make our dearly-beloved and faithful Saher de Quinci to have the land beyond the wall of the city of Leicester, which was the Earl of Leicester's, because we have committed them to him for guardianship, unless it be of the honour of Grentemenuill or of the dower of the Countess of Leicester, the land of the Countess of Leicester being reserved, which we have enjoined to be returned to her in exchange for land of the honour of Grentemenuill, which the same earl gave to the Lord of Lincoln by agreement made between them for that land; and the land of the Canons of Leicester being secured, which the same earl gave to them by his legal power, which we have enjoined

---

[1] Rotuli Litterarum Clausarum, vol. i. p. 24 *b*.

to be returned to them. I myself attesting at the Tower of London, on the 28th day of April, (in the 6th year of the reign, A.D. 1205.)"

"*The King to the Barons of the Exchequer, health in the Lord.*—We command you that you may have respect to Saher de Quinci for four score and ten marks of silver, which are due from him at the Exchequer for the debt to Aaron the Jew and others, so long as he shall have been in our service beyond sea, with horses and arms, by our precept. I myself attesting at Clarendon, on the 28th day of May. Per eundem et per Justiciary."[1]

"*The King, et cetera, to Geoffrey Fitz-Peter, et cetera.*—We command you that if Amicius, the son of the Earl of Leicester, should have retired from England, immediately after his retiring you may make Saher de Quinci, or his seneschal, to have all the land of Winterburn and Stoke, with appurtenances. I myself attesting at Portsmouth, on the 7th day of June. By Hugo de Neville."

"*The King, et cetera, to the Barons of the Exchequer, et cetera.*—Know that we have pardoned our dearly-beloved and faithful Saher de Quinci three hundred marks of the debt which he owes to us at the Exchequer; and therefore we command you to make him acquitted of the aforesaid three hundred marks. I myself attesting, on the 21st day of June, at Dartmouth, (A.D. 1205.)"[2]

It is commanded the Sheriff of Buckinghamshire to allow Saher de Quinci to have his scutage remitted in his bailiwick. It is likewise commanded other sheriffs in whose bailiwicks he has lands.[3]

---

[1] Rotuli Litterarum Clausarum, vol. i. p. 34 *b*.
[2] Ibid., p. 38 *b*.
[3] Ibid., p. 43 *b*.

King John of England. 233

"*The King, et cetera, to the Barons of the Exchequer, et cetera.*—We command you that, of the three hundred marks which we have pardoned Saher de Quinci, in the 7th year of our reign, at Dartmouth, placed to him for the thousand marks which he at first had promised to us, as he says, you may make to be placed to him for all his debt,—to wit, for six thousand marks by which he levied a fine with us,—to have the land of Robert, Earl of Leicester, which fell to him on the part of his wife, and for having the honour of Hinket. But, nevertheless, he may have three hundred marks from the Exchequer, which may be placed to his account anyhow thereat as one hundred marks. I myself attesting at Porchester, on the 25th day of May, in the 8th year of our reign."[1]

Here we find Saher de Quinci is pardoned 300 marks at the Exchequer on the 21st of June, A.D. 1205. Here, on the 25th of May in the following year, A.D. 1206, the 300 marks, that had been placed for the 1000 marks which he really owed to the Exchequer, are now made to stand for his whole debt of 6000 marks. But yet after this he may have lent to him at the Exchequer 300 marks more, which are to be entered to him, or against him, at the Exchequer as 100 marks lent to him. This man was constantly obtaining assistance for the payment of his debts from the Government; and when the power of Government failed to raise the half-yearly payments for the baronial and knightly feudatories of the Exchequer, the greatest disorganisation of society arose. The King must be insulted, and spendthrifts of high degree must repudiate their just debts at Runnemead under the shadow of the grand charter of *British liberty!*

"*To the Sheriff of Wiltshire, et cetera.*—We enjoin upon you to give without delay to our dearly-beloved and faithful Thomas de Sanford and G. de Neville full seisin of the lands of Saher de

---

[1] Rotuli Litterarum Clausarum, vol. i. p. 71.

Quinci in your county, which we have given to them. I myself attesting at Newtington, [in Kent,] October 2, (A.R. 17, A.D. 1215.)"

In the early part of the reign, Saher de Quinci appears to have been under the greatest obligation to King John for debts paid for him to the Jews; but when an invasion was threatened from France, Saher de Quinci appears to have joined the invading party against his sovereign, and so lost his favour, as the above and following writ will verify, by the enforcement of the confiscation of his lands.

"It is commanded the Sheriff of Suffolk that he should give to Gilbert de Kentwell the land which was Robert de Veer's in Werdelinton, and the land of Saher de Quinci in Tudeham, and the land of Peter de Thelnetham in Thelnetham, and the land of William de Wadingefeld in Pridinton, and the land of Thomas de Muleton, and the land of John de Goding in Buckeshall, and the land of Cecilie Carbonel in Loneham, and the land of Roger de Markeshall, which they, enemies of the lord the King, held of the fee of the said Gilbert, to be held as long as it shall please the lord the King. Attested by the King at Malling, on the 8th day of December, (A.D. 1215.)"

"*The King, et cetera, to Roger [de Laci,] Constable of Chester, and Henry de Rolleston, et cetera, Castellans of Rock Andely, on the Seine.*—We command you to permit one sea-going ship ascending to France, and another sea-going ship descending from France to Normandy, with wine from France, which are Robert Fitz-Walter's, to ascend and descend acquitted from blackmail. I myself attesting at Rouen, on the 14th day of February, A.D. 1203, and A.R. 4."[1]

"*The King, et cetera, to Robert Fitz-Walter, et cetera.*—We

---

[1] Rotuli Normanniæ, p. 78.

command you that you put forth all our stretch of power and blackmail in our castle of Valle Rodol. I myself attesting at Pons Aldom, on the 23d day of February. By Peter de Pateshull." [1]

"*The King, et cetera, to Geoffrey Fitz-Peter, et cetera.*—We command you that without delay you free to our dearly-beloved and faithful Robert Fitz-Walter the castle of Hertford, which we have given him to guard, as we have commanded you by our other letters; and in testimony of this we send, et cetera. I myself attesting at Chinon, on the 28th day of August, A.D. 1202." [2]

"*The King, et cetera, to all people, et cetera.*—Know that Robert Fitz-Walter and Saher de Quinci have returned the castle of Valle Rodol to the King of France by our order. And therefore we command you, and enjoin that they, and all those who were with them in that castle, may be on that account acquitted of blame. William Marshall [Earl of Pembroke and Earl Marshall] attesting at Rouen, on the 5th day of July, (A.D. 1203, and the 5th year of the reign.)" [3]

This is the writ which brands Robert Fitz-Walter and Saher de Quinci traitors to the King and realm of England. These men were Castellans of Valle Rodol, an important castle on the Seine, which they delivered up to the King of France without striking a blow, and received the thanks of the Government of England for their fidelity and promptness in obeying orders from Government.

When writing on these traitors, Roger de Wendover observes,[4] "that the French king came to Ruyl, a noble castle, which he surrounded with engines of war; but after he had arranged them in order, even before he had made one assault, Robert Fitz-

---

[1] Rotuli Normanniæ, p. 80.
[2] Rotuli Litterarum Patentium, p. 17 b.
[3] Ibid., p. 31.
[4] Chronicle, vol. ii. p. 207. A.D. 1203.

Walter and Saher de Quinci, the noblemen to whom the charge of the castle had been intrusted, delivered it up uninjured to the French king; and as the least stone of that castle was not damaged, so not one hair of the heads of the garrison was hurt."

These two men were, in the hands of Stephen Langton, the traitorous Archbishop of Canterbury, the main instruments of carrying Magna Charta, twelve years after the surrender of the castle of Ruyl. For these twelve years they were aiding and abetting Louis of France for the invasion of these realms, and this at a time when they were peers of the realm of England. We will look into these twelve years, and see how these two traitors conducted themselves therein. We must keep in view the fact that Saher de Quinci's debts were paid to the Jews by King John's Government before the custody of the castle of Ruyl was intrusted to the care of him and his partner in treachery and treason, Robert Fitz-Walter.

"*The King, et cetera, to all men, et cetera.*—Know ye that we shall consider as ratified all that which William d'Albini may do in the sale and invasion of the lands and incomes of Robert Fitz-Walter, under the seal of the said Robert, for his redemption from the prison of the King of France, saving our service. And in testimony of this thing, et cetera. I myself attesting at Danfront, on the 21st day of November, A.D. 1203-4."[1]

The King being Lord Paramount in the above case, and Robert Fitz-Walter being his vassal, holding by baronial or knight's service, no sale or invasion of the tenement could take place without the consent of the lord.

"*The King to Robert Fitz-Walter, et cetera.*—We command you that securely you may come to England, according to the form of the apostolic mandate; because we afford peace and security

---

[1] Rotuli Litterarum Patentium, p. 37 *b*.

to you, according to the form of the apostolic mandate. And in testimony of this thing we send to you, et cetera. Attested by the Lord Peter, Bishop of Winchester, at Wingham, on the 27th day of May, in the 15th year of our reign, (A.D. 1213.)"

In the same manner it is written to Eustace de Vesci.[1] Before and after the date of the above writ (for a fortnight or three weeks) the King was at Canterbury, Ewell, Dover, or Wingham. This was the time when he became a vassal of the Pope, and broke the peerage of England, by converting them in a body into copyholders. This was the time when that step was taken which, as we have seen, invalidated the legislative power of the baronage of England, and rendered worthless the great legislative enactment of Magna Charta. John ceased to be Lord Paramount in England, and had to receive and obey commands from his superior lord. The first command which he received from the new Lord Paramount was to pardon certain traitors, then in France exciting an invasion from France, of England. King John obeyed. He signed the order of recall for these traitors; and here we have two of them, *Robert Fitz-Walter* and *Eustace de Vesci, pardoned.*

" *The King to all his faithful subjects, health in the Lord.*— Know ye that we have ordered that full restitution of all their immovables and liberties be made immediately, without impediment, to Robert Fitz-Walter and Eustace de Vesci, and their adherents, without delay, after we, or those to whom we may commit the charge of our kingdom upon this business, shall have been required to do it, before Christmas-day. And if by chance, which God avert that it should be, we grant and concede not in good faith; that it may be left to our venerable father, Stephen, Archbishop of Canterbury, to reduce us, our appeal being rejected, to the same state in which we were before the form of peace was accepted by

---

[1] Rotuli Litterarum Patentium, p. 99.

us. And in testimony of this thing we have made our letters-patent on this business to be granted to you. I myself attesting at Winton, on the 19th day of July, in the 15th year of our reign, [A.D. 1213,] with all faith in Christ."

"*The King to William de Harecurt, et cetera.*—We command you that, immediately on these letters being seen, you may pick out for freedom Thomas de Clare, the man of our dearly-beloved Robert Fitz-Walter, who was taken on the occasion [1] of the aforesaid Robert, and who is in your custody at Corfe [Castle.] And in testimony of this thing we send to you on that account these our letters-patent. I myself attesting at Winton, on the 20th day of July, in the 15th year of our reign."

In the same manner it is written to Robert de Leveland for Randulph de Greinville, who is in his custody at the Bridge of the Flete. "Teste eodem." [2]

"*The King to Saher, Earl of Winchester, [a Baron of the Exchequer,] et cetera.*—We command you that you may restore to Alicia Peche, his daughter Alicia, with his other hostages, whom he has delivered to us on the '*occasion*' of Robert Fitz-Walter his brother, and who is in your custody, because we have restored them to him, to be returned to us at our command. And in testimony of this thing we send to you these our letters-patent. I myself attesting at Winchester, on the 21st day of July, in the 15th year of our reign." [3]

---

[1] The "*occasion*" here alluded to is the rumour of a conspiracy formed in the year before, or A.D. 1212, to assassinate King John, or deliver him a prisoner to his enemies, the Welsh. An investigation took place, and hostages were demanded, in sons, daughters, and nephews, from the nobility; when Robert Fitz-Walter and Eustace de Vesci absconded,—the former to France, to join the traitorous bishops there,—and the latter to the King of Scotland, his brother-in-law. — Roger de Wendover, vol. ii. p. 258.

[2] Rotuli Litterarum Patentium, vol. i. p. 101 *b*. A.D. 1213. [3] Ibid.

The Liberation of a Castle.

"It is commanded John de Bassingeburn to free the castle of Hertford, with its appurtenances, to Robert Fitz-Walter, as his right."[1]

No attestation here; but the writs above and the writs below are attested by the King himself at Windsor, on the 23d day of June, and in the 17th year of the reign. This was about five weeks after the signing of Magna Charta at Runnemead.

According to Roger de Wendover,[2] the barons who held London in an insurrectionary manner, under Robert Fitz-Walter, "*the Marshal of the army of God and the holy Church,*" put off their treasonable gathering at Stamford from the 29th of June for a week later, at Staines Wood and Hounslow. This was done through fear of losing London by a surprise.

"*The King to the Guardian of the Honour of Eye, [in Suffolk,] health in the Lord.*—Know ye that we have returned and quitclaimed, to our dearly-beloved and faithful Robert Fitz-Walter, Fulcard the prisoner, who is in our prison of Eye, [in Suffolk;] and therefore we command you to free without delay the same Fulcard to the same Robert Fitz-Walter, on his certain messenger bringing these letters; and you may permit him to depart acquitted. And in testimony of this, et cetera, we send to you. Attested as above, (at Winchester, June 30, in the 17th year of the reign.)"[3]

"*The King to the Sheriff of Hertfordshire, et cetera.*—We enjoin upon thee that without delay thou wilt make Walter le Buk to have full seisin of the manor of Benington, with all its appurtenances, which we had committed to Robert Fitz-Walter to

---

[1] Rotuli Litterarum Patentium, vol. i. p. 144 b.
[2] Chronicle, vol. ii. p. 328.
[3] Rotuli Litterarum Patentium, vol. i. p. 146.

guard, when he was for our peace. I myself attesting at Berkhampstead, on the 3d day of April, (A.D. 1216.)"

Robert de Goldingham, clerk, has letters of presentation to the church of Disce, (in Norfolk,) with its appurtenances, which is vacant, et cetera, by reason of the land of Robert Fitz-Walter being in the hand of the lord the King, and letters are directed to the official of Norwich.

It is given at the same time, and the same year, (Corfe Castle, July 10, in the 18th year of the reign, A.D. 1216.)[1] *July 10. - 18 John* *John died 19. 10. 1216.*

"*The King to the Archdeacon of Durham and Philip de Ulecot, et cetera.*—We command you that, immediately on these letters being seen, you make the castle of Alnewic to be dismantled, and you see that this be done with all haste, and that it be so prostrated that Eustace de Vesci can do nothing with it for the future. And in testimony of this thing we send to you our royal letters-patent. Attested as above "—yes! on the 27th day of May, at Wingham, near Dover,—where John had been for some time, a fortnight at least, and where he met Pandulph the legate and surrendered his crown to the Pope, the future Lord Paramount of England, and where he signed writs on the same day, this 27th of May, for the pardon and privilege of return to England to Robert Fitz-Walter, Simon Langton, the brother and tool of Stephen Langton, and the above-named traitor, Eustace de Vesci.[2]

Alnwick Castle was the feudal holding of Eustace de Vesci, the brother-in-law and adherent of the Scottish king. When the owner of Alnwick Castle became involved in treason with Robert Fitz-Walter, and had to abscond in consequence, Alnwick Castle was seized, and held by the King as a forfeited possession.

Eustace de Vesci being pardoned by the Pope, the new Lord Paramount of the Alnwick fee, did not prevent the tenant-in-chief,

---

[1] Rotuli Litterarum Patentium, vol. i. p. 190 b. [2] Ibid., p. 99.

King John, dismantling the copyhold before he returned it, or allowed the pardoned rebel to take possession.

"*The King to Geoffrey de Neville, et cetera.*—We command you to arrest Robert de Ros and Eustace de Vesci, especially if William, the son of the same Robert de Ros, shall have come to you. We will not take him nor will we molest him, especially if he should have come to our dearly-beloved Peter Fitz-Herbert. Yea, we will liberate William himself without redemption, his acquittance to be borne by the aforesaid Robert de Ros; and in testimony of this thing, et cetera, we send to you. I myself attesting at Reading, on the 9th day of April, and the 17th year of the reign, (A.D. 1216.)"[1]

"*The King to Geoffrey de Neville, Chamberlain, et cetera.*— Know ye that we have not desired so much to take money from the barons of England who were against us, as we have desired their good and faithful service; and therefore we command you that, if Robert de Ros, Eustace de Vesci, and Peter de Brus should have wished to give security to us for tendering their good and faithful service to us, and that without this we may take some money from them, it is our pleasure that they may come to us in safety and securely; and in testimony of this thing we send our royal letters-patent to you. And we send also to you our letters-patent for making a safe-conduct to the same Robert, Eustace, and Peter; by which, if they should wish, you may conduct them to us securely, and by which again they may return to their own country in safety, if it be their wish to do so. I myself attesting at Reading on the 11th day of April, and the 17th year of the reign."[2]

"*The King to all men, et cetera.*—Ye may know that we have received under our safe and secure protection Robert de Ros,

---

[1] Rotuli Litterarum Patentium, vol. i. p. 175.   [2] Ibid., p. 176.

Eustace de Vesci, and Peter de Brus in coming to us, in returning and tarrying with us, for giving security to us for his faithful service, as our dearly-beloved and faithful Geoffrey de Neville, our chamberlain, may tell them on our part, who shall conduct them to us, at the same time with the protection of our faithful John Constable of Chester and Gerard de Furnival. And if it should happen that these three may not be able to come for the conducting of the aforesaid Robert de Ros and Eustace de Vesci and Peter de Brus, two of them may bring them to us in safety; and if by chance two of them may not be able to come for the aforesaid conducting, one of them may conduct the same Robert, Eustace, and Peter. And therefore we command you, firmly insisting, that to the same Robert, Eustace, and Peter, with their attendants who may come with them, neither in coming nor in returning may you offer, or allow to be offered, any molestation or hindrance. And in testimony of this thing, we have caused to be granted to them these our letters-patent. I myself attesting, at Reading, on the 12th day of April, and in the 17th year of our reign, (A.D. 1216.)"

As these men, Robert Fitz-Walter, Saher de Quinci, Eustace de Vesci, and Robert de Ros are so mixed up through the whole reign with the King's kindnesses, and their own ingratitude and traitorous conduct, and this over a period of sixteen years, it is impossible to classify them. They were all of one class, and were frequently found together in one pardon, one benevolence, or one traitorous conspiracy. This is our only excuse for not bringing the dates into stricter consecutive order. We have, as much as possible, endeavoured to make one character follow another.

"*The King, et cetera, to the Barons of the Exchequer, et cetera.*—You may know that we have acquitted Eustace de Vesci, for compassion sake, for the 300 marks which he has owed to us, for the plea which was pleaded between him and Richmond de Hunfrauvill; and therefore we command you that you may make him to be acquitted on that business. Attested by the Lord

Peter, Bishop of Winchester, at Guildford, on the 28th day of December, (A.D. 1207-8.)"

"*The King, et cetera, to the Barons of the Exchequer, et cetera.*—Ye may know that we have acquitted Robert de Ros for the 300 marks which he has owed to us for the fine imposed for the privilege of having the guardianship of Thomas de Bekering. And therefore we command you to make him acquitted on that business. Attested by the Lord Peter, Bishop of Winchester, at Guildford, on the 28th day of December, A.D. 1207-8, and the 9th year of the reign."[1]

"*The King to the Sheriff of Yorkshire.*—We enjoin upon you to make Hugo d'Averench seisin of the guardianship of the land which was Reginald de Capetoft's in Sepinton, and of the heir of Reginald himself, on account of this being disseised on occasion of the ill-feeling which we have had against Eustace de Vesci. I myself attesting, at Nottingham, on the 3d day of September, (in the 15th year of our reign, and A.D. 1213.)"[2]

"*The King to his dearly-beloved and faithful E., Archdeacon of Durham, and Philip de Ulecot, et cetera.*—We command you that without delay you return to Eustace de Vesci the oxen and horses which ye have of his, and his arms, which were in the castle of Alnwick, [when dismantled by the above two officials in May, or about four months before this time.] I myself attesting, at Durham, on the 15th day of September, A.D. 1213."[3]

"*The King to Randulph de Normanville, et cetera.*—We enjoin upon thee that thou shalt make Alan de Tilly to have such seisin of his land in thy bailiwick, as he had of it on the day in which he was disseised *on the 'occasion'* of Eustace de Vesci.

---

[1] Rotuli Litterarum Clausarum, vol. i. p. 99.   [2] Ibid., p. 149.
[3] Ibid., p. 150 b.

Attested as next above, (at Westminster, on the 13th day of October, in the 15th year of the reign, and A.D. 1213.)"[1]

In the above roll we have another allusion to the "*occasion*" of Eustace de Vesci's absconding, along with Robert Fitz-Walter, on the alarm being given at the King's court that certain traitors were there, and that certain treasonable deeds were about to be perpetrated against the person of the King. This was the "*occasion*," when certain retainers of Robert Fitz-Walter and Eustace de Vesci suffered confiscation and imprisonment, on their lords absconding as confessed traitors.

"*The King to Geoffrey de Neville, his Chamberlain, et cetera.*—We command you that you make without delay our faithful Brian de Insula to have full seisin of all the lands with their appurtenances, which were Eustace de Vesci's and William de Mobray's in your bailiwick. I myself attesting, at Winchester, on the 30th day of May, (A.R. 18, A.D. 1216.)"

Vesci.

"*The King to Philip de Ulecot, health in the Lord.*—Ye may know that we have granted to our dearly-beloved and faithful William de Harecourt, our seneschal, one mediety of the land which was Eustace de Vesci's—namely, the barony of Alnewick, which he claims to be his right and hereditament; and we grant to you the other mediety, as we have commanded you otherwise. On which account we command you, that, on the inspection and testimony of legal men, you may immediately make the aforesaid William to have the mediety of that land with the aforesaid barony, with all its appurtenances, in your bailiwick, to be held for our use—the other mediety, with all its appurtenances, [to be held for your use.] I myself attesting, at Walton, on the 14th day of September, (in the 18th year of the reign, and A.D. 1216.)"

---

[1] Rotuli Litterarum Clausarum, vol. i. p. 153.

"And it is commanded Geoffrey de Neville, Chamberlain, Philip Mark, and Nicholas de Hay, that they make William de Harecourt to have one mediety and Philip de Ulecot the other mediety, of the land which was heretofore called Eustace de Vesci's, with all its appurtenances, on the inspection and testimony of legal men, as was ordered before. Attested by the King at Walton, [in Buckinghamshire,] on the 15th day of September, *anno regni* 18th."

The above writ was written only a month before the King's death. Eustace de Vesci had died some time before this; but, in the confusion of the times, his property might not be immediately adjudicated upon by the government.

These documents may be safely left to speak for themselves. We know not what evidence is if they do not furnish, on the one hand, proof "strong as Holy Writ," of a needy, greedy, mean nobility, ever hanging upon their King with leech-like cupidity; and, on the other, the King against fearful odds, and with the poorest resources and instrumentalities, standing erect and chivalrous, and moulding circumstances to the welfare of his country.

CHAPTER XXII.

JOHN'S ALLEGED LOW ASSOCIATES—LUPESCAIRE AND ALGAIS.

KING JOHN, in his war in France, carried on against the lord-paramount for the Norman and other fees in France, laboured under great disadvantages; as the Lord-Paramount set free from their allegiance, on the tenant-in-chief of Normandy, Anjou, Tourain, and Main, all sub-infeudatories, copyholders, sockmen, et cetera.

The feudal system was a reality after the type of the laws of the Medes and Persians, which alter not. The lord-paramount was lord-paramount, the freeholder was freeholder, the copyholder was copyholder; and no papistical conjurings, bowings, or grimaces could alter it; for there the FACT stood, far above the machinations of priestly incantations and dispensations. The Church of Rome could not dispense with the provisions of feudalism, for the feudal system stood above and beyond its reach. The lord-paramount set the sub-infeudatories free from their allegiance to the tenant-in-chief, and they were free. All English barons or knights holding French fees were set at liberty from their allegiance to the King of England when in France, or acting in accordance with those feudal tenures.

Thus King John's feudal position in France was damaged by the arbitrary act of his lord-paramount. They were set free from their allegiance to the King of England by the King of France, and *they became free.* This was *feudalism.*

In this position, John was driven to raise his armies for the Norman wars; not, as heretofore, from the sub-infeudatories of his dukedom or earldom in France, but from England,—and these from *volunteers*. The feudal system was broken in France about A.D. 1200; and in England, at Dover, in the year A.D. 1213, as we have told.

John's position in France was a most delicate and difficult one to maintain; and he had to maintain it—difficult as it was—as he best might, by raising forces in England, Brabant, Poland, and even Portugal and Spain. His Norman forces were collected from the ends of the earth; as he could, by the power of money, paid in bounties and wages, collect and bring them together. Troops he must raise, and troops he did raise, for Normandy.

John had his French principalities, provinces, counties, hundreds, with their several earls, vice-counts, bailiffs, and constables, to provide for and protect.

Appointments and promotions, in and from all grades of society in rank, knowledge, and general civilisation, had to be made, to fill all offices civil and military, as the exigencies of the King's position in France required.

John had no choice in the matter. He had to carry on the war with France in France, as best he could, and with such means as he could secure.

Amongst a host of aspirants for glory and promotion, two knights arose upon the military surface of contention and strife, — one named Lupescaire, and the other Martin Algais; and these two represented by the Chroniclers of the age to be from Bragançon in Portugal, though we think they came from Brabant. Be this as it may, these Norman wars attracted adventurers and soldiers of fortune from every State of Europe, and perhaps even some stragglers from Africa; for the crusades of Richard I. had thrown upon the world a class of men who were only too glad to enlist under any flag, in any field of strife and contention. Martin Algais was promoted to the office of Seneschal of Gascony and Perigord, which trust he held for a considerable time—three or four years, or more. Lupescaire held Falaise also as Governor, for the King.

The fact of King John having selected these two knights for promotion and confidential positions in the government of Normandy, has been seized upon by the monkish writers to weight their charge against the King of relishing LOW COMPANY. We all know King John has been represented for six hundred and fifty years, without any contradiction, to have been partial to vulgar and low associates, and brutal pursuits and pastimes. This charge proceeds from the King's promoting these Bragançons to high places of military trust in Normandy, and from this alone.

We would now show by what process King John invited the low acquaintance (so called) to his society.

The following letters-patent supply full information on the subject:—

Summons.

"*The King, et cetera, to all his Beloved and Faithful of the Land of Hainault and of Flanders holding Lands or Fees of the King of England, [as Tenant-in-Chief,] et cetera.*—We command you, as ye love the lands and fees which ye hold of us, to come to us and do us the service which unto us ye owe; so that ye be with us at Rouen by the approaching feast of Saint John the Baptist, [Monday, June 24,] equipped in such wise that we may owe you our thanks, and we will gladly do unto you that which we ought to do. Witness ourself at Le Héron, on the 25th day of May, (A.D. 1202.)"[1]

Such is the historical FACT as to how King John was brought into such close contact with the 'low associates and brutal companions' so obnoxious to the Chroniclers of the thirteenth century.

King John's summons brought to his standard from time to time, as we have already seen in former chapters, all the spend-

---

[1] Introduction to Rotuli Litterarum Patentium, vol. i. p. 7.

thrifts, adventurers, and soldiers of fortune, of Europe; and these being more than a match for Robert Fitz-Walter, Saher de Quinci, and Eustace de Vesci, in bravery and generalship, they very naturally took the position assigned to them by merit and good leadership, and the chapter of accidents.

The two Brabanters, or Bragançon knights, Lupescaire and Martin Algais, more specifically, were attracted, along with the great European crowd of adventurers, to Normandy. They became eminent military leaders, and obtained deserved promotion in consequence, which greatly excited the envy of the English and Norman knights in the service along with themselves of the King of England. One effect was, John was forthwith charged with favouring unworthy flatterers and low companions, and promoting to high office, place, and dignity men quite unfit for the confidence he placed in them.

This charge of liking for low company was first historically made in the Margan Annals, A.D. 1232, as your modern historians allege; but when we turn to the venerable authority, it proves a myth. Nor is this an unfrequent thing with the Chronicle writers of the fourteenth and fifteenth centuries. They are ever quoting, at second and third hand, some manuscript Chronicle which they never had the chance of seeing.

Moreover, coming down to more modern days, how many generals and admirals, and even bishops, have we not heard of who passed full muster officially, but yet were not first-rate characters in private life; and this without bringing any charges of low-companionship against the reigning sovereign on account of their promotion?

But, setting monkish Chroniclers aside, let us turn to the Patent Rolls of the Record Commissioners' Reports for the date, A.D. 1202, where we shall find the following writ:—

"*The King, et cetera, to Americus de Trevaloy.*—We command you that without delay you free to Lupescaire the castle of Lymville, with its appurtenances, and with the crops of autumn standing; and in testimony of this transaction we send to you these our letters-patent. Attested by myself at Chinon, on the 5th day of August, A.D. 1202." [1]

In the above Writ we have a castle taken from the enemy, and probably from a feudatory in rebellion, and given, as hundreds of castles and manors were given, to some minister of the Crown, court-favourite, or general commanding the successful expedition against it. Another Writ of letters-patent, from p. 21 *b* of the same work, we give next :—

"*The King, et cetera, to all Constituted Authorities throughout Normandy, et cetera.*—We command you that you should conduct in safety through Normandy the plunder of our dearly-beloved Lupescaire, and the men of the said Lupescaire conveying that plunder; nor may you allow any annoyance to be offered to them. I myself attesting at Bures, on the 16th day of December, A.D. 1202."

The above letters-patent present nothing but what occurred an hundred times in such a warfare as was carried on in Normandy in the years 1202–1206, et cetera.

Another writ of letters-patent we give from p. 24 of the same work :—

"*The King, et cetera, to all Bailiffs of Normandy, et cetera.*— We command you to guard and maintain by force the plunder of Lupescaire, and to cause it to be conducted through our land, not doing, nor permitting to be done, in any thing molestation or injustice. I myself attesting at Sogz, January 26, 1203."

Again :—

"The Prior and Canons of Saint Barbe have letters-patent of the lord the King, on the protection of John Marisco and Lupescaire; and that if anything should be taken from them, they should cause that to be restored to them."

From the above, it would appear that the spoils taken in this

---

[1] Rotuli Litterarum Patentium, vol. i. p. 15 *b*.

war required the royal protection, especially when the commander of the expedition was a Bragançon—one not very particular in distinguishing friend from foe in a raid for plunder.

Geoffrey de Lucy and Peter de Maulay have letters directed from the lord the King, on the protection of Lupescaire in his land of Amenesch.

Here follow a series of writs from the same book:—

1. (P. 28 *b*.)—" Peter Gascon, the man of Lupescaire, has letters-patent from the lord the King for safe conduct through the whole land and power of the lord the King."

2. (P. 30.)—" *The King to Martin Algais, the Seneschal of Wascon, et cetera.*—Know ye that we have committed to our dearly-beloved and faithful Lupescaire, Riberiac, and Albeterre, to sustain him in our service as long as we have assigned to him a certain garrison; and therefore we command you that you make him to have them. I myself attesting at Rouen, on the 27th day of May, A.D. 1203."

3. (P. 32 *b*.)—" The Earl of Leicester has letters-patent from the lord the King for simple protection directed to Lupescaire and William le Mercer; and it is stated in their fine that they should not require from him, nor from his men who are in his bailiwick, assistance for foss-work, or other works."

4. (P. 35.)—" *The King, et cetera, to Lupescaire and his Companions, et cetera.*—Truly understand, that as our Norman barons have sworn that they guard, and defend, and hold by force you, therefore we command you to guard and defend all the lands, things, and men of our dearly-beloved and faithful J. de Pateshull; and chiefly his lands of Conde upon Black Water, and his other lands; and you may not do, nor permit to be done, annoyance or injury to his things in any way. And if you have taken anything from the lands or things of the said John, that you make to be restored to him without delay; for you well understand how he and our other barons are held to guard and control you, and in the same manner you are held to guard and defend

them. I myself attesting at Herbtot, on the vij day of November, (A.D. 1203.)"

The following charter, from the "Rotuli Chartorum," (vol. i. part I., page 105,) we give, as it is on the same subject :—

Carta Lupescara.

"*John, by the grace of God, et cetera.*—Know you that we have given and conceded, and by our present charter have confirmed, to our dearly-beloved and faithful Lupescaire, White Land, with its appurtenances, to be held by him, and kept well and in peace, freely and quietly, as long as we have assigned to him his garrison in another place. Attested by R., Earl of Leicester, William, Earl de Ferrars, William de Breosa, Geoffrey de Saucy, William d'Albini, G. de Fornivall. Given by the hand of John, Archdeacon of Worcester, at Pons Archies, on the 5th day of June, anno, et cetera, quinto, (A.D. 1203.)"

As Martin Algais, another Bragançon, (Brabanter?) also barbs the charge of King John's taste for low associates, we must investigate his position as a leader, general, or seneschal of Gascony and Perigord, and see what is what. So we return to the 'Records :'—

1. "*The King, et cetera, . . . by the same grace, of Burdegalen, and H. Xancton, Bishop, A., Earl of Engoleme, A., Vice-count of Toarc, William de Rupibus and Robert de Turnham, Martin Algais, et cetera.*—We command you that you have faith in those whom our dearly-beloved and faithful William, Earl of Salisbury, our brother, and Peter de Pateshull may point out to you on our part, for promoting our business. Attested by myself at Belencumb, on the xvij day of May, (A.D. 1202.)"

2. "*The King, et cetera.*—Know ye that we wish that Berenger Berave and Raymund Berave and Bartram Berave, merchants of our dearly-beloved Martin Algais, and theirs of the merchant class, may be acquitted through all our land; all customs apper-

taining to the liberty of the city of London being saved. Attested by myself at Bonport, on the 23d of July." [1]

3. "*The King, et cetera, to Robert de Veteriponte.*—We command you that without delay you free to our dearly-beloved Hugo de Gornac all the French prisoners taken in this war,—those whom you have,—the prisoners whom Martin Algais has taken being excepted; and in testimony of this thing, I myself attesting at Rouen, on the 17th day of July, (A.D. 1202.)"

Again, from the same, p. 17 :—

4. "*The King, et cetera, to all Bailiffs in Normandy, et cetera.* —We enjoin upon you that, to the bearers of these presents,— Hugo de Bosevill, our servant, and Peter de Arkay, the servant of Martin Algais, conducting the spoil of the said Martin in Normandy,—you permit no toll, nor annoyance, nor injury to be done, by which they may be impeded in their going or returning."

Again, from p. 20 *b* :—

5. "*The King, et cetera, to all who are with Martin Algais, et cetera.*—After our war began, no misfortune occurred which we could have felt more annoyingly than this which happened to our dearly-beloved and faithful Martin Algais, because against him, God bearing witness, we were vehemently excited and disturbed, but that by his counsel, and that of his men, we have more fully improved our condition, than you may dare to canvass. Nevertheless, we command you that, as far as seeking our service, you diligently and fervently pay attention to his commands as hitherto ye have done, because the service of your men, at the command of the said Martin, shall be remunerated to you. And know ye that for the service of the said Martin, before the service of any one else, we pray. I myself attesting at Saumur, on the 13th day of November, (A.D. 1202.)"

From the royal protection required by these Portuguese soldiers of fortune for their booty, obtained in their various excursions into

---

[1] "Salva libertate civitatis Londinensis." Rotuli Litterarum Patentium, vol i. p. 15.

the enemies' lands, it appears that they were unpopular as soldiers. What Bragançon troopers might be in the year 1202 we have no means of knowing; but we should suppose anything but what a king, free to choose, would have chosen for friends or associates. Their unpopularity as soldiers was quite sufficient for the monkish writers to link them and the King together, in order to damage the reputation of John by the association.

Again, from p. 21 of the same book :—

6. "*The King, et cetera, to all Bailiffs in Pictavia and Wascon, et cetera.*—We command you that you should guard and defend the plunder of Martin Algais which Bernard Buche may have the conveyance of; and we have undertaken that you shall not permit annoyance or injustice to be done to them in any way, on account of the aforesaid plunder, from Thursday next before the Feast of the Blessed Andrew the Apostle, (November 28,) in the fourth year of our reign, even to the day of the Nativity next following. I myself attesting at Chinon, on the 28th day of November, (A.D. 1202.) By Thomas, the Clerk of the Chamber."

The same Martin Algais had other letters-patent, in the same form, concerning the plunder which Peter Com and Reimund Bertram convey, and during the term granted by this letter, from the Vigil of the Blessed Andrew, (November 29,) even to the Feast of the Purification of the Blessed Mary, (February 2, A.D. 1203.)

It is quite evident that these soldiers of fortune from the King's friend and ally, the King of Navarre, and the Emperor of Morocco, were very unpopular with the Christian troops engaged in the Norman war. In the year A.D. 1202-3, Normandy swarmed with monkism and priestism in all the impure purity of Catholicism, and their lust of accumulation of property. Hence they would afford a fine field for plunder for a brigade of Zouaves, or Moors, or Arabs of full or half cast, Spanish or Portuguese; or what would be as bad, or worse, wild Poles from Livonia.

The monastery, church, chapel, cell, and grange of friend or foe, French or English, would, under ordinary circumstances, share alike when presented as a spoil to these organised Pagan or Mohammedan savages. It is not difficult to understand how they needed the 'royal pass or letters-patent.'

Another charter we give from the same work, p. 23 *b* :—

7. "*The King, et cetera, to the Bishop of Agen, Abbots, Archdeacons, Archpresbyters and Chaplains, and Universal Clergy located through the Bishoprick of Agen, et cetera.*—It may be known to you, dearly-beloved, that we were prepared to grant all those petitions which the Earl of Toulouse had directed to us by Reimund Berner. And, above these, he conspired to make treasonable combinations with our enemies against us. On which account we entreat you so far as to summon all the barons, knights, burgesses, and men universally of the bishoprick of Agen, that they return to our allegiance. From whence he may receive the greatest good with honour, both he that shall henceforth do nothing for the aforesaid earl, or for his subordinates; and he who [shall do] for Martin Algais, who is for us in Wascon, as well when there may be attentive seneschals as others who may come into their places. And know ye that if the Earl of Toulouse, or any other constable having any evil intention, may wish to perpetrate that evil through all council-chambers, and through all other places, we will be defenders. Attested by myself at Cenom, on the 22d day of January (1203.)"

Again, from p. 27 of the same book :—

8. "*The King, et cetera, to Emeric Catto de Campania, Geoffrey Heliers, and Elie de Molendinare, et cetera.*—We command you to come to us securely with our dearly-beloved and faithful M[artin Algais,] Seneschal of Wascon and Perigord, and those who may come with you, by the counsel of Akenbald, Vice-count of Cumbor, may come securely in the county of the same seneschal. We grant you, and those who may come with you, a secure passage, and the space of eight days for returning to their own country before the same seneschal come to us, and be in conference

with us; or more time may be granted for safe conduct in returning to their own country, if the same seneschal should consult us on this business. Attested by William de Breosa at Rouen, on the 5th day of April, (A.D. 1203.)"

Again, another charter from p. 27 of the same book :—

9. " *The King, et cetera, to Master Burdegal, the brother of P. de V'nol, and Martin Algais, Seneschal of Wascon and Perigord, et cetera.*—We refer the gracious actions upon this business, which you so diligently and devotedly have so often sent, to your discretion, on the friendship between us and our dearest brother, Alfonso, the illustrious King of Castile, to be renewed and confirmed. And we command you, so far as by the faith in which ye may be held to us in this business according to which we enjoin upon you, when upon this question in the same business he should be drawn, ye may proceed to other things between us and you, our honour being secured; because, according to the tenor of that discourse which you may agree upon, for the honour of God, and that of the aforesaid king, our dearest brother, and ours, we will hold ourselves bound. Attested by William de Breosa at Rouen, on the 5th day of April, (A.D. 1203.)"

Again, another charter on the same parties we give from p. 28 *b* as follows :—

10. " *The King, et cetera, to the lady the Queen our mother, and the Lord Burdegal, Archbishop, and Robert de Thornham, Seneschal of Pictavia, and Martin Algais, Seneschal of Wascon and Perigord, and B., Seneschal of Anjou, and Hubert de Burgh, Chamberlain, and brother Peter de Vernol, and William Maingus, and William Cocus, health in the Lord.*—We send to you brother John de Valnt, who has seen those things which are carried on around us, and who will be able to certify to you of our condition, in whom ye may have faith in those things which he may tell you from hence; but nevertheless, by the favour of God, it shall stand better with us than he is able to give account of to you, and than we have given to you by mission; and you may

have faith in the same John in those things which he may tell you on that business. And we command you, Robert de Turnham, that the money which we send to you be not divided, but under the inspection and counsel of our Mother and William Cocus. Attested by William de Breosa at Faleis, on the xvj day of April, (A.D. 1203.)"

The Brothers of the Militia of the Temple of Rupella have letters-patent of the lord the King, directed to the Archbishop of Bourdeaux, Robert de Turnham, and Martin Algais, and another letter, of a like character, directed to Amoravic, for protection only.

Once more, we give another charter from p. 36 *b* of the same book :—

11. " *The King, et cetera, to all his Barons, Knights, and faithful Subjects of Wascon and Perigord, et cetera.*—We command, as far as you are held in fidelity to us, that you seek, on every stated occasion, to prepare yourselves to come into our service, so that you may be prompt, and prepared with soldiers, horses, and arms, for the summons, which our venerable Father the Archbishop of Bourdeaux and Brother P. de V'nol, and Martin Algais, our Seneschal of Wascon and Perigord, or two of them, might send you on our part, if all of you be not able to be present; and we, by the aforesaid Archbishop and Brother and Seneschal, or by two of them, will provide you with money, so that ye may be able to sustain our service well when ye have come to us. And if by chance disputing should arise amongst any of you, you shall reinstate peace amongst yourselves, or make a truce, by the counsel of the aforesaid. Your coming in thus to us, in this our necessity, is so praiseworthy, that it behoves us to commend your fidelity graciously. Attested, et cetera."

Again, we give another charter from the same, page 36 :—

" *The King, et cetera, to the Clergy, Knights, and Pagans from the Land of La Bord, et cetera.*—Know ye that we have set over all our land of Wascon and Perigord, as seneschal, our dearly-beloved and faithful Martin Algais,—and through forgetfulness we have omitted to send letters to you,—that you obey him as our seneschal. Nevertheless, we command and firmly enjoin upon you to be attentive and obedient to him as our seneschal; and that you perform to him, as to our seneschal, honour and civility. I myself attesting at Barbeft, on the 28th day of November, (A.D. 1203.) By Brother P. de V'nol."

This charter on Martin Algais being really Seneschal of Wascon and Perigord, and addressed to clergy, knights, and "*pagenis de terra de Labord,*" or pagans from Livonia, the extreme northern point of Poland, bordering on Russia, shews a considerable amount of uneasiness to have existed in Wascon and Perigord with respect to the recognition of Martin Algais, a soldier of fortune from Portugal or Brabant, with his ranks filled with pagans from Livonia, in Poland, and perhaps from Africa.

Alfonso, King of Navarre, married King John's sister, and the King of Morocco was closely allied to the Navarre family. These are the reasons why the King of England was so connected, by treaty, with Spain and Morocco. These Spaniards, with their pagan troops, found their way into King John's service through the above alliances—European and African.

How the pagans from Poland came to be connected with Martin Algais is beyond our comprehension, without substituting *Brabanter* for Bragançon. Perhaps they had been connected as mercenary fighters in other battles, and under other paymasters. King John, as we have seen, driven as he was by his feudal tenants in England and Normandy to fight against France with such troops and such weapons as he could procure, could only fall back upon the pagans of Labord, and the Hagareens of Africa, with half-casts from Spain and Portugal. One can picture the dismay, the uttermost terror which these barbaric hordes must have excited in all the ranks of monkery and priestism. Certes they would have slight discrimination in seizing the spoils of castle or monastery, or sacking city, town, or hamlet.

Still another charter on the same subject we give from page 43 of the same book :—

13. "*The King, et cetera, to all his Bailiffs and faithful subjects appointed throughout England, health in the Lord.*—We command you that all merchants of Pictavia and Wascon and Perigord, coming into our land with their merchandise, and bringing with them letters from Martin Algais, our Seneschal of Wascon and Perigord, or letters-patent of brother P. de V'nolius, and both testifying that they and their merchandise were from the aforesaid lands, then you may permit them freely, and without impediment, to go and return to our land, and there to negotiate, by doing it according to the custom of England. Attested by Earl Geoffrey Fitz-Peter, at Winton, on the 19th day of June, (A.D. 1204.)"

Again :—

14. "*The King, et cetera, to all, et cetera.*—We command you to give credit to those things which our dearly-beloved son Geoffrey and Sanaricus de Maloleon and Martin Algais, our Seneschal of Wascon, by the counsel of the head [man,] and upright men of Rochelle, or of the aforesaid Geoffrey and Sanaricus, by the counsel of the aforesaid head man, and upright men of Rochelle, where Master Martin will not be able to be present, they may have told you, on our part, for your honour and convenience and ours ; and we have held firmly to you that which the said three, or two of them, to wit, Geoffrey and Sanaricus, by the aforesaid counsel of the chief man and upright men of Rochelle, where the aforesaid Martin Algais may not be able to be present, they will take counsel with you on coming to, and standing by, our service. Attested by myself at Windsor, on the 26th day of April, (A.D. 1205.)"

Further, we give another charter from the same page, 53 *b*, and regarding the same parties :—

15. "*The King, et cetera, to all advisers and friends of Reymund de Planewes, et cetera.*—Know ye that from the time when the brother of Reymund de Planewes and his first-born son, or his second-born son if the first-born has not lived, shall have come

with letters testimonial of Sanaricus de Maloleon and Martin Algais, our Seneschal of Wascon, [Gascogne,] that they may remain as hostages for the said Reymund, we will liberate the body of the said Reymund. And if, in the meantime, the lot of humanity should fall to the said Reymund, we will grant that the aforesaid brother and his son may return in safety to their own country. I myself attesting, at Windsor, on the 30th day of April, (A.D. 1205.)"

Such is the documentary evidence extant in the Public Records on King John's conduct with respect to these two Bragançons. Comment were sheer waste. The remainder of the charge rests upon one unknown Chronicler entirely—one Albericus, a monk. Roger Hoveden, the most trustworthy of the class, was dead before those Portuguese appeared upon the stage. Roger de Wendover, the next in succession, makes no allusion to them. His copyist and embellisher, Matthew of Westminster, never alludes to them, neither does Henry Knyghton, a still later Chronicler. The whole charge of taste for low company rests upon an unknown writer, " Albericus, the monk of the Three Fountains," and this man introduced by Mr Thomas Duffus Hardy, F.S.A., of the Inner Temple, a writer and publisher under the Record Commission. We will quote him :—

" KING JOHN'S FRIENDS AND ADVISERS.

" On the subject of King John's associates and intimates, history creates the impression that his court was chiefly composed of such nobles, ecclesiastics, and other influential persons, whose interests were identified with his own. It was not, however, from amongst these that he selected his confidential friends and advisers, but from mercenaries, with whom he is said to have been surrounded; and it is stated that he retained about his court, and kept in pay, reputed bravoes, and others of like infamy. That John was not particular in his choice of such characters as public functionaries, or for private intimacy, is apparent from the dignities and other rewards which he lavished on two notorious individuals of that period, Lupescaire and Martin Algais, mercenaries of Bragançon, both of whom are stigmatised for their baseness by the historians of that day. In the absence of all evidence in support of their having merited such munificent remuneration, by honourable service to the crown, it is not unreasonable to suppose that they received these extravagant rewards chiefly from having administered to the King's vices."

So much for the writer on the Patent Rolls of the Tower of London, Mr Thomas Duffus Hardy, F.S.A. Mr Hardy charges King John with retaining about his court, and keeping in pay, "reputed bravoes, and others of like infamy," and this on the authority of Roger Hoveden. Roger Hoveden, the chaplain of Henry II., and truthful historian, died A.D. 1202; and Martin Algais and Lupescaire were acting their part in Normandy and elsewhere in the years 1203–5, and perhaps even 1206. It is a pity that any one connected with the Record Commission should lend himself to any party purpose. The conduct is altogether unworthy alike of Mr Hardy and of the Record Commission. Simple remembrance of dates demonstrates that the quotations from Roger Hoveden, as made by Mr Hardy, are miserable aftermonkish interpolations. Roger Hoveden is similarly alleged on every period and incident of John's chequered life—falsely alleged, seeing the worthy monk

> "Was gone to dust,
> His soul with God, I trust,"

at the time he is said to write disparagingly of John. We daresay sufficient has been adduced to dispose of our King's alleged "low company;" and so we proceed in our Vindication.

CHAPTER XXIII.

'WALLET' OF HISTORICAL MEMORABILIA.

HAVING vindicated King John from the several charges with which mendacious monks and credulous modern historians, (so-called,) have traduced his illustrious memory—resting our disproof not on opinions or rhetoric, but on extant and irrefragable evidence, stored up in the Tower Records, and other of our national MSS.,—we propose in this concluding chapter to bring together a great mass of incidental materials that have necessarily accumulated in the progress of our researches. These give most interesting and important confirmation to our estimate of the actual King John, as distinguished from the phantasm who for seven centuries has usurped his name. They reveal, as we have often had occasion to observe, a marvellous ubiquity of personal oversight, a self-consuming application to duty, a rare nicety of accuracy in pecuniary transactions, down to the smallest details, a generous carefulness in recompensing merit, a resolute adhesion to right, and above all, a masterly prescience of character and of issues. These venerable documents will also be found to present a singularly rich contribution to the illustration of national manners, customs, habits, and gradual progress.

With these remarks, we proceed to translate our 'Records.'

On the 14th of October, A.D. 1200, the King himself writes from Esseleg, or Ashley, in Hampshire, to the Mayor of Winton; and on the 24th of the same month he writes to the " Præpositus,"—constable or reeve of the manor,—on the venison being sent from

Winton to Marlborough. Whether the mayor of Winton were a merchant tailor or not, we cannot decide; but we should suppose that he was, and that he made clothes for the King, and perhaps his court, when they were staying at Marlborough Castle—one of the King's favourite residences. John's employing a Wilton tailor, and writing to the man,—the mayor of the town himself,—about these clothes, and no measurements being given in the letter, but merely the class of clothes required, we must naturally suppose that the tailor had his measure, and the measure also of his son Walter.

In his letter to the Mayor of Winton, John requests the bearer of the note to be supplied with one cassock of green, with rabbit fur; one pellice of rabbit skins, and one cape of russet woollen cloth, with lamb fur; and two robes of russet, with a riding-coat of lamb skins; and thirty yards of linen cloth; and three pairs of hose; and two pairs of mailed-hose for foot-soldiers—for our son Walter, (who was he?) " and the cost of these articles shall be reckoned to you at the Exchequer. *Teste meipso*, ap. Esseleg, xiiij die October, (A.D. 1200.)" [1]

N.B.—The two pairs of mailed hose, for foot-soldiers, for our son Walter, household captain, must have been made to measure, which shews that the Mayor of Winton was tailor for Captain Walter of Marlborough Castle as well as for the King.

We find, on the 26th day of October, A.D. 1200, that King John was at Melkesham writing to the Constable of Winton for a hundred pounds' weight of wax for the Queen, then staying at her castle of Marlborough,—the bill for this wax to be made out and taken to the Exchequer, where it would be paid; "*teste meipso*," —as was the case in hundreds of cases—being the signature.[2]

On the 12th of October of the above year, the King himself writes to William de Saint Michael, commanding him to make for the King's dearly-beloved Norman four cups with covers to them,

---

[1] Rotuli de Liberate, p. 2.   [2] Ibid., 2 Johann., p. 8.

which the King wished to send into Normandy, and the account to be taken to the Exchequer. The usual "*teste meipso*" gives validity to the order.[1]

On this same day, the 12th of October, the King himself, with his usual "*teste meipso*," writes to his dearly-beloved and faithful Treasurer and Chamberlain of our Exchequer, requesting him to free £50 from the Treasury to Lupillunus, our crossbowman, to acquit his securities, and those other crossbowmen, his companions. Dated at Kildeford, [Guildford.][2]

On the 2d day of November of this same year, the King himself wrote to W., the Treasurer, and G. and R., Chamberlains of the Exchequer, requiring them to free from the Treasury to our brother Emeric, Master of the Temple, fifty marks of silver, to be paid to him, which the King owed for his queen-mother for making her will,—the common "*teste meipso*" accompanying the above order, dated from Saint Briavell [Castle, in Gloucestershire.][3]

We shall continue our translations of these old 'Records' in chronological order, leaving them to speak for themselves:—

"*Rex, et cetera, to Geoffrey Fitz-Peter, et cetera.*—We had lost the precious stones and our jewels which we were accustomed to wear around our neck, which Bertholet, the bearer of these presents, has found, and has brought them liberally and faithfully to us; and we, on account of his service, have given to him at Berkhampstead, where he was born, xx shillings of return; and therefore we command you that you should assign those xx shillings of return to him without delay at the same place. *Teste meipso*, at Moreton, xij day of November, A.D. 1201, 3d Johann."

Another writ on church patronage, promised on a vacancy occurring, follows:—

"*The King, et cetera, to Geoffrey Fitz-Peter.*—We command you to give to Peter de Cresk, clerk, from the first churches which

---

[1] Rotuli de Liberate, 2 Johann., p. 2.   [2] Ibid.   [3] Ibid., p. 8.

may happen to be vacant, one from our gift; and if by any means one should be vacant [at this time,] you may give him that; and if no vacancy should fall out, you may give him x marks at our Exchequer [yearly] during the years in which there was any vacancy in this promised church preferment. *Teste meipso*, at Orbec, vij day of December, (A.D. 1201, 3d John.)"

Another draft upon the Exchequer for the Corpus Christi Vincit Anthem, sung before the King at Argentum, as follows:—

" *The King*, *et cetera*, *to William, the Treasurer, and the Chamberlain of London, et cetera.*—Free from our Treasury to Robert de Durham and Roger de Southampton, our clerks, xxv shillings, because they sung before us at Argentum on Christmas-day a Corpus Christi Vincit. *Teste meipso*, at Argentum, xxviij day of December, (A.D. 1201-2.)"[1]

" For sewing x pairs of linen shirts for the use of the lord the King, iij shillings and iiij pence. For sewing three shifts for the use of the same, ix pence. For j urinal, j penny. To Geoffrey de Calet, knight."

" *The King, et cetera, to Geoffrey Fitz-Peter, et cetera.*—We command you that you place Philip Russell in some abbey until some prebend of two denarii, or three, vacate by death, which we wish to be assigned. *Teste meipso*, at Arches, xviij day of May. Per P. de Stoke."[2]

These abbeys were nice honourable asylums, or jails, for certain doubtful characters, where they could be registered as prebends on the monastic muster-roll, for commons, and honourable confinement.

" *The King, et cetera, to the Barons of the Exchequer, health in the Lord.*—Reckon to the Vicecount of Gloucester xviij marks, for vij tuns of wine bought for our use, of which iiij were sent to Bridgenorth, and iij to Worcester, and viij shillings and viij

---

[1] Rotuli de Liberate, p. 25. [2] Ibid., p. 32, A.D. 1202.

pence for their carriage; and for the carriage of our breams from our pond, from Henley even to Marlborough, xlvij shillings and five pence halfpenny; and for linen cloth, vj shillings and vij pence; and for xviij barrels, iiij shillings and vj pence; and also for linen cloth placed in the barrels and tuns, and in weights and thread, iij shillings and iij pence halfpenny. Attested by Geoffrey Fitz-Peter at Bridgenorth, et cetera."

The sending breams to Marlborough Castle from Henley-on-Thames, and from the Severn at Tewkesbury, was common at this time. The breams at Tewkesbury now attain to a weight of seven lbs., and the fish are very abundant.

"*The King, et cetera, to the Vicecount of Gloucestershire, et cetera.*—We enjoin upon you to find carriage for iiij^{xx} of breams, even to Marlborough; and for Peitevin and Adam Scott, who may lead them hither, at their reasonable cost for victuals; and it shall be computed to them at the Exchequer, et cetera. I myself attesting at Worcester, on the xvj day of May (A.D. 1204.)"

"*The King, et cetera, to the Vicecount of Gloucestershire, et cetera.*—Find Peitevin and Adam, our servants, the bearers of these presents, what are necessaries of life to them according to reasonable custom, for taking seven score breams from Theokesburgh even to Marlborough, and it shall be reckoned to you at the Exchequer, et cetera. Attested by Peter de Stokes at Marlborough, on the xxxj day of March, (A.D. 1204.)"[1]

"*The King, et cetera, to the Vicecount of Worcester, et cetera.*—Free from thy farm to the sacristy of Worcester Church two marks for a certain cloak which it had accommodated us with, by offering at the same place, and it shall be reckoned to you at the Exchequer. I myself attesting, at Wudestoke, on the xix day of March, (A.D. 1204.)"

---

[1] Rotuli de Liberate, p. 88.

By the above writ it would appear that the King, when at Worcester, had to borrow a cloak for some public occasion. He wished to make a return, but had not the money in his pocket; so he wrote to the Sheriff of Worcestershire, requesting him to lay down the money for him, and carry the account to the annual settling with the Government. This kind of payment being universal, for even the smallest sums, does not indicate any pursy covetousness on the part of the King.

"*The King, et cetera, to the Vicecount of Oxfordshire, et cetera.*—Free from your farm to John Salvage x marks for the reparation of our bakehouse of Wudestoke, and it shall be reckoned to you at the Exchequer. Attested by Geoffrey Earl of Essex, at Wudestoke, on the xix day of March, (A.D. 1204.)"[1]

"*The King, et cetera, to the Barons of the Exchequer, et cetera.*—Reckon to the Vicecount of Dorsetshire xj pounds, xij shillings, and ij pence, which he expended in refreshing paupers on the entrance to our house of Gillingham. Attested by Geoffrey Fitz-Peter, Earl of Essex, on the viij day of April, (A.D. 1204.)"

This was a housewarming at Gillingham Castle, on taking possession by the King of his new property. Here paupers were entertained by the King, and the Vicecount of Dorsetshire paid for the feast the sum of £11, 12s. 2d., and took the account to the Barons of the Exchequer for repayment at the Christmas audit of accounts.

"*The King, et cetera, to the Bailiffs of Southampton, et cetera.*—We enjoin upon you, on these letters being seen, immediately to buy L pounds of the best cheese, and fit for provisioning a castle, on the view and testimony of Thomas, the nephew of Gervas and Walter Fortin; and you shall make it to be conveyed in a good vessel even to Rouen, and there to be

---

[1] Rotuli de Liberate, p. 83.

freed to Richard de la Mora, on the inspection of Peter de Patc-. shull, [a chamberlain of the Exchequer;] and it shall be computed to you at the Exchequer what you may have paid, as well for the expense in buying as in the carriage, et cetera. Attested by Geoffrey Fitz-Peter, et cetera, at York, on the xxvj day of February."

This cheese, purchased at Southampton for Rouen, would imply that England made better cheese in the year 1204 than was made in Normandy.

"*The King, et cetera, to the Vicecounts of London, et cetera.*—Liberate ye from your farm x pounds to William Fitz-A'dr for the repairing of our palace of Westminster, and of our houses, on the inspection of legal men, and it shall be computed to ye at the Exchequer. Attested by Geoffrey Fitz-Peter, at Westminster, on the xxvij day of March."

"*The King, et cetera, to the Bailiffs of Sorham, et cetera.*—Find a passage for Thomas de Cambridge, our clerk, with viij horses, and it shall be computed to you at the Exchequer. Attested by Geoffrey Fitz-Peter, at Winton."

"On the Sabbath day, [June 27,] at Clarendon, for harness bought for the use of the lord the King, as well for the great stable as for the stable of the chamber, by Walter de Saint Aldoen and Nicholas de Well, of which a particular account may be given on the back of the roll, xlj shillings and ix pence halfpenny."

On Sunday, May 13, A.D. 1201, the King himself wrote to Wm. Briwerr, the treasurer, and also to G. and R., chamberlains of the Exchequer, requesting them to liberate from the treasury xxv shillings to Jacob of the Temple and Hugh of Hereford, his clerks, who had sung a Corpus Christi Vincit on the day of Pentecost, at Porchester, before him.[1]

"*The King to Geoffrey Fitz-Peter, et cetera.*—Ye may know that, in accordance with the petition of our mother, we have

---

[1] Rotuli de Liberate, p. 14.

granted to Osbert, her man, the first prebend of any after this time which may happen to be vacant; and, therefore, we command you that you give him it. I myself attesting at New Castle, at Sarta, ix day of September, (A.D. 1201.)"

It is commanded Geoffrey Fitz-Peter to give to Alen the Welshman, who slew his antagonist in the service of Lord Richard, j denarius by way of return, whom in the first case he may place in some abbey.

Charity Given.

"*The King, et cetera, to Geoffrey Fitz-Peter, et cetera.*—We command you that you make William and Nicholas, the sons of John le Broc, our servant, to have the prebend, which was Roger le Tort's, who is dead, as is said, because we have given it them. I myself attesting, at Montfort, on the ij day of October, (A.D. 1203.)"

"The King has conceded to the nephew of Bric, the chamberlain, xv. marks of revenue in an ecclesiastical benefice when they should become vacant; and he has written on this business to the Justiciary."[1]

"*The King, et cetera, to Geoffrey Fitz-Peter, et cetera.*— We command you that you make, without delay, Thomas de Landa, our vadlet, to have the prebend of three denarii, which a certain chaplain, who is dead, had by our gift, at Chelford. I myself attesting, at Rouen, on the iiij day of October, (A.D. 1203.)"[2]

"*John, by the grace of God, et cetera, to the Vicecount of Buckinghamshire, health in the Lord.*—We enjoin upon you to make Alexander the harper to have the prebend of one penny, which Passemer had the arrears of, for the whole time before the same Passemer died. Attested by G., et cetera."[3]

"At the same place, [Freitmantell,] to William, the man of

---

[1] Rotuli de Liberate, p. 65.   [2] Ibid., p. 65.   [3] Ibid., p. 92.

Adam Crok, who brought vj heads of Welshmen, the servants of Cadewallan, cut off, to the lord the King, at Rochester, vj shillings by the King."

"For the restoring of seven long linen night-shirts of the lord the King, vij pence. For repairing dog-slips, vj pence. For j quiver for the use of the King, xij pence. For two pairs of summer boots for the use of Robin de Samford, [the master of the horse,] iij shillings. For j great sack of skin for the use of William, the tailor, in which to place the linen of the lord the King, and small matters, xiij shillings and x pence."

"For three yards of soft cloth from Syria, for the use of the lord the King, ij shillings and vj pence. On the same day, [May 6, 1210,] at Sutton, in Surrey, to a certain messenger going with letters to xij sworn men, and to the council of Bayona, half a mark. By the King."

"At Odeham, for cords bought at Winchester, to bind the leather bow-strings to the bows which the lord the King made to be brought from Winton, v pence."

"Also, on the day of Venus next, [Friday, May 18, A.D. 1212,] at the Tower of London, to Henry de Saint Helena, the goldsmith, for buying precious stones to place in a crown of gold, which the said Henry was about to make, by the precept of the lord the King, C marks by the King, freed to the same Henry by John Fitz-Hugo."

"*The King, et cetera, to the Constable of Windelsour, health in the Lord.*—We enjoin upon you to give Girald, the crossbowman, his acquittances for the day, iiij pence and an obolus, [a halfpenny,] and besides you give him yew-wood and strings, and horn to make crossbows, on the view and testimony of legal men; and it shall be computed to you at the Exchequer. Attested by Geoffrey Fitz-Peter at the Tower, London, on the xxix day of January. By Robert de Veteriponte. (A.D. 1204.)"[1]

---

[1] Rotuli de Liberate, p. 79.

"*The King, et cetera, to William the Treasurer, and G. and R., Chamberlains, et cetera.*—Free from our treasury to John, the crossbowman of Genoa, four marks, for the crossbows which he has brought for us from Genoa. Attested by Peter de Rupibus at the Tower, London, on the xxx day of January. *Per eundem.*"

"*The King, et cetera, to William the Treasurer, and the Barons of the Exchequer, et cetera.*—Reckon to Hugo de Neville xiv shillings, for three robes which he has given to three crossbowmen by our request. Reckon to him the discharge which he gave to Peter Sarazcen the crossbowman, each day ix pence, from the viij day of December, in the fifth year of our reign, even to the iij day of March; and from the iij day of March, until the same Peter received his discharge, you may make to be reckoned for each day ix pence. By Peter de Rupibus."[1]

"To Richard, the son of the presbyter of London, for j pair of panniers for the carrying of wax-tapers in, viij shillings."

"To John Long going with letters to Robert de Ros and Eustace de Vesci, vij pence."[2]

"For making a cope of scarlet, furred with green cloth from Syria or Spain-coton, xj pence."

"For thread for the use of William Scissor, ix pence."

"To Ivo de Lascelle, knight, the companion of Peter de Croun, as a gift, x marks. By the King."

It is commanded the Treasurer and Chamberlains to free to Ruffo, the archer of Genoa, x marks, in restitution of his loss which he had when he came to the King.

Genoa at this time (A.D. 1204) appears to have stood high for its crossbows, crossbowmen, and archers; for it is frequently mentioned in these writs in connexion with these implements and skilled warriors.

The wages paid to the better class of such men amounted to as

---

[1] Rotuli de Liberate, p. 94.   [2] Ibid., p. 97.

much as 9d. a day, when an ordinary smith, carpenter, or skilled artisan received only one halfpenny a day; the great mass of the population receiving no money-wages.

"*The King, et cetera, to the Vicecount of Wiltshire, et cetera.*—Find Roger, our crossbowman, abiding in our castle of Salisbury, his acquittances, namely, vj d a day, and give him j mark of silver to liquidate the arrears of his expenses, and j robe, and it shall be reckoned to you at the Exchequer. I myself attesting at Winton, on the xix day of May, (A.D. 1204.) By Peter de Rupibus."[1]

"On the day of the Sabbath next, at the same place, [the Tower, London,] for vij swords, and two polished daggers, and vj arrows for the crossbows similarly polished, by William Scissor, ij shillings and vj pence."

"At the same place, [Lambeth,] in the hiring of a boat bearing the harness of the garde-robe beyond the Thames, between Westminster and Lambeth, when the bridge of London was broken, iiij pence; by William Scissor and Ivo the hostler."

"At the same place, [the Tower, London,] for j pack-saddle, or pair of panniers, bought to carry the relics, by the command of the lord the King, iiij marks; freed to Robert de Abendon, clerk of John Fitz-Hugo."

"At the same place, for the party-coloured cloaks bought for the garde-robe by the hand of William Scissor, xv shillings."

"For a skin, and the making it into two sacks, besides the sack for the clothes, xij pence; by the same, William Scissor."

"For the acquittances of iiij sumpters and iiij coachmen of the garde-robe, who went from Chertsey even to London with the harness of the garde-robe, each of whom had ij pence a day, and there remained for one day, in which the lord the King threw, [at Ditton, the residence of Geoffrey Fitz-Peter, Earl of Essex, the Chief Justiciary,] according to custom, the Chief Justiciary, [in a wrestling-match,] the sum of xvj pence."

---

[1] Rotuli de Liberate, p. 101.

"On the day of Mercury next after the feast of Saint Barnabas the Apostle, [June 13, A.D. 1212,] at Rothwell, to John de Canterbury, the messenger, going with letters to Master Richard de Marisco, [Chancellor,] and William Briwerr, [Treasurer,] at London, xv pence."

"On the day of the Moon next after the Nativity of Saint John the Baptist, [Monday, June 25, A.D. 1212,] at Carlisle, to Wilekin de Meinnill, the vadlet of Philip Marc the vicecount of Nottinghamshire, who carried to a female friend of the lord the King a chaplet of roses from Ditton, the manor of Geoffrey Fitz-Peter, since the lord the King was hospitably entertained there by him."

This crown of roses was the trophy won in the wrestling-match by the King, and sent after him, even to Carlisle, by his vanquished opponent the Chief Justiciary of England, Geoffrey Fitz-Peter, Earl of Essex.

"*The King, et cetera, to Geoffrey Fitz-Peter, et cetera.*—We command you that immediately, on the day on which the bearer of these presents—Roger Wascelin—shall come to you, these letters being seen, you make to be acquitted without any delay, through the hand of the same Roger Wascelin, for C and lxvj pounds and xv shillings of sterling money, for the merchants of Pictavia and Wasconia, for wines taken from them for our use; but nevertheless, you will manage this business so that they may be able to congratulate themselves on their acquittance, and that they again may bring to us their wines more freely; because, if they at this time be freely satisfied, for the future wines might come into our land from their parts; but if otherwise, a paucity of wine might come through them to us. I myself attesting at Montfort, on the xxvij day of August, (A.D. 1203.)"[1]

We stop one moment to inquire here who were with the King at this time in Normandy. On this day William Marshall, Earl of Pembroke, signed a writ at the same place—Montfort. A few

---

[1] Rotuli de Liberate, p. 60.

days before, August 18th, the King and John Gray are connected in the same writ at Cambray.

On the 21st August, John Gray attested writs at Cambray; and Peter de Pateshull also attested writs on the same day, at the same place.

On the 23d of August, the King attested a writ at Tianus; and the day following, William Marshall, Earl of Pembroke, attested another writ at the same place.

From the above, it is evident that William Marshall, John Gray, and Peter de Pateshull, were ministers in attendance upon the King in Normandy in the month of August, A.D. 1203.

"On the Sabbath-day next, [Saturday, March 14, 1210,] at the same place, [Saint Bridget's, Clerkenwell,] in play by the lord the King, who was beaten with John Buqurinte, citizen of London; when playing against Warin Fitz-Gerold, v shillings and ix pence."

"To William the Berner, and Adam, men of the Earl of Winton, who brought breams to the lord the King; as a gift, v shillings. By the King."

"On the day of Mercury, [July 8, 1209,] at the same place, [Bristol,] to Gervase, the draper, for xix yards of green precious stuff, L shillings and viij pence, in a whole piece; for one yard, ij shillings."

"At the same place, for two linen monastic vests for clothing of the lord the King, iiij shillings. By the Bishop of Winchester."

"For two scabbards of skin, and three scabbards of cloth listings, bought at Gloucester, to place upon the arms of the King, iij shillings and ix pence."

"To Eimeric, the armourer, for his expenses for two days, xv pence," [7½d. a-day.]

"At Kenilleworth, to Robert de Sutton going to the Constable of Hereford for the platted bed of the lord the King, vj pence."

"To Alberic, going with the letters of the lord the King to Geoffrey Fitz-Peter, and the Lord Bishop of Winchester, and the

Lord Bishop of Bath, and the Lord 'Elect' H. of Lincoln, and the Earl of Arundel, and William Briwerr, being at Dover, [July 26, A.D. 1209,] v shillings." [1]

"*The King, et cetera, to the Vicecount of Wiltshire, et cetera.*— Find for Waleran, our servant, whom we send to you invalided, and his man and his two horses, what shall be necessary for him from your farm until he be recovered, and it shall be reckoned to you at the Exchequer." [2]

"*The King, et cetera, to the Barons of the Exchequer, et cetera.* —Reckon to the Vicecount of Worcestershire lxvi shillings, which he expended in purchasing viij cows, which he sent to us at the Feast of the Paschal Lamb at Wudestoke."[3]

"*The King, et cetera, to the Vicecount of Devonshire, et cetera.* —Find from your farm carriage for ij thousand marks from Winton even to Exeter; and find for our chaplain, Robert de Turnham, one robe of green, with a cloak of rabbit-skin; and it shall be reckoned to you at the Exchequer. Attested, et cetera."[4]

The remains of the rabbit-skin cloak may be seen, even in our day, cut down into a mere strip of fur, and decorated with a lining of white silk, crimson, or scarlet, which we take to have more to do with priestly ostentation than the inclemency of the weather.

"To Robert de Turnham, as a gift, CCC marks. By the King."

"On the same day we have freed, for travelling expenses, one hundred and fourscore and two pounds; for xviij mounted crossbowmen who came from Pictavia, C marks, on the vision of Robert de Turnham and Geoffrey de Neville, and sent to hunt. By the King." [5]

"For one fur of lamb-skin for the sure-coat of Robin de Samford, iiij shillings."

"*The King, et cetera, to the Bailiffs of Sorham, et cetera.*—

---

[1] Rotulus Misæ, p. 123.
[2] Rotuli de Liberate, p. 90.
[3] Rotuli de Liberate, p. 94.
[4] Ibid., p. 102. [5] Rot. Misæ, p. 142.

Find a ship, without regard to price, for the Master of the Knights of the Temple, and H. de Well, our clerk, whom we send for our messenger into Normandy, and it shall be reckoned to you at the Exchequer, et cetera. Attested by Geoffrey Fitz-Peter, Earl of Essex, et cetera, at York, on the xxvj day of February, (A.D. 1204.)"[1]

From the above writ, it would seem that the Master of the Temple possessed the full confidence of the King and his Ministry during the Norman contest.

"*The King, et cetera, to the Barons of the Exchequer, et cetera.*—We command you that you reckon to our venerable father, John, Bishop of Norwich, that he have, for the custody of the castle of Oreford which he has in charge, that which you may have been accustomed to reckon to others for the guards of the same castle. Attested by Hubert, Archbishop of Canterbury, at Portsmouth, on the xj day of April, (A.D. 1204.)"

Hubert Walter, Archbishop of Canterbury, was the foster-father of John Gray. These two were eminent Ministers of State to King John till the days of their deaths,—the one in 1205, and the other in 1214,—but nothing of setting the ordinary course of law at defiance ever occurs in the conduct of these great statesmen.

"*The King to the Vicecount of Devonshire, et cetera.*—Find, without regard to cost, a good and secure ship to transfreight the Bishop of Pampilon, and it shall be computed to you at the Exchequer. Attested by William Briwerr, at Winton, on the xiij day of April, (A.D. 1204.)"[2]

"It is commanded Geoffrey Fitz-Peter to give Gerard de Furnivall a certain feast at Newport every year for two days,—to wit, in the vigil of Peter and Paul, and in the daytime, unless it should be to the hurt of neighbouring feasts."

---

[1] Rotuli de Liberate, p. 81.   [2] Ibid., p. 90.

"The lord the King has granted to the Earl of Albemarle j feast at Shalingford of three days' duration,—namely, on the Vigil of Saint Cross, and ij days following; and j market at Waneting on the Monday, which formerly was on the Lord's-day, 'nisi sit,' et cetera."

All these grants of marts and feasts contain the '*nisi sit*,' it be to the injury of some neighbouring mart, fair, or feast.

"*The King, et cetera, to Geoffrey Fitz-Peter, et cetera.*— We command you that you make Earl Roger Bigod to have a feast at Haneworth every year of three days' duration,—namely, on the Vigil of the Blessed Bartholomew, and two following days, unless it should be to the injury [of other parties,] et cetera. I myself attesting at Rouen, on the xxx day of August." [1]

"The lord the King has granted to Roger de Thoney j market to be held at Southampton each day of Mercury, nevertheless provided it be not to the injury of others, et cetera."

"*The King, et cetera, to the Vicecount of Lincolnshire, et cetera.*—We command you that you make Roger de Thoney to have lxxvj pounds and xv pence of land at Saint Botulph, and a feast, with all appertaining to the same land, as we have freed those other lands to Peter de Nereford. I myself attesting at Windesore, on the xxvij day of March, (A.D. 1204.)"

"Also, Adam to one Parmenter of Winton, for two outer cloaks for xj shillings; for a fur cape of the lord the King, of escallarius, lx shillings."

"On the same day, at the same place, for making robes and sewing linen clothes and stockings for the use of the King, xiij shillings and vij pence, freed to William, the tailor, by Peter de Maulay."

"To Fulcher, a secret messenger, who came from parts beyond seas, half a mark. By Roger de Veteriponte."

---

[1] Rotuli de Liberate, p. 61.

"To Aleis de Xanton, a certain spy, half a mark. By the Elect of Lincoln."

"On the day of Mars next, [June 9, 1209,] at Orset, we have liberated to Reginald de Cornhill [the Government banker] xxxiiij pounds vj shillings and viij pence, to take charge of what monies may come from the monks of Fountains."

"On the day of the moon next, [June 1, A.D. 1209,] at the same place, [Knep Castle,] we have freed to Reginald de Cornhill one hundred marks, for guarding what monies may come for the fine of the Archdeacon of Durham. By the King."

"To Eimeric, the armourer, for two cases of leather for placing the cuirasses in, and leather for keeping the helmet of the lord the King, v shillings and vij pence halfpenny; and for two great sacks of canvas for the packing of eight cuirasses, ij shillings."

"On the same day, [Sunday, June 21, 1209,] at the same place, [Westminster,] to Buske and Nicholas, men of Absolom Dacus, who brought Spanish goshawks of Asturia; as a gift, ij marks. By the King; freed to Hugo, the clerk of Philip de Wilecot."

"On the day of Jove, [June 25,] to John de Bassingburn for making the foss at Tickhill, xx marks. By the King; freed to Matthew, his vadlet."

"*The King, et cetera, to Geoffrey Fitz-Peter, et cetera.*—Know ye that we have received, through the hands of Richard and Gilbert, servants of William de Saint Michael, a thousand fat pigs, and seventy-two does of fallow deer, which ye have sent to us; and, therefore, we command you that you on that account should be acquitted. *Teste, et cetera.*"[1]

"On the same day, at the same place, [Woodestoke,] for six sacks 'de Grisenge' for the clothes, furred to the treasury patterns, each sack of four yards bought and made at Oxford by William Scissor, the sum of twenty-four shillings and twopence."

---

[1] Rotuli de Liberate, p. 31, A.D. 1202.

"To Walter de Hauville, the falconer, xl shillings, by the Bishop of Winchester."

"*The King, et cetera, to the Barons of the Exchequer, et cetera.*—Reckon to Hugo de Neville one hundred bacon pigs, which he has given to Robert de Veteriponte, to victual the castle of Salisbury, by our precept. Attested, et cetera, by Peter de Rupibus."

"To John Cointance, Adam Le Viel, Adam Le Bel, Luke, Hugo, five sumpters of the garde-robe, for shoes, v shillings.

"To Adam and Gervase, coachmen of the garde-robe, ij shillings."

"To Florence, the laundress, for shoes, xviij pence."[1]

"On the same day, May 13, at Bath, to William de Pavilly, for one pair of jack-boots of cow's-hide, for the use of the lord the King, iij shillings; for two pairs of jack-boots of calf-skin, v shillings; for two pairs for summer, calf-skin, iij shillings and iij pence; for two pairs of small shoes, vj pence.

"The lord the King has pardoned Fulcon de Kantilupe fifty shillings of the ten pounds which are owing to our Exchequer; by our letters-patent, at Chinon, the xix day of August, A.D. 1201."

"Geoffrey Fitz-Peter, et cetera, is commanded to make all the lands, things, and men of Richard Morin to be in peace [with the Crown with respect to all taxes and demands upon them] as long as he was with Alan Basset, in the service of the lord the King, with horses and arms."[2]

"*The King, et cetera, to Geoffrey Fitz-Peter, et cetera.*—Know that we have acquitted Brien, our porter, of ij palfries which he owes to us, and therefore we enjoin upon you to permit him to have peace on that business. I myself attesting at Westminster, on the xxv day of March. By Hugo de Neville."

Noster Ostiarius and Brian Ostiarius frequently occur in these writs, and shew the confidence in which he was held by the King.

"The lord the King has pardoned the church of Saint Michael,

---

[1] Rotulus Misæ, p. 110.   [2] Rotuli de Liberate, p. 61.

at Oxford, and Master John, Archdeacon of Oxford, and his successors, xxxij pence and j quarter, in perpetuity, for the soul of the queen our mother."

"To Randulph Parmenter, to buy small necessary things for the use of the lady the Queen, v shillings."

"For panniers to place fruit, for the use of the King, for a good while, [*per pleres vices,*] viij pence."

"To the five boys of Robin de Samford, for shoes, ij shillings and j penny."

"On the day of the Sabbath, [Saturday, April 24, 1210,] at the same place, [Nottingham,] for xj yards of woollen cloth, [de grisenc,] to make a cloak, when we went to the army in Scotland, x shillings."

"On the day of Mercury, [April 21, 1210,] at the same place, [Wakefield, in Yorkshire,] out of respect to the lord the King; for a great deal of flesh-meat, [bought and given away, or consumed in a great dinner,] xj shillings and viij pence, by Robert de Veteriponte.

"*The King, et cetera, to Hugo de Neville, et cetera.*—Know ye that William Briwerr has paid a fine to us of one hundred marks for disforesting the manor of Felton, and, therefore, we command you that it be disforested, according to the tenor of our charter, which you may make him to have on that business; you knowing that the aforesaid fine he has paid to us; and you may enrol him acquitted on that business. I myself attesting, at Montfort, on the xxiij day of July (A.D. 1203.)"[1]

Exchange of Land.

"*The King, et cetera, to Geoffrey Fitz-Peter, et cetera.*—Know ye that we have committed to Philip of Worcester, by the convention which is agreed upon by us, Feireford, with its appurtenances,

---

[1] Rotuli de Liberate, p. 51.

pig, and venison, and wild-fowl; so that he shall not be able to take venison, nor sell wild-fowl, unless by our wish and command. But we grant to him that, although we may place pigs in our woodland, likewise he may place pigs in it; and therefore we command you that you make him to have seisin of the aforesaid lands, with carts and chattels appertaining to those lands; but nevertheless, when we wish to make the exchange back again to the same Philip for the aforesaid land,—to wit, CC pounds of land, as is covenanted between us,—that he shall return to us as many carts and chattels, and those lands as well stocked, as he received them; and besides, we have granted the herbage of those lands, the seignorage being reserved to ourselves when he has returned those lands to us; and we have placed our servant to guard the porkers and the venison and the wild-fowl. I myself attesting at Rouen, on the ij day of September, (A.D. 1203.) And it is enjoined upon Hugo de Neville that he may place a keeper there."[1]

The King always appears to be very tenacious of his seignorages when the herbage for pig-runs are granted in the forest; and even partial fowling, hawkings, and huntings are tacitly allowed in the tenants of the Crown; but the selling of wild-fowl, or taking it in decoys within the limits of royal forest or marsh, appears to have been strictly forbidden. Perhaps this restriction had something to do with the ancient system of flapper-driving in the fens.

"*The King, et cetera, to the Vicecount of Southampton, et cetera.*—We enjoin upon you to find a good and secure ship to carry our bucks [of fallow-deer] even to Barfleur; and it shall be computed to you at the Exchequer. I myself attesting at Marleborough, on the xj day of December, (A.D. 1203.)"[2]

"*The King, et cetera, to Hugo de Neville, [Chief Ranger of the*

---

[1] Rotuli de Liberate, p. 62.   [2] Ibid., p. 75.

Royal Forests,] *et cetera.*—Inquire into the necessary expenses of the Queen my wife and her family, under the inspection of Robert de Veteriponte, [a chamberlain of the Exchequer,] as long as she remained at Marleburgh and at Wudestoke; and it shall be computed to you at the Exchequer. I myself attesting at Burbage."

"For one outer great-coat, of various colours, to protect the furred tunic of the lord the King, xx shillings."

"For a membrane [grisio] for certain gauntlets of the lord the King, ix pence."

This grisio was probably buckskin or doeskin, dressed in some expensive manner; for the price of ix pence was that of the best parchment,—and that ix pence a sum, in the year 1209, equal to fifteen shillings of our time and money.[1]

"For two good parchments to make rolls for episcopal matters, xviij pence."

"*The King, et cetera, to Geoffrey Fitz-Peter, et cetera.*—We command you that without delay you make the Earl of Arundel [William d'Albini] to have all the land which the wife of John de Humet held in feud of the said Earl. I myself attesting at Lexovia, on the viij day of September, (A.D. 1203.)"[2]

Under the same form it is written for the Earl of Leicester, respecting all the land which the aforesaid wife held in Angoleim from the feud of William de Silly.

The above two writs refer to Norman confiscations and re-grants to court officials. William de Braosa and William d'Albini were both connected with the ministry. The Earl of Leicester was another grantee. He married the daughter and co-heiress of Blanchman, Earl of Leicester, and took that title in right of his wife. His name was Simon de Montfort—a Norman by birth;

---

[1] Griseus or Grisium, in Du Cange's Dictionary, is rendered "pellis animalis cujusdam," which the Galls call 'vair.' We suppose it to have been any ornamental skin,—as goat, badger, or deer, —with the hair left on, for ornament.

[2] Rotuli de Liberate, p. 62.

and he was the father of Simon de Montfort, the patriot who headed the barons against Henry III., and fell at the battle of Evesham with his son Henry and eleven barons. The second Montfort, Earl of Leicester,—the hero of Evesham,—married Eleanor, the widow of William Marshall the younger. She was the second daughter of King John, and sister of Henry III.

Land Given.

"*The King, et cetera, to Geoffrey Fitz-Peter, et cetera.*—We command you that you should make Pollard, our servant, to have a certain house at Northampton which is called Lardarius, unless that house should have a greater value than ij shillings a year. I myself at Lexovia, on the viij day of September, (A.D. 1203.)"[1]

The above shews a freehold tenement, of the value of ij shillings a year, given as a reward to a servant.

Land Granted.

"*The King, et cetera, to Geoffrey Fitz-Peter, et cetera.*—We command you that without delay you make our venerable father, John, Bishop of Norwich, to have the manor of Snaffam, which was the Earl of Brittany's, in its integrity, with herbage and other chattels, and all its other appurtenances. I myself attesting at Tiasnus, on the xj day of September, (A.D. 1203.)"[2]

John Gray was one of the King's great Ministers of State. He was foster-grandchild of Randulph le Glanville, the great Justiciary of Henry II. If Arthur Plantagenet had been murdered, it must have been known to this man, and he would hardly have received a portion of the estates of the murdered man, as (so-called) history babbles.

" It is commanded the Vicecount of Rouen to send to Radepont

---

[1] Rotuli de Liberate, p. 62.   [2] Ibid., p. 63.

xiij sheaves of maple-tree shafts, and xij dried, and a hundred pikes, and five hundred pectorels of good iron, and the custom shall be remitted to him."

"*The King, et cetera, to all, et cetera.*—Know ye that *Robert, the son of Robert*, the mercer, lost his ear at Chateau-neuf-sur-Sart in our service, and not on account of felony. And this we certify to you that you may know it. Witness ourself at Montfort, the 23d day of July, (A.D. 1203.)"

Roger Chennel has the King's letters-patent in the same form.

"For burnishing two spathas [long two-edged and two-handed swords] of the lord the King, xxij pence."

"For iiij pairs of shoes of iron for the use of the same, xvj pence, freed to William de Dun."[1]

"On the day of Mercury, [March 31, A.D. 1210,] at Pickering, in play by the lord the King at tables, x shillings, which he lost against the Earl of Salisbury, [William Plantagenet, the Admiral of England, base brother to King John, and son of fair Rosamond Clifford."][2]

These losses at tables, even down to fourpence, are all paid by writs upon the Exchequer, and the parties so influential in the Government as to render the transaction perfectly ludicrous, if measured by our standard of kings and courts.

"To Wilekin Bloiet for shoes, xviij pence."

"In repairing the box for the pennies, iiij pence halfpenny."

"To the lord the King at play with the Earl of Salisbury at tables, iiij shillings and x pence; and on another occasion at play with the same, iiij shillings and xj pence."

Mem. 3.

"*John, by the grace of God, et cetera, to all his Bailiffs and faithful subjects, health in the Lord.*— Know ye that Hawisa,

---

[1] Rotulus Misæ, p. 151.   [2] Ibid., p. 159.

Countess of Albemarle, hath made a fine to us of five thousand marks [1] for her hereditary property, and dowers which appertain unto her; and that she should not be constrained to marry herself; so that if she should wish to marry herself, she would do it through our instrumentality. And the aforesaid five thousand marks may be returned to us at the times which we have appointed for her, and caused to be enrolled; and in testimony of this thing, we have caused this our charter to be executed for her on that account. These attesting—Lord P. Winton, Bishop; William, Earl of Salisbury, our brother; Geoffrey Fitz-Peter, Earl of Essex; William, Earl of Arundel; William Briwerr; Hugo de Nevill; Peter Fitz-Herbert. Given under the hand of Master Richard de Marisco, Archdeacon of Northumberland, [Chancellor,] on the iij day of November, in the xiiij year of our reign, A.D. 1212-13."

And so our

VINDICATION
of
KING JOHN OF ENGLAND

draws to a close. Our 'Epilogue' is a simple request that the reader compare the FACTS of our Narrative with the Monkish mendacities and modern trivialities. Let this be done, and we hesitate not to affirm that, on the one hand, the nearer you get to the living and actual John, the more will he be found a TRUE MAN, patriotic, brave, generous, thoughtful, vigilant, full of noble impulses, sagacious, self-sacrificing, and, in short, the very antipodes of the historical John: and that, on the other hand, the more near you get to the John of "Chronicle" and monkery, the more is the unveracity, unreality, phantasm character of the

---

[1] Rotuli Chartarum, p. 189. 5000 marks = £3333, 6s. 8d.; and the latter, multiplied by 20 for our time and money, will give £66,666, 13s. 4d. for Hawisa, the last of the Romilys of Skipton Castle, not to be blessed with the felicities of a fourth husband.

portrait discerned. That John had the infirmities of our common humanity we seek not to gainsay; but they are as nothing to his substantive greatness and lustre, take him all in all. And so " hail and farewell," right noble King!

NOTE A., Page 3.

We had intended giving here illustrative documents and details of the famous, or, on the Bishop's side, infamous, "disputes" alluded to *supra;* but, on examination, they prove too bulky and entangled for convenient exhibition in the space at our command. We prefer delay until an after-opportunity, should another edition of our book be called for; and meantime those interested may consult Hoveden and Wendover, and the other early authorities and references enumerated in our Index.

INDEX OF CHIEF MATTERS.

A

Absolution of John, 78.

Advocates, clerical, 132.

Aids, 95, 97.

Albans, St, John at, 116.

Albini, William d', 18, 114.

Ale, 101.

Alexander, King of Scotland, 109.

Alfred, 7, 49.

Algais, Martin, 34, 246, *seq.*

Andelys, 44; siege of, 51.

Archbishop, election of a successor to Hubert Walter, 61–78.

Arthur, Duke of Bretagne, his claim to the English crown, 5; supported by Philip of France, 5; in arms against John, 5; French possessions of England demanded for, 45; taken at Mirabeau, 46; privately executed, not murdered, 46, 48; various accounts, 46; *seq.*

Articles of Magna Charta. (See Magna Charta.)

Assize, circuits of, 15–17. (See Circuits.)

Associates of John, 273, 274.

Athyes, 105.

B

Bailiffs, 21, *et alibi*.
Barhuch, 19, 20.
Barons of Exchequer, 21, 37.
„ of England, friends and foes of John, 84, 85.
„ the, 131–140; their position in Feudalism, 131.
Becket, Thomas à, 133.
Benedictines, 62.
Berkhampstead, 195, *seq*.
Berner, 38, 182.
Borrowing, 95, 149.
Bowmen, 105, 166.
Brady, Dr, 124.
Bread, 59.
Breams, 266.
Briwerr, 30, 35.
Brittany, Duke of. (See Arthur.)
Bucks, 281.

C

Canterbury, archbishopric of, disputes concerning, 62; to be appointed by the Pope, 62; Langton appointed, 62.
Carriages and horses, 19, 20; charges, 20, 21, 22, 174.
Castles given to John, 3.
Cave, 125.
Charter. (See Magna Charta.)
Chaucumbe, 214.
Cheese, 267.
Chronology forgotten by John's detractors, 1.
Church, English, to be free, 91, 113, 148.
Churchyard Parliament, 133. (See Folkmote.)
Cinque Ports, 58.
Circuits of Assize, 15; John's attention to, 15; places of, 16, 17; persons with John, 18, 19, 26, *seq*.

Index of Chief Matters. 291

Clarendon, Statute or Constitution of, 133, 134, 137, 138.
Clergy, advocates, 132, *seq.*; outwitted by surrender of the Kingdom, 140.
Clergy, the 97.
Cloak, 266.
Coachman, 38.
Cole, Henry, 28.
Collingham, William, 121.
Conqueror, William the, 161.
Constance, mother of John [Arthur], 5.
Copyholders not barons, 143.
Corn, 151.
Councils, (see Folkmote); second, 40; various, 41, *seq.*
Cowardice and like charges, 43, 56, 61, 67, 162.
Crusades, 52.

D

Dansker, 160.
Dead bodies, 64.
Debts, 93, 95, 149.
Discipline, 38.
Dogs, 176, *seq.*
Dover, surrender of England at, 70.

E

Ear, lost, 284.
Ecclesiastics. (See Clergy.)
Edward the Confessor, 79; liberties of, 81.
Eleanor, 45.
Election, John king by, 7–12.
Eminent officials of John, 29–42.
Ethelwolf, 7.

Eustace of Ely, 66.
Excommunication, 64 ; of John by name, 65 ; of the Barons, 114, 115, 116.

F

Famine, 224, *seq.*
Fee-farm, 101.
Fee, lords of, 151.
Felony, 99.
Feudalism, smitten, 143 ; what it was, 158, *seq.* ; illustrated by Writs, 162, *seq.*
Feudatories, 79, 144.
Fleet of France destroyed, 77.
Folkmote, 4.
Forest, 103.
France, invasions of, 50.
Freeman, 97, 148.

G

Gambling, small, 284.
Geoffrey, son of Henry II., 1.
Gervas, 133, 136, 138.
Giraldus Cambrensis in Ireland, a noticeable fact, 2.
Gray, John, Bishop of Norwich, 31 ; appointed Archbishop of Canterbury, 61, 62. .

H

Harding, 58.
Hardy, T. D., 17, 32, 222, 223, 260, 261.
Hare-hunter, 177.
Harness, 21.
Hawks, 173.
Hearne, 125.

Heirs, 91, 172.
Henry, Dr, 133, 134; partisanship of, 136, 137.
Henry II., family contentions, 1; son of, 1; death of, 3; a lawyer, 132; character, 136.
Henry, son of John, Inter-chapter on, 126–130.
Henshall, 46.
Higden, 123, 147.
Holinshed, 147.
Homage, 76, 155.
Honiton, 26.
Honours conferred on John by Richard, 3.
Horses, 19, 20, *seq.*, 197.
Hose, 263.
Hoveden, Roger de, 3, 11, 139, 186, 261.
Hume, 46, 47.
Hunter, Joseph, 18.
Hunting, 173, *seq.*

I

Infeudatories, 144.
Innocent III., 8, 49, 63.
Interdict, Papal, over England, 64; no effect on John, 65.
Invasion of England, 66.
Ireland, John in, and alleged conduct there, 1, 2.
Isabella of Angoulême, 13; issue of, 13; crowned, 14; Writs concerning, 190, *seq.*
Itinerary of John, 14, 18.

J

Jewels, 264, 270.
Jews, affairs of, 31, 32; *custodes Judæorum*, 32; debts to, 94, 95; John's alleged cruelty to, 204, *seq.*; Jew at Bristol, 204.

John, King, birth, 1 ; knighted, 1 ; in Ireland, 1 ; recalled, 2 ; created Earl, 3 ; slandered by Bishop of Ely, 4 ; popular with the people, 5, 6 ; King by election, 7–12 ; opposed to Papal claims, 8 ; in Normandy, 8 ; crowned, 8, 9 ; character on accession, 11, 12 ; divorce from Isabel, 12, 187 ; marriage to Isabella, 13 ; re-crowned with her, 14 ; authority real, 29, *seq.;* served by the best men, 42 ; rapidity of, 46 ; "stuff" of John proved, 48 ; refuses Langton, 63 ; bravery in meeting threatened invasion of England, 67, *seq.;* popularity with the people, 83 ; closing incidents, 122–125 ; death, and questions about, 123, *seq.*

Judges, 26, *seq.*

Justiciary of England, Chief, 30.

K

Kindness of John returned by ingratitude, 229, *seq.*

Knighton, Henry de, 47, 199, *et alibi.*

Kydells, 101.

L

Laci, Roger de, 51.

Laci, Hugo de, complaints against, 2.

Langtoft, 123.

Langton, Stephen, 62 ; a traitor, 66, 79, 80 ; suspended, 115.

Legates, 64.

Leland, 46, 47, 51, 125.

Leo the Jew, 208, *et alibi.*

Letters-patent, 72.

Lingard, 187, *seq.*

Liverpool, 59.

Llewellin, 109.

London, taken by the nobles, 82.

Longchamp, 3 ; dispute with John, 3, 4.

Louis of France, 120 ; invades England, 121 ; threats, 127.

Low-born men, alleged, 42, 246, *seq.*
Lupescaire, 246, *seq.*

M

Madox, 30, 31, 32, 173.
Magna Charta, treason, 84, *seq.;* barons on each side, 84, 85; meeting at Runnemead, 84; agreed to, 86; remarks on, 86, 87; in Latin, and Translation, 88–113, (see fac-simile in pocket;) character of the men, 114, *seq.;* a farce, 114; the fruit of a conspiracy, 120; title invalid, 141, *seq.;* details, 148–162; real design of, 152.
Marisco, Deputy-Chancellor, 32.
Marriages, 164, 165, 167.
Marshal, William, Earl of Pembroke, 4, 31, 134.
Measures, 101, 150.
Merchants, 101, 102, 103.
Mill, 163.
Ministers of the Crown, discipline of, 38, 39.
Mirabeau, siege of, 45.
Mirrour for Magistrates, 49.
Money, 169.
Movement, incessant, of John, 27.

N

Nationality of England saved, 71, 162.
Neville, Geoffrey de, 241, *seq.*
Neville, Hugo de, 30, 39.
Newark Abbey, 125.
Nobles at coronation of John, 9, 10; ignoble, 48, *seq.*, 50, 52; defection, 53, 55; treason, 81, 82.
Normandy, John in, 15; difficulties in, 43–57; successes in, 55.

O

Oath, a reality to John, 12.
Officials of John, 29–42.

P

Palfrey, 164.
Pandulph, 66, 68, 69.
Paramount, Lord, 146.
Pardon of nobles, 113.
Paris, Matthew, 187, *seq.*
Pateshull, 31.
Paul's, St, Folk-mote at, 4 ; another meeting, 79.
Pegge, 123, *seq.*
Peter de Rupibus, 20, 28.
Peter, Geoffrey Fitz, 9.
Philip II., 43 ; conference with John, 44 ; proclaims John a traitor, 48 ; effect of capture of Arthur, 50 ; outwitted, 76, 77.
Plantagenets, 34, 36.
Poisoning, alleged, of John, 201, 202.
Poor, John's care for, 223, *seq.*
Pope, (see Innocent III.,) Popery, a reality, 69 ; Lord, 143.
Priestism smitten, 139.
Prisoners at Mirabeau, 48.
Problem before John, 69, 70.
Prophecy, alleged, of John, 186, *seq.*

Q

Quinci, Saher de, 48, 209, 229, *seq.*

R

Randulph de Diceto, 13.
Recklessness, alleged, 170.

Index of Chief Matters.

Richard I., accession, 3; crusader, 3; return, 5; slain at Chalus, 5; assigns crown to John, 5; inference from, 5.
Roads, 19, 28.
Roses, crown of, 273.
Rotuli de Liberate, 21, 23, 40, 115, 117, 171, 174, 175, 176, 177, 178, 208, 210, *seq.*, 226, *seq.*, 266, *seq.*
Rotuli Litterarum Clausarum, 194, *seq.*
Rotulus Misæ, 21, 22, 24, 179, 180, 181, 182, 183, 184.
Rochester Castle, 114.

S

Sandford, 187.
Scutage, 95, 150.
Seignorages, 281.
Selden, 131.
Seltford, 213.
Seneschal, 258.
Shakespeare, 46.
Sham, 154.
Sheriffs, 36, 38.
Shoes, 284.
Skulking, alleged, 220.
Soc and sac, 168.
Southey, 87.
Spelman, 131.
Spendthriftness, alleged, 170.
Sports, details of, 173, *seq.*
Strickland, 188, *seq.*
Stutevill, 33, 42.
Succession, designated, 8.
Sureties, 93.
Surrender of England, 54, 69, 70; documents, 70-78, 164, *seq.*
Swineshead Abbey, 124; Prioress of, romance about, 201.

U

T

Tailors, 263.
Tanner, 125.
Teuton, 194, 195, *et alibi*.
Thomson, 87.
Title of Magna Charta, 140, *seq*.
Tooth-drawing nonsense, 205, 217, 218.
Tower Records. (See Writs.)
Traitors, 60, 140, *seq*.
Tribute, 41.
Tyes, 192, *et alibi*.
Tyranny, alleged, 199.

V

Vacillation, alleged, 8.
Valtrars, 181.
Vassal, John becomes a, 143, 156; vassalage, 158, *seq*., 161.
Vavasour, 49.
Vesci, Eustace de, alleged seduction of wife of, 199, *seq*., 237, *seq*.

W

Wales, 107, 109.
Walleran, 127.
Wallet, memorabilia of, 262, *seq*.
Walter, Hubert, Archbishop of Canterbury, 4; speech, 9, 10, 28; details of, 58–60.
Walter, Robert Fitz, 118, 237, *seq*.
Warden, 92, 93.
Washes, 123.
Wendover, Roger, 3, 10, 43, 47, 54, 62, 63, 65, 66, 69, 74, 75, 76, 77, 79, 81, 83, 115, 116, 118, 119, 120, 121, 129, 153, 154, 156, 235.

Westminster, Matthew of, 144, 146.
Widows, 93.
Wight, Isle of, 221, *seq*.
William I., 131, 132.
William of Malmesbury, 132, 135.
Willis, 125.
Windsor besieged, 121.
Wine, 101, 150.
Woman, 107.
Wood, 99, 195.
"Worry," 79, *seq*.
Writs, illustrative of Feudalism, 163, *seq.;* poor, 225, *seq.;* Saher de Quinci, 229, *seq.;* Lupescaire and Algais, 246, *seq*.

Y

Yeomen, 144.

☞ Attention is respectfully invited to the emblazoned facsimile of the *Magna Charta*, which is placed in a pocket of the front board of our volume. *This was not in the book when I bought it.*

BY THE SAME AUTHOR.

THE LIFE AND TIMES OF DANIEL DE FOE.

1 vol. 8vo. Portrait. 10s. 6d.

LONDON: J. R. SMITH, 36 SOHO SQUARE.

BALLANTYNE AND COMPANY, PRINTERS, EDINBURGH.

www.ingramcontent.com/pod-product-compliance
Lightning Source LLC
Chambersburg PA
CBHW022103230426
43672CB00008B/1264